A
Palo Alto
Dreamer

The 60/70 Sparkling

A Palo Alto Dreamer

The 60 / 70 Sparkling

First published in the United States 2009

Published by Lulu.com

Cover design and book formatting by Jane Horton
Printed in the United States of America

Special Thanks to Liz and Gretchen
for
Encouragement, Love, and Friendship

For information or comments contact Jane Horton
janehorton@earthlink.net

First Edition, December 2009

ISBN 978-0-557-19084-3

The first part of the story has been put down on paper. That was the easy part...the part about The 50/60 Kids, growing up in Palo Alto in the 1950s and early 1960s.

Writing this sequel was much harder. I struggled over what to write and what to leave out, how to make sense of the 1960s and early 1970s while sharing the vibrancy, the intensity, the hope, and the connectedness.

I still protected the dreamer in me, but my world was expanding and society exploded with sex, drugs, and rock n' roll. I was committed to social justice and had great faith that the wrongs of society would be righted by my generation.

Gretchen said, "Write the next part of your story... I want to know what happened to that little girl."

So here is the next part of my story...the story of a generation caught up in the sparkling revolution of the 1960s and early 1970s.

Dedicated to my family, my lovers, my friends...some living and some gone, who remember or were part of

"The 60 / 70 Sparkling."

Contents

Prologue

It felt like sixth grade was suddenly going to be over too soon. Marie and Christine and I had been friends for a long time; Marie and me since kindergarten, and Christine and me since she had moved to Palo Alto in the third grade. Next year I would go to a different school, to Ray Lyman Wilbur Jr. High School. I would not be the tallest girl in school anymore, and I would not know my teachers and everyone in my classes. I would take a school bus to school, and have different teachers and a P.E. uniform and be in seventh grade, the youngest class at junior high. It was scary in a way, but it was time.

I didn't know what things would be like next year. I had finally figured out how some things worked, what some of the rules were and who were the good and bad guys. But I didn't know if I would ever kiss someone, or fall in love, or be an art teacher, or have kids, or have a boyfriend, or if some day I would be beautiful like my Auntie Jan.

I was thirsty to learn, and the world was so exciting with poetry and writing and ways that I could help other people. Maybe I would be a social worker; maybe I would be an artist. I thought that I would like to live in a helicopter or in a school bus that was all fixed up inside like a house on wheels. Maybe I would live along the Amazon River for part of the year and collect insects, and then maybe I would live in the desert for a while, landing wherever I wanted to land in my helicopter.

All I knew was that I had my life ahead of me, life that was exciting and amazing and funny. I wanted so much to grab hold of what it was that meant something and that made a difference in the world and to figure out who I was and why I was on this Earth.

Things were sure to change.

The Last Day of Sixth Grade
The 50 / 60 Kid

Summer Family Camping

During the summer between sixth and seventh grade my family went camping at Big Basin. Big Basin Redwoods State Park is California's oldest state park, established in 1902, and it is famous for ancient coastal redwood trees. Redwood trees are the largest living things, and we were lucky to live so near to a redwood forest; it was only an hour-and-a-half drive from our Palo Alto house. The last hour of the drive was car-sicky, with a very winding road. At least it was shady because of the trees, but sometimes it seemed that the front of the car would meet the back of the car, the road twisted so! We drove our recently-purchased Plymouth station wagon. Most families had station wagons to provide room for the family AND a lot of other things. When we arrived at Big Basin, we agreed that driving the curvy road had been worth it, as Big Basin was so beautiful.

We pulled into the campground Saturday morning with a plan to have our family tent pitched by lunch time. Compared to Palo Alto, the sun felt hotter, the sky was bluer, and the dust in the air was sparkly. Pitching the tent meant finding the most level part of the campsite, picking up all the rocks, and raking the area where the tent would be until the ground was smooth. We would then spread out a tarp, carry the tent from the car and unfold it. My sisters and I would sit on the tailgate of the station wagon while we watched my parents pitch the tent. The tailgate was the door at the back of the car that folded down to make it easy to load things inside the station wagon; things like the tent, ice chest, folding chairs, firewood, and other camping gear. My older sister, Judy, had just finished ninth grade and my baby sister, Jennifer, was going to start third grade in September. The three of us sat close to each other on the tailgate, swinging our legs as we tried to stay out of our parents' way

The Pink Tent

We had the only pink tent in the entire universe. My parents bought it at a Sears' "Closeout Clearance Special." I am sure if my parents had not bought that pink tent that the Sears store in Mountain View would have paid someone to take it away. However, we girls had learned the value of the pink tent, because to any boys we met we would just say, "Oh, we're at the pink tent." That was all they needed to know, because no one ever saw such a tent before or after. It must have been that the fabric for something else had slipped into the manufacturing line for tents, and when their mistake was discovered they said, "What the heck, let's see if anyone will buy this crazy pink tent!"

We girls would sit on the tailgate watching my parents, and each time it went like this: Daddy would crawl inside the tent with the umbrella-like metal pole that went inside the flattened tent, and lying on his belly he would put one end of the pole into the round hole on the tent floor, and the other end into the hole in the tent ceiling. Then Daddy would slowly open up the pole by turning a handle. It never worked the first time, and the whole thing would collapse. There would be a lot of swearing and then my mom would try. My dad, who would be outside the tent, would give advice until maybe the tent got a bit higher before it collapsed, then there would be some more swearing and then they would each have a beer, taking a break from trying to pitch the tent.

My parents would sit in our folding lawn chairs in the warm sun, drinking cold beer from the old aluminum ice chest. We girls would wander off together. Sometimes we would meet other kids or just watch the deer. The deer were so tame that we could feed them by hand. My mom had visited Big Basin when she was a little girl, and the deer had been very tame even then. The smell of the redwood forest and the noontime heat felt almost hypnotic and I was glad to be alive and able to go to such a beautiful park.

By the time we got back to the campsite either the umbrella pole which stayed on the inside of the tent would be up, or my parents would still be sparring over how to get it to stay up. Then we girls would go away for a while until they got it figured out. It was a whole lot of work to pitch that tent.

When my parents finally got the tent pole up, there were ropes to put through the outside rings on the tent, and stakes to pound into the ground to hold the tent up. Finally it was, "Wipe your feet, close the zipper, and don't touch the tent pole..." There was a tent flap that had two holes in it, and a rope would go through each hole, and we would tie the ropes around two trees. If there were no trees we pounded tall stakes into the ground and used those instead. That made a shady overhang that covered the tent opening. At night we would untie the flap and it would cover up the door of the tent.

When our tent was pitched we could go for a hike or take a nap or play cards or go to the visitor center or go to the creek. If the creek was warm and we put our feet in the mud we might get a leech on us. Leeches were creepy! Even though I was almost a teenager, if I got a leech on me I would run screaming to Daddy for him to take it off! Daddy called them "bloodsuckers." When he was a little boy in Kansas swimming in the creek, Daddy said the boys all swam naked and hated it when the bloodsuckers got on them, but that was part of swimming in a warm creek.

I will never forget the next morning. It was Sunday, and we were trying to sleep in. But the birds were loud, and there was something about sleeping on an air mattress and how the light came in through the pink tent that forced me to get up once I was awake. The campground dust made my nose stop up, so with sliding around on an air mattress and not being able to breathe, I just gave up trying to sleep in and got up.

Daddy was already up, and pretty soon we girls and my mom were up too. Daddy went to the park store to get the Sunday newspaper, and then Daddy came back, almost running back, with the Sunday paper. He threw the paper on the picnic table, and the big, big headlines were that the famous movie star, Marilyn Monroe, had died.

We could not believe it. Marilyn Monroe was beautiful and all the girls wanted to look like her, and how could she be dead, dead at age thirty-six?! She was the same age as Daddy; how could someone who was thirty-six just die like that? Our camping trip instantly deflated as we sat around the picnic table and read the newspaper out loud. We could feel that same somber feeling over the entire campground as other campers read the newspaper, with feelings of shock, perplexity, disbelief, and of disillusionment.

It might be hard to understand, but in those times there wasn't a bombardment of information the way there is today. Marilyn Monroe was the Blonde Bombshell. Period. One never had to sit down and think, "Uh, which one is Marilyn...." because there was a clarity about those whom we idolized: Willie Mayes, Marilyn Monroe, Lucy and Ricky, and the moment their name was said, a person knew exactly who that star was and what they were doing and why.

Marilyn Monroe was the name we had whispered since we were little. It was as if we knew and understood something about her, something forbidden and perhaps nasty, but forbidden and nasty in a way that little girls tried to figure out what exactly Marilyn did to make everyone want to be like her. Older girls wanted to copy her. Even if the older girls didn't understand it, they knew that women who looked and acted like Marilyn Monroe were movie stars who sang to presidents and were rich and very happy. Her sudden death was a tragedy.

In the weeks that followed Marilyn's death, there were rumors and speculation and many newspaper articles and magazine stories. Her death was a part of daily conversation. People were shocked and sorry that she had died. But then school started in September, and Marilyn Monroe's death was no longer a priority discussion among us new junior high students. We had other things to learn and other things to talk about. We didn't really understand that the death of Marilyn Monroe changed how women would view themselves, that when Marilyn died it was the end of the "Blonde Bombshell" role model. New role models were going to take Marilyn's place.

RAY LYMAN WILBUR
JUNIOR HIGH SCHOOL

PALO ALTO   CALIFORNIA

Dedication

The 1964-1965 Ray Lyman Wilbur Junior High School
Yearbook is dedicated to the spirit of the Wilbur Warrior
and to the ideals which that spirit represents. Among these
are character, loyalty, courage, strength, honor, dependa-
bility, and good citizenship. As we have done in past years,
let us endeavor in the future to keep this spirit alive and
meaningful.

The Yearbook Staff

Junior High

Our junior high school had seventh, eighth and ninth grades, and was named Ray Lyman Wilbur, "Wilbur" for short. Some years later the name was changed to Jane Lathrop Middle School. Junior high was a time of growing up and of the world changing very quickly in a very short time. I was no longer the best in anything, which was a big change for me because I had always been the smartest, the ugliest, the fastest runner, the best drawer, the tallest...there were a lot of "ests" in my life that were gone. And the reality of "the popular kids" vs. "everyone else" hit home as well. Initially I struggled to fit in, to copy, and to be like everyone else, but I had an epiphany a few months after seventh grade started.

I had worn my favorite jumper to school...a red corduroy jumper that Gramma Gigi had made for me, with a tight waist and full skirt. The corduroy wales were narrow and the jumper was the perfect shade of red. I wore a pink blouse with it, the only pink blouse I have ever owned. The fabric had pink and white squares on it that were so tiny you had to look closely to see that it was not solid pink, and there was lace at the collar. The jumper covered most of the blouse, and I really liked the way the two looked together.

It was lunch time, lunch in the cafetorium. No one who was popular brought their lunch from home. Students who brought their lunch from home were at the very, very bottom of the social pecking order. Bringing lunch from home meant that your mom must have packed it, and stood at the door and handed it to you because she didn't trust you with lunch money and making your own choices about what to eat. Or it meant that you didn't have lunch money at all. There were a few benches where the really unpopular kids ate their lunches from home; mostly boys who would laugh until milk came out their noses and who acted disgustingly.

Who you sat with at lunch indicated your social standing and if you were accepted or not. So I went, tray in hand, and sat down at the same table with all the popular kids...after all, Mary was in my home room because our last name's started with "R." Students were assigned to their home rooms by the beginning letter of their last names, so I thought that I kind of knew Mary. Well, there was absolute silence at the table the moment I sat there.   I had committed a great social indiscretion, and didn't know the rules. Mary looked at me disdainfully and in a loud, scornful voice said, "Red and pink! Who would ever wear red and pink together?!" Then she got up and left the table, and so did her whole crowd, leaving me at the table by myself.

I could feel everyone looking at me, so I got up, looked around the cafetorium, and saw a girl who was sitting by herself. I went over and sat down with her; she smiled, then I smiled, and then for some reason we started to laugh, and kids at some of the other tables started to laugh, almost like everyone was relieved. I decided from that point forward that I would wear whatever the hell I wanted and sit wherever I wanted with whomever I wanted and screw the popular kids!

From that day onward, I made it my mission to look around and see who was by themselves and to just walk up and sit with them, or walk with them, and to talk with them and find out about who they were. And I made a lot of interesting friends that way, meeting people every day. I would introduce my new friends to each other, and if someone was fat or lonely or unhappy it didn't matter, because I was listening to them and learning from them, and I think they learned from me too.

I met my friend Susan by just going up to her and introducing myself, and it turned out that she lived right down the street from me. Susan asked me over to spend the night one time, but we had a horrible overnight. Susan's mom knew that Susan hated tomatoes but served them up anyway, and then neither Susan nor I could leave the table until Susan ate the tomatoes. When her mom finally left the table, I whispered for Susan to give me the tomatoes, that I would eat them, but her mom came in and said that I was NOT to eat them, Susan had to eat them. We both fell asleep at the table and spent the night there, asleep in our chairs at the table. I never imagined in my entire life that someone would MAKE someone else eat an entire plate of food that they hated, plus punish the sleep-over friend at the same time, all the while smiling as if they were justified. And I never would have imagined a friend who would be so stubborn to make me suffer all night! She could have just sneaked the tomatoes to me! I was shaking my head in disbelief the entire next day…a very sleepy day.

Susan was adopted and was part Chinese or maybe Filipino, but her parents were white, and when Susan was about twelve her parents adopted a younger girl that was Chinese. Susan knew more about boys and sex than I did, so a lot of times we would hang out with boys at her house when her parents weren't home. We would listen to music and take cigarettes from her mom's dresser drawer, and boys would come over and we would hang out in the garage. We read movie magazines and smoked and Susan and I became good friends.

Seventh grade was different from elementary school because I took a yellow school bus to and from school. The bus stopped right down the street at the corner of Louis Road and Loma Verde. Walking to the bus stop in the morning felt like being on display, because there were always kids already at the bus stop who would watch as other students walked down the sidewalk. Everyone would stare at the next kid who walked up. Sometimes Sandy Jensen from next door and I would walk together, and that was less daunting. The Jensens still lived next door to us, the same family that had lived there since I was four or five years old. They had three girls too, but we were all different ages so we had never been in the same classrooms at Palo Verde Elementary School. But now in junior high, I became closer friends with Sandy, because riding the bus gave a person the chance to meet students in other grades.

I got off to a rather embarrassing start with the whole school-bus-riding experience, having tripped and fallen upwards on the bus steps during the first week of school. I was carrying a violin in its case, plus my books and I tripped going into the bus in the morning, skinning my knees and spilling my books down the bus aisle. Then one of the ninth grade boys sat next to me and tried to kiss me. All I could think about was Mr. Burns from sixth grade telling my class that he better not hear about us making out behind the bleachers! I turned my head away from that ninth-grade boy, but secretly I was flattered that he wanted to kiss me.

The bus was a microcosm of society, with the lonely bus driver responsible for safely driving the bus, as well as being the enforcer who had to tell students to sit down, to cut it out, or to move to a different seat. He was the person who established and maintained some form of sanity and order on the bus.

It usually was not possible. The older boys always wanted to sit next to girls and try to kiss them. It was hard deciding what was worse: having the boy next to you hassling you or not having any boy think you were worthy of being hassled and kissed. I would just look out the window and tell those boys to go away, because I still wasn't sure about that "having babies" thing. I didn't want to take any chances kissing boys. But sometimes a boy would kiss me anyway, right there on the bus! It was a different world, a world with loud and rowdy kids who didn't care what the adults thought and some kids who didn't even care if they got kicked off the bus for causing trouble.

Nylons

Nylons were sheer stockings that were held up with garter belts. Panty hose were not around when I started junior high, and girls either wore nylons and flats and tight skirts with kick pleats in the front, or they wore no nylons with really ugly saddle shoes or even the uglier white suede tie shoes that were called "bucks." Bucks came with a little powder puff bag to whiten the shoes at the end of each day.

My first year at junior high I was sent to school wearing white bucks. Christine had flats. Marie had flats. Everyone that I attended class with had flats and I didn't. And there were two kinds of nylons to wear with flats: mesh nylons or sheer nylons. Mesh nylons were made so that they would not tear or run; even if they got a hole in them, they would not run! One pair of mesh nylons would probably last a century. The threads were woven back and forth and across so that you could not even see through them and they made the person who was wearing them look like their legs were coated with old-lady pale-brown thick layers of unfashionable old-style stockings. Mesh nylons were what I was allowed to wear to church on Sunday. My skirt would stick to those stockings; they were so rough that the skirt material could not slide across them.

And then were the sheer nylons. Gloriously beautiful, sheer nylons! They were see-through and slippery and shiny, and so thin that they seemed weightless. The color that everyone wanted was the color called "cinnamon." Cinnamon nylons made legs look like they were really, really tan, and smooth and shiny, and they were so delicate and sheer that even a tiny hole would spread instantly up and down the nylon stocking, making a long hole called a "run." All sheer nylons ran really easily…not like mesh nylons, which you could actually cut with scissors and they would still not run. Sheer nylons were good for about one wear, and then they would get a run. When they ran, all the girls would put a drop of nail polish on the end of the run to stop it. Girls didn't care if they had a run in their sheer stocking, because it showed without a doubt that they were, in fact, actually wearing nylons!

About a block away from our house was a YWCA, the Ross Road YWCA. The YWCA stood for "Young Women's Christian Association," but people just called it the "Y." It was a building that had a gym in it and meeting rooms and was part of a global organization focused on social programs and providing women with leadership training and shelters from domestic violence. But we just thought about the "Y" as a fitness center.

If I decided to walk to school instead of taking the bus, I would go down Ames Avenue, turn on Ross Road, and walk right to the YWCA. So I started a life of two existences, at least as far as junior-high fashion was concerned: I would walk to school some days, just so that I could change my appearance at the "Y" on the way to school. I would leave my house wearing the clothes that were longer and less fashionable than I liked, but that my mom allowed me to wear. It was a good thing that really big purses were in style, because in my purse I could carry everything that I needed to change my looks! No one carried a back-pack in those days, as students had lockers at school and would carry home only the books they needed that night for homework, but girls did carry big purses.

When I got to the "Y" I would roll my skirt...girls would roll the waist band of their skirt to make their skirt shorter. I would then put on nylons...nylons I had bought at Bergman's

Department Store with either my allowance or with babysitting money I had earned. I would put on flats...the flats I was supposed to only wear at church but would put in my purse before I left for school. The pointier the toe of the flats, the better they were! I actually had a pair of red, very pointed-toe flats for church, so I would hide those in my bottomless purse and put them on at the "Y."

And there was makeup. I wasn't allowed to wear makeup, so when I was in the restroom at the "Y," I would put on very black eyeliner, very black mascara, blue or green eye shadow, skin-colored face-makeup from a bottle, face powder from a compact applied with a powder puff; rouge on the cheek bones, and lipstick by using a lip pencil and outlining my lips and then filling them in with lipstick from a tube. The fashionable lipstick was a very shiny, very pale, almost-white shade of pink.

Then my hair. We all wanted to "rat" our hair...to back-comb our hair and spray it thick with hairspray, and finish it off by combing our hair smooth over the whole thing. I would do my hair, ratting it up high and smoothing it down and finishing it off with hairspray and a little fabric bow in the front.

I would leave the "Y," walking to school, looking like the other girls, with my skirt shorter and my white bucks and anklet socks packed securely in my purse. At least I looked like I was in junior high! I would pass the golden-domed Russian Orthodox Church on Ross Road, the fire station at the corner of East Meadow and Middlefield, and walk on past Mitchell Park, the park where I had played as a child.

On the way home I did the whole thing in reverse: I combed out my hair, took off my makeup, unrolled my skirt, took off the nylons and the flats, and dressed how I had looked when I left the house.

I started smoking in seventh grade. A lot of the kids that were older smoked and I liked smoking too. I liked having a cigarette in my hand, and I loved to blow smoke rings. It was pretty easy to buy cigarettes even though the law was that a person had to be eighteen to smoke. Either the shops would sell cigarettes directly to kids, or someone's older brother or sister would sell them to us. So when I walked to school I would smoke a cigarette, or two or three. Of course, if I rode the bus, none of this was possible, so I planned to walk pretty often, and would only take the school bus if it was rainy or I didn't feel like walking. Some of the braver boys would light up cigarettes if they were sitting in the back of the bus, but then the bus driver had to stop and that made everyone late, so smoking on the bus was pretty rare.

Judy's friend, Sylvia, used to walk home from school sometimes too. If I saw Sylvia walking home I would walk really slowly because I didn't want her to see me. She was my sister's friend, and I was afraid she would tell on me, afraid that Sylvia would see me dressed up like the other kids and smoking and tell my sister. I knew that Judy would then either tell my mom or hold it over my head in the "I-am-your-sister-let-me-blackmail-you" way that seemed to be our sisterly default.

Of course the inevitable happened: My mother was waiting at the front door one day when I returned from my walk home…returned from changing back to the proper, conservative, boring and unhip clothes that I had worn when I left home that morning. It was purse inspection time, with my mom angrily dumping everything out of my purse onto the kitchen table and confronting me with it.

"Is this yours?!" about my makeup.

"Yes."

"How about this?!" about my cigarettes.

"Yes."

And this went on and on, until we got to the hairspray, which I honestly could say was my friend's, because I had borrowed it. You would have thought that I was a murderer, that there was no other criminal act ever committed in the history of the world that compared to my crime of trying to dress like all the other girls.

"The hairspray isn't mine," I said defiantly. And then my mother didn't say anything. She was at a loss for words, as if her handbook on raising children had skipped this chapter. When I was smaller and younger, it would have simply been, "Get me the wooden spoon," and I would have been spanked with the wooden spoon until she felt that her point had been made. But things had now changed; I had grabbed the spoon away from her. I was almost 5' 4" tall, which was taller than my mom, and I wasn't going to be hit any more. So when I defied her rules my mom didn't know what to do. Judy had not yet defied the rules, so this was a pivotal moment for a teenaged girl who was waiting for her mother to come up with a suitably unfair and unjust punishment, a punishment that certainly was beyond the scope of the crime and totally undeserved.

Well, my mother just looked at me, put all the stuff back in my purse, and walked away. That was it. Just walked away.

The next morning I left the house wearing flats, cinnamon-colored nylons, makeup, and with my hair styled the way that I wanted. I took the bus, not having to walk to the "Y" and change. "Does your mom know that you are wearing make-up?" one of my friends asked me. "I left the house like this," I said. It was a good feeling to sit on the bus with my friends, all of us wearing the style of clothes that we liked and the right make-up and hair style, and all to be sitting together.

I was mad at Sylvia though. I figured she had stopped by my house and told on me.

In seventh grade most of the music we listened to revolved around love and teenagers and high school and unfairness and at getting back at people. There was *Dead Man's Curve*, the sad car-accident song, *Last Kiss*, and *Tell Laura I Love Her*. Those songs put a lump in my throat when I listened to them because young love in all those songs had come to a tragic end. *Teen Angel* was SO SAD! It was about a girl who was out with her boyfriend and their car stalled on a railroad track. But after her boyfriend pulled her out of the car to safety, she ran back to the car, and a train hit the stalled car, killing her. The boy's high-school class ring was clutched tightly in her hand; the ring was the reason that she ran back. It was so romantic and so tragic, and in junior high, the thought of this type of young love was the model, the ideal of how sacrificial love should be.

I would listen to these love-tragedy songs, and in my mind I could see the story, the incredible sadness of people that were so much in love, of how one had died and the other was left to live the remainder of their long life in a fog of sorrow. Their entire life from that moment onward was a loveless and loyal existence, because their only true love was gone. I would feel the pain in the songs, and they really affected me.

And then Diana Ross and the Supremes sang, *Where Did Our Love Go?* Well, the words were similar to the sad songs, except when a person listened to Diana Ross, pretty soon that person would be walking with the beat, and it was impossible to be sad to a song by Diana Ross! There was *Baby Love*, *Back in his Arms Again*, and *Where Did our Love Go?* There were a lot of other songs about love, and making people love you, and not being able to live without the other person. But the Supremes' songs were perfect to dance to, and the sadness became secondary to the beat. I couldn't sit still and be sad while listening to those songs!

The song, *Judy's Turn to Cry*, told about Judy dancing with another girl's boyfriend, but at the end of the song the boyfriend goes back to her, so then it was Judy's turn to cry.

The Beach Boys sang about the little surfer girl, about the little old lady from Pasadena, and the Mamas and the Papas sang about *California Dreamin'*.

For Christmas in seventh grade I got a transistor radio! A transistor radio was so small that a person could carry it around and listen to music any time that they wanted to…well, any time that the radio would pick up a station. When a person traveled around town the radio stations would fade in and out. The radio had a dial that turned to find the stations, so when a station faded away it just meant turning the dial a little bit to find music again, as there were no digital readouts. When the music faded away there would just be scratchy sounds instead of music.

The coolest thing about my radio was that it had an ear plug! It had one end that plugged into a little hole in the radio, and the other end was an earpiece, and I could walk down the street holding the radio and listening to the music through my ear plug! My radio had a brown leather case, with little holes in front of the speaker so that I could still hear the music through the case. The case protected the radio.

One result that happened because of the transistor radio with the earplug was this: Before the radio with the earplug, people walking down the street had no excuse for not looking someone in the eye and saying, "Hi." And for teenagers this was not always comfortable. But now I didn't have to look a stranger in the eye, or a boy from another school, or someone that I didn't want to talk to. I had a transistor radio that everyone could see, and an earplug with a wire plugged into the transistor radio, so if I didn't look at someone or say, "Hi,"...well, that was okay, because the assumption was that listening to my music was taking all my attention. I now had an excuse. Socially it was now okay to ignore others in public, because the radio wasn't bothering anyone else, and people were polite to keep the music to themselves. It allowed and gave us permission to be less social and ignore others.

The first time I heard the song *Puff, the Magic Dragon* by the folksinger group Peter, Paul, and Mary, I was mesmerized. I stopped in my tracks and did nothing until the song was over. It was a really sad fairy tale sung straight into my heart. And every time it came on, it was still very, very sad. I couldn't believe that this song was actually on the radio. Peter, Paul, and Mary were starting to be on the radio frequently, singing folk songs. They also sang a song, *If I had a Hammer*, and suddenly everyone knew the words to that song and everyone wanted those bells of freedom to ring all over the land:

"If I had a hammer, I'd hammer in the morning
I'd hammer in the evening, all over this land
I'd hammer out danger, I'd hammer out a warning,
I'd hammer out love between my brothers and my sisters,
all over this land.

If I had a bell, I'd ring out danger, I'd ring out a warning
I'd ring out love between my brothers and my sisters,
all over this land.

If I had a song, I'd sing out danger, I'd sing out a warning
I'd sing out love between my brothers and my sisters,
all over this land.

Well I got a hammer, and I got a bell,
and I got a song to sing, all over this land.
It's the hammer of Justice; it's the bell of Freedom,
It's the song about Love between my brothers and my sisters, all
over this land.

It's the hammer of Justice; it's the bell of Freedom,
It's the song about Love between my brothers and my sisters,
all over this land."

My mom listened to radio station KNBR all day long, and the people on the radio were her window to the world. But if you were cool in Palo Alto, you listened to radio station KYA 1260 on the radio dial.

KYA was the leading "Top 40" music radio station in the Bay Area until KFRC switched to Top 40 music. Kids in junior high identified themselves by which radio station they listened to. Either it was KFRC, KYA, or KDIA, the soul station in the Bay Area. KDIA helped launch the career of the musicians Sly and the Family Stone. KYA had a disc jockey named "The Moose." After a while of listening to the same station it felt like I knew the disc jockey. And when KYA transferred The Moose to the night shift, he became "The Captain of the All-Night Flight on Super Freak 1260." His flight

took off at midnight and touched down at six o'clock in the morning, and along the way, The Moose invented a free-form FM-style before FM radio came along. My friends and I all would stick our transistor radios under our pillows at night and listen to this radio show. The Moose might decide he was sick of a certain song, and instead of following a script, he would change everything and maybe stop the record and bomb it with sound-and-voice effects.

Later, when the Vietnam War was on everyone's mind, The Moose would help rally people for protests, for civil rights, and free speech. He praised long hair and drugs and spoke up against war, and at night he played free-form rock 'n' roll.

Before Wilbur Jr. High was built, the land was owned by three farmers by the name of Diss; they sold the property to a man named Joseph Eichler. Joseph Eichler was an architect, and he donated the land for both Wilbur and for Fairmeadow Elementary School, which was next door to Wilbur. Eichler houses were all over Palo Alto by the time I was in junior high. The homes were known for their atriums, radiant heat, and open living spaces.

Our mascot at Wilbur was the Wilbur Warrior and our school colors were scarlet and gray. There were two other junior high schools in town: Jordan and Terman. The classrooms at Wilbur were considered state-of-the-art, with tri-level lighting, a sloped roof, a large number of windows, and long buildings called "wings." We had special classrooms for home economics (home ec.), language learning, music, wood shop, metal shop, band, choir, orchestra, drama, and art. The library was divided into two rooms: a reading room, and a room with tables and chairs for work. The cafetorium was a cafeteria/auditorium combination with an attached kitchen and it included a stage.

The gym had a girls' side and a boys' side, and each side had locker rooms indoors. There was a big locker for our street clothes, and we had a small locker to keep our gym clothes in during the week. It was just ours; we didn't have to share it with anyone. The gym had an equipment room, a wrestling room, a dance studio, a classroom, and offices for the teachers.

Before the school year started, a letter came to the house telling us about the required P.E. uniform. All girls had to wear the same uniform. The letter told us where to buy the uniform, and that all students had to put their name on the back of the uniform. The format for the name was that it had to be the first initial, then a period, then the last name. The only deviation would be if there were two students in the same P.E. class with the same last name and same first initial…then they had to write their first name. Well, not really write it. It had to be three inches tall and either embroidered in white thread or sewn on with white cloth letters. We were not supposed to just write our name on the back. Geeze.

The uniforms were so ugly that no one wanted to wear them. They were bright blue cotton one-piece uniforms, with short sleeves and metal snaps up the front, and shorts that ended mid-thigh. They had elastic all around the waist, so that the shorts looked like old-fashioned bloomers from the 1920s! And every new seventh-grader stood out on the field as a novice in her bright blue, spanking new P.E. uniform, especially with her name so carefully embroidered on the back.

All the eighth graders removed the elastic from their uniforms, so they hung in a baggy, saggy style. The uniforms had to be taken home every Friday and washed, and the teachers checked on Monday to make sure each student came to class with a clean uniform. If not, the teacher marked it down in her book as a demerit and the guilty student had to do extra exercise as a punishment. But after nine months of weekly washing, the bright-blue uniforms faded to a much milder color and the cloth lost its crispness. Embroidery began to fray and come off, so the eighth graders often had only half a name on their back. The ninth graders' uniforms were worn thin and faded to a lighter blue, and their names might not even be on the back of their uniform any more.

If you had an older sister who had the same first initial and last name – well, you had it "made in the shade" because you started P.E. in a worn-out uniform instead of a stiff, crisp and bright blue uniform. My older sister, Judy, didn't participate in P.E. because of her kidney problems, so I had started seventh grade in the bright-blue uniform. But at least my younger sister, Jennifer, inherited a well-used uniform when she started Wilbur!

In elementary school our physical education had been a lot of fun. There had not been many highly-organized feats to accomplish or learn...we ran around the field and played informal games or the teacher would organize dodge ball or steal the bacon. Mostly we ran and played and had a good time.

Our P.E. Uniform — The Girl's Track & Field Team

In junior high all of that changed. We had to go to the locker room, and then change. There was no privacy, and most of us were not used to undressing down to our underwear in front of strangers. What was worse, there were some of the girls who should have worn bras but their parents didn't allow them to, and so when they undressed everyone was embarrassed. Girls would rush to the gym and change quickly, putting street clothes into lockers and then hurrying into the gym.

The gym teacher took role by yelling our last name and we had to yell back "PRESENT!" If we didn't yell "present" then we got marked absent. The other embarrassing thing was that if we were on our period we had to add "MP!" after we yelled "present." The teacher would mark it in her book and that would get us excused from running around the field or from doing this horrible exercise called "burpees." Burpees meant you stood straight, then leaned over and touched the floor, kicked out your feet behind you, went flat to the floor, did a push-up, then stood up and clapped, then started it all over again. Most of the girls in seventh grade had not yet started their periods, and it was embarrassing to yell "MP," because everyone looked at whoever yelled it.

There was a variety of sports that we were required to practice, including field hockey, which I hated. Girls were always hitting other girls in the shins with the hockey sticks, and we had to learn the rules and take written tests about it. The same happened with golf and softball; there were lots of rules to learn and written tests, based on how well we had learned the rules. All the fun was taken out of P.E. because we had tests and rules to learn instead of just having a good time and getting rid of our energy and playing together.

Wilbur had a swimming pool – the same pool where I had taken swimming lessons as a kid and had hated those lessons! Now that I was in junior high, synchronized swimming was offered in P.E., and I had a lot of fun in that class.

No matter what sport we took, at the end of the P.E. class we had to take a shower. The gym teacher sat on the top of the stall by the showers and marked in her grade book that students had taken a shower. If our shoulders were not wet enough the teacher would say we hadn't taken a shower and the teacher would send us back again to wash. We used the gym towels to dry off after our showers, and the towels were about as big as a wash cloth and really scratchy.

We had less than ten minutes to shower, dress, and arrive at our next class. We had to hurry and put on our street clothes, lock up our P.E. uniform and shoes, and rush! On Friday the teacher made sure we took our uniform home to be washed. She actually stood by the exit door and marked in her grade book that the uniform was in our hands before she would let us leave P.E.

Wilbur had a snack bar and snack machines, which was completely different than Palo Verde! At Wilbur's brunch sliced sourdough French bread, dripping with real butter, was sold for a dime a slice. It was so groovy that we had a twenty-minute brunch time in the middle of the morning!

If a junior high student was on the honor roll, then that student would be expected to be one of the hall monitors, a member of the "Scarlet Guard."

The honor roll qualifications were that a student had a high grade-point average, usually a 3.80 or higher, and no discipline problems or trouble at school. A student who was a hall monitor got to leave class five minutes early and wore a special vest and was responsible to monitor the area of the hallways to which they were assigned.

I became a member of the Scarlet Guard. I was assigned to watch a specific hallway and corridor during the five-minute break between classes. This meant that if someone was running in the corridor because they were late or for any other reason, I was supposed to write them a ticket and they would be assigned detention as the consequence. I also was supposed to keep my eyes on the row of lockers, because sometimes students had their lockers broken into or vandalized.

At first I really liked being a monitor. But it became more difficult because these were my friends, and if they didn't run they would be late to class. Sometimes a student's class was on the other side of the campus and it was impossible to get there on time without running. My internal conflict grew.

So I just quit giving out tickets. After a week or two the teacher who sponsored the Scarlet Guard called me into his office to ask why I hadn't been giving out tickets. He didn't think that students had changed their behavior, and he suspected that I wasn't doing my job. I told him with all my heart and soul that I didn't feel right giving other students tickets and making them go to detention when they were just trying to get to class on time. I poured out my heart to him, passionately promising that I would give a student a ticket if they were shoving or yelling or being disruptive, but that I believed that getting to class on time shouldn't be a reason to give someone a ticket and detention. I was sure my intensity and conviction would sway him, that he would understand the moral dilemma that I was caught in. I wasn't going to punish people because their schedule placed them on opposite sides of the campus and made it almost impossible to get to class on time without running.

Well, the teacher did not agree with me. He told me that to be a monitor I had to conform to what the rest of the monitors did. I couldn't make exceptions, because then students would not know what to expect or what the rules really were. Everyone had to be uniform in the way tickets were issued or there would be anarchy on the campus between classes. If one monitor gave out a ticket and the next monitor didn't, but the situation was the same, then the lack of consistent discipline would cause anarchy.

Anarchy? Anarchy because one monitor didn't give out tickets for running in the corridor?! I had the power to create ANARCHY in my junior high because I wasn't giving out tickets to people who ran? What power I had! I'd had no idea up to that point that being an honor student and consciously rationalizing the difference between purposeful disobedience and disrespect vs. circumstances beyond one's control would be so complicated and would allow me the opportunity to cause anarchy in my junior high!

The teacher explained that otherwise all students would start running. Unless there was some kind of punishment to keep the rules enforced, students would become anarchists and we would be debased to a school that was out-of-control. Well. I didn't agree. I believed that people would only run if they were late. Students wouldn't run just because there was no punishment for running...that made no sense to me!

Several weeks later I completely changed my monitoring style. My duties had taken on a mission, a purpose, a test for me as one small student in the gears, the cogs, the machinery that comprised the rules that enabled things to be as they always had been and as they always would be. When it was almost time for the tardy bell to ring, I started yelling at the students: "The bell is going to ring...you better run!" I yelled, "Hurry up! Run! You are going to be late! Hurry!"

The Scarlet Guard sponsor was standing right behind me one day. He had decided to check on me, since I still wasn't issuing tickets. And I was marched off to his office and then my vest, whistle, and ticket book were taken away. I was told that not only was I banned from being a hall monitor, but that I couldn't go on the end-of-the-year honor roll and hall monitor picnic, which was an event where qualifying students spent an entire day away from school at the Santa Cruz Beach Boardwalk.

It all turned out for the best, because I really hadn't been looking forward to the day at the Boardwalk anyway.

Going Steady

"Who Are You Going With?" I was starting to have a lot of boyfriends. Having a boyfriend in junior high meant that the boy asked the girl to go steady, and if she accepted, then the girl was "going with" the boy. It was more a public display of togetherness than it was a relationship. It meant that the couple was seen together. The boy would walk the girl home and carry her books; they would hold hands and talk, sometimes whispering. After the couple was used to walking home holding hands, they would start walking home with their arms around each other's waist or shoulders. At school they would sit together at lunch and spend as much time with each other as their schedules permitted. I worried that I would have sweaty hands or I would smell bad or the boy and I would walk with conflicting rhythms. With some boys it was easy to walk the same-sized steps and be synchronized, and with other boys I could never find the right rhythm.

Everyone at school had a locker, and therefore the only things that we brought home with us at the end of the day were our binders and the book or two that we needed that night. Usually we carried home only one or two books and some worksheets. Teachers would mimeograph worksheets instead of giving us new workbooks to use. Worksheets were easier for a teacher to quickly correct than if each student did their work on a separate piece of paper, and duplicating pages was cheaper than buying new workbooks for each student.

Mimeographing was one processes utilized to duplicate papers before there were copy machines at schools. When I had been in elementary school it had been amazing and fun to watch how the teachers made the master for creating the mimeographs, but now that I was older it was no longer interesting. The school also used ditto machines to make copies... all the kids loved to put the freshly-dittoed papers up to their noses and inhale the aroma!

Even though the boy that I was going steady with would carry my books, the few books and worksheets were still light enough that he could carry his books and my books and have his arm around me or we could hold hands. We were not old enough to go anywhere or do anything on our own, and most kids' parents had forbidden them to go steady, so it made going steady all the more attractive. My parents had forbidden me to go steady, but how were they to know or find out? Unless Judy or one of her friends told on me, my parents wouldn't even know that I was going with a boy.

I went steady with a bunch of different boys: Mike MacDonald, who had two different colored eyes, one blue and one green and who was on the football team; a boy named Greg who was in the eighth grade when I was in the seventh grade and Bobby Lloyd, who I ran and ran with in elementary school. Kissing was a new experiment with all these boys, as we would kiss awkwardly, afraid that our noses would bang together. But we liked everyone to see that we were "steadies" and that we were going together.

The boy always gave the girl a Saint Christopher medal when they were going steady. I don't know exactly why, except that Saint Christopher was supposed to protect people. So when other girls would see me with a Saint Christopher medal, they would crowd around and ask who I was going steady with....girls frequently checked to see who was going steady. I would do the same with my friends; we kept track of who was "going" with whom, just because it was important to know! But when I was walking home and got near to my house, I would always tuck the Saint Christopher medal inside my blouse so my parents wouldn't see it.

Usually after a few weeks of going steady, couples would break up and then start going steady with someone else. That way nothing REALLY serious could happen.

The summer between seventh and eighth grade I took tennis lessons at Wilbur Jr. High. There were a lot of students, mostly girls, taking the lessons. We thought that our teacher was really cute, and I didn't care if I learned to play tennis or not. Tennis was hard and as I was really uncoordinated, I had no hope or expectation of excelling in the sport. It was just fun when the young and handsome tennis teacher stood behind me and held my arm and then held my other arm to show me how to hit the ball. And the worse a player was, well, then, the teacher spent more time with that player, so who would want to get any better anyway?

There was another girl named Jane in my summer tennis class. Jane lived right by the railroad tracks. After tennis there were three of us who would walk over to the other Jane's house.... three of us who were in tennis lessons together and were madly infatuated with our tennis teacher. We would walk to the other Jane's house in our new Keds tennis shoes, our tight short shorts and our white sleeveless blouses.

At the other Jane's house, no parents were at home and it was a lot like being at my friend Abby's house. No parents, an older sister, a whole lot of boys, loud music...but at this house there was a lot of cigarette smoking, a lot of beer drinking, and sometimes there were people getting high on pot.

Getting high on pot. This was new. This meant people rolling joints, which was what we called the marijuana cigarettes, and smoking pot, which was what we called marijuana. We were not sure if it was legal or not...but everyone smoked cigarettes, including me, and smoking pot was just a really smooth transition. I didn't like it all that much because it always made me hungry and I felt like my allergies were ten times worse when I smoked pot than when I didn't, but it made me laugh and the world seemed funnier when we sat around and smoked pot. It was just something that people did when they became friends and there was really nothing wrong with it.

Adults could drink and party and have fun, but kids were not allowed to drink...besides, when we did drink, most of the time we just threw up until we were exhausted. Smoking pot never made any one throw up. The grown-ups were hypocritical: They could smoke cigarettes and drink alcohol and it was okay, but lawmakers put an age limit on a piece of paper, arbitrating a numeric age barrier between legal and illegal. It was as if turning one day older would cause a person to be responsible and deserving because of their age! Well that made no sense to me. It was nonsense, especially when it was all these old people making the laws. It didn't seem like a democracy when there was an age limit on participation.

Of course those old people would side with the rest of the old people...they didn't care if younger people had the same rights as adults.

The laws kept teenagers and young adults powerless. Eighteen-year old boys could be required to go to war and kill or get killed, but could not get married without their parents' permission. And a person could not drink legally until they were twenty one, so smoking pot made as much sense as any of the other laws. The adults would not listen because they were too old to understand anyway.

I met some boys at Jane's house that summer, and went steady with some of them. It was fun hanging out, listening to music, laughing and joking around. But in all of it there was an undercurrent of discontent, a feeling that I was not really getting it, that there was something bigger in life. Drinking and getting high with my friends was fun. Messing around with the boys was fun and kissing felt good. I had found out that my nose didn't get smashed when I kissed. I had been afraid that I would squash my nose into the other person, but now I knew better.

The look to have in 1963

I enjoyed the laughing and fun that resulted from smoking pot and drinking, but I thought that there had to be something else in life waiting for me. And it was not my tennis teacher or those boys, many of whom were just trying to get their hands inside my bra or inside my panties...there had to be something else that was more important in life.

Some more '60s ads from American Girl Magazine.

A girl's best friend is Betty Crocker Mix!

Babysitting

I was doing a lot of babysitting. There were many young parents in our neighborhood and also young parents who attended the Congregational Church, and all it took was one of those parents telling their friends that I was a good babysitter, and soon I had as many babysitting jobs as I wanted.

Most of the time it was fun to babysit. The parents would be in good moods because they were going to the movies or out to dinner or perhaps to a lecture at Stanford or even up to the City to meet friends. The little kids always liked me and I enjoyed playing with and feeding them, then helping them get ready for bed. Once they were asleep I would watch TV or talk on the phone with my friends. But I had to be careful talking on the phone, because in those days there was no call-waiting or answering machines; if a parent needed to call me they might be calling from a phone booth and they would not appreciate it if they got a busy signal when they called their home. And if they were at their friend's house they wouldn't want to have to keep asking if they could use the friend's phone to call me – it would look like they had an irresponsible babysitter.

There used to be phone booths at every gas station, outside of every store, phone booths at street corners and at schools. To use the phone from a booth, a person just had to put in a coin and the phone would return change if needed. A person needing help with anything just had to dial the "O" for "Operator" and an operator (usually a woman) would come on the line and help with whatever was needed. An operator would help a caller make a collect call if the person needed to call someone but didn't have any money. The operator dialed the number and asked the person who answered if they would accept the charges and if they said, "Yes," then the call went through. The charge would later show up on the phone bill of the person who had accepted the collect call.

When I was babysitting I didn't usually talk on the phone after ten o'clock at night, because that would be when the parents might call to say that they would be late. When the parents were late it was both good and bad; I would get paid time-and-a-half for when they were late, but it also was hard to stay up and not fall asleep.

When I was at Wilbur the going rate for babysitting was fifty cents an hour. A good night would be when I started at five o'clock and the parents said they would be home at eleven o'clock, but didn't get home until midnight. Then I would earn at least four dollars for that one night.

I loved babysitting for one family that had three little boys. They lived near Wilbur and I would walk with them to Mitchell Park and play in the sand and on the swings with them. When they were really tired I would take them back to their house, feed them dinner, give them their baths, read to them, and put them to bed. It was hard in the summer because it was light until around nine-thirty at night and the kids wanted to stay up until it was dark. But I wouldn't let them, because that was what their parents trusted me to do. Besides, I always had a nagging fear that one of the parents might get sick or they might not like the show they were attending and therefore they would come home early. And if they did, I wanted to be sure I was doing what the parents had requested.

Even if kids were bratty sometimes or were testing me by ganging up on me, I always seemed to win them over and have a good time and they liked having me babysit.

One thing that I really liked about babysitting was seeing what other people ate. I babysat for people from Germany, Japan, the mid-west, New Zealand and England, and everyone had different kinds of foods. They had different kinds of books, furniture, and even dishes. I read *Who's Afraid of Virginia Woolf* at one of the houses; some of the houses had *Playboy* magazines and one house had magazines about questioning authority and practicing vegetarianism. My Auntie Jan had *Playboy*, and I had always been curious about it. Auntie Jan was my mom's only sister and she was seven years younger than my mom; my mom had no brothers. Auntie Jan was my only aunt in California. Daddy's brother, my Uncle Jack, was married to my Aunt Bernie, but as they lived in Kansas, we seldom visited them.

When I was babysitting and saw *Playboy*, I overwhelmingly wanted to read it. *Playboy* had photos of naked ladies in it and a lot of interesting articles and also cartoons of naked people. Some of it was embarrassing, but I still wanted to see what it was all about. Most of the articles were boring, but I didn't believe that people looked at *Playboy* for the articles.

One of the best things about babysitting was that after the kids had gone to sleep I could watch whatever TV show I wanted to watch. There were only four channels that the TVs in Palo Alto received, so there weren't a lot of choices. However, I liked being able to decide what I was going to watch, even if I would have been watching the same program at home. Of course, there was no such thing as a remote control and the TV pictures were black and white, but we loved TV. At midnight the TV stations would play the national anthem, show the American flag waving in the breeze, and a voice would announce that the TV station was signing off the air. TV was not broadcast around the clock. After midnight it was hard to stay awake, without a TV show to watch.

One night when I was babysitting, my friends kept calling me because the band, the Rolling Stones, was going to be on TV that night! The Rolling Stones were from England and their lead singer was Mick Jagger. All of us girls had opinions as to whether he was cute or not. I thought he was kind of ugly and skinny, but he sure could dance! I turned on the TV that night and I got to watch the Rolling Stones sing, *Satisfaction*, and when I went back to school on Monday everyone was talking about the Rolling Stones and what they thought about that song and what it might really mean.

Many times I was near enough to my house to walk home after babysitting. I didn't like getting a ride home with the father after babysitting because a lot of times the father had been out to eat and had been drinking and he would be really stupid and ask me questions like, "Do you have a boyfriend," or "Do you think I am attractive?" I would just say nothing and get out of the car as fast as I could. I don't think those married men remembered being so jerky because the next time I would see the husband who had asked me those questions, he would act like everything was normal.

The one family I disliked babysitting for lived right across the street from my house. This family had two babies; one was tiny and slept most of the time. The other one was two-years-old and the minute his parents left he would cry. But before his parents left the mom would lecture me. She would talk really slow like I was stupid, and each time she would tell me the same things: Where the little boy's diapers were, what to feed him, how to open the high chair, where his clothes were, where the list of emergency numbers were – EVERY TIME! As I lived across the street, I figured in an emergency I could go home or go the Jensen's. I didn't need the tutorial each time!

When the mom finally was done talking and she and her husband left, the two-year old would cry and run around screaming. He would do that for hours, screaming and crying and running, through the house for hours without stopping. He would only stop if he made a mess in his diaper. Diapers were made from cloth and I would have to rinse the diaper in the toilet and then put the dirty diaper in a diaper pail. I had to hold this struggling little boy down to put on a clean cloth diaper, and the cloth diaper had to be safety-pinned on.

Safety-pinning a diaper is tricky and if the child is squirmy, it is easy to poke them with the pin. If I accidentally poked a baby with a pin, they would cry and I would pick them up to cuddle them; either the diaper would fall off and I had to start all over again or maybe the baby might pee while I was holding it! If I didn't get the diaper on tight enough, it fell off, and if the diaper was too tight…well, the baby screamed about that! Plastic pants had to go over the diaper. Without plastic pants, the cloth diapers would leak everywhere, and even with plastic pants the diapers would still leak. If I babysat a girl, then I folded a separate diaper inside the other diaper to pad the back. For a boy, the extra diaper padded the front of the diaper.

Watching infants and toddlers was a lot of work, and included putting on their bibs and feeding them. Some of them, especially the wild boy across the street, just wanted to shake their head while spitting out food! I would put the little boy in his high chair to feed him, and he would just spit out everything and make a big mess. But if I didn't attempt to feed him the parents would think their child had been neglected and left hungry all night.

Baby bottles were made from glass and the bottle's nipples were made from rubber, and babies drank "formula." Baby formula was made by mixing milk and corn syrup together and then heating the mixture in a pan on the stove to just the right temperature. The temperature was correct when a person sprinkled a drop of formula on their wrist and they could not feel it because it was the same temperature as their body. Most of the families would leave formula in their fridge so that it only had to be heated in a pan of water on top of the stove, but if they forgot to leave formula, I would have to make it.

Some nights the people across the street were two or three hours late. I suspected they were glad to get away from their little boy. There were some nights when that loud little boy never did go to sleep. As his babysitter, it was really hard to be nice to him when all he did was cry and scream, cry and scream, cry and scream.

Frequent babysitting meant that were some months I earned thirty dollars!

One night when I was babysitting, Judy was taken to the hospital. She was paralyzed. During her stay at Stanford Hospital the doctors could not figure what caused her sudden paralysis. I thought Judy was going to die; when she was little the doctors didn't expect her to live and she still took daily medication for her health problems, but it was a mystery why she was unable to walk.

When Judy came home from the hospital she was better, but she finished the remainder of the school year studying at home with a tutor that the school district provided.

Smoking

Wilbur Jr. High had an open campus. Open campus meant that students could leave and return to campus when they wanted to. If students were smoking cigarettes on the Mitchell Park side of the path between Wilbur and Mitchell Park, the school administrators would not do anything about it. Not many seventh graders smoked, but the students in all three grades who were smokers would hang out together on the Mitchell Park side of the path.

This was the time for the smokers to socialize. What was neat was that everyone, no matter what grade, all got along if they had smoking in common. Most of the students who smoked were really clean cut; the boys had short hair and wore button-down plaid shirts with slacks. The girls wore their knee-length A-line skirts with cinnamon-colored nylons and pointy flats, their hair coiffed and hair-sprayed with a little bow centered in their hair over their forehead. But there were the beginning of undercurrents of social unrest. Kids were not legally old enough to smoke, but it was a battle that the school administrators fought only on campus... and the side of the path that was on campus.

Many kids smoked because smoking was very popular and common with adults. There was no such thing as public "smoke-free" areas. If people were not smokers themselves, they still would have ash trays in their homes for smokers. Most shops, stores, and restaurants gave away match books to anyone who wanted them; they were inexpensive and useful advertising.

Busting students for smoking at the park wasn't a battle that seemed worthwhile to the school administrators. Teachers and administrators tolerated students' smoking as long as students followed the conventions that had been set during the previous years: Smoke on the side of the path that was not school property, put out the cigarette if someone in charge headed their way, and don't litter.

On campus, I would smoke in the restrooms while school was in session. The restrooms had tall ceilings and even if it was really hot outside, the bathrooms were still cool and full of echoes. There would always be some girls inside the bathrooms smoking.

Wilbur's vice principal was in charge of discipline, but every morning he would just ride his bike past the smokers at Mitchell Park. Many of the teachers lived near Wilbur, and just as Mr. Burns at Palo Verde had ridden his bike to school, Wilbur's vice principal rode his bike to school, too. Before the school day started, and there were no students on school grounds, the vice principal would just say, "Good morning," and keep on riding his bike. He didn't make a big deal out of what students were doing when it came to smoking near school. We knew if we stood on the side of the path that was Mitchell Park that our vice principal would not do anything.

But students on the Wilbur side of the path would get suspended for smoking - no question about it. It seemed really stupid to me that a few feet would make such a difference, and that the existence of rules was more important than if the rules made any sense.

I knew former high-school kids that had graduated, and as soon as they had that diploma in their hand they had to go to fight in the Vietnam War as part of the draft. They were age eighteen, but they could not vote until they were twenty-one. A person could be a soldier, be married, have kids, but still not be old enough to vote! We were starting to feel a fear about the war and disbelief that some of our other friends might go off to Vietnam and never return alive, and many of us were beginning to question the rules relating to age and legality.

"The Big Bust on the Hill"

The Palo Alto Police Department had a program called "Narcs on Bikes" which was a program they piloted to try to catch students who were smoking pot, but they were happy to bust cigarette-smokers as well. The Big Bust rounded up Mitchell Park pot smokers after school one afternoon. I think there were about twenty students taken to juvenile hall who had that infraction on their permanent record. The threat of, "It will be on your permanent record" was one that had hung over our heads since day one, and now students were being rounded up in force because of a non-violent "crime" they were committing. As if a herd of stoned teenagers was somehow a threat to the town of Palo Alto.

Okay, so remember the boundary? Wilbur, the path, and Mitchell Park? One lunch period two eighth-graders climbed up a tree to have their lunchtime smoke. The tree was actually on the Wilbur campus, but climbing a tree and sitting in it to have a smoke was a routine experience. Unfortunately, girls were denied this experience because we were not allowed to wear pants or shorts to school, and there was no way we could have climbed in our skirts, flats and nylons. But we could certainly cheer the boys on and appreciate that the male gender could climb trees and smoke at the same time. A P.E. coach from

Wilbur saw those two boys smoking in the tree, ran to the tree and yanked both the boys down from the tree by grabbing their feet until they crashed to the ground!

The students on the Mitchell Park side saw this happen and started shouting, "Teacher brutality!" The coach began marching the two offenders to the office, and he challenged the crowd to come with him. The students who had been smoking on the other side of the path began following, building up a crowd on the way to the office. By the time the crowd arrived at the administration offices, there were at least fifty students milling around shouting, "Brutality...Brutality!" The offending students were ushered into the principal's office and the door was shut. Then an unplanned "sit-in" happened right in front of the administrative offices.

The sit-in...it was a new, non-violent method to try to force change to happen. If there were a lot of people just sitting in a doorway, or sitting in an office, or sitting in a corridor...well, one person by themselves might not make a change, but when there were twenty or thirty or hundreds of people all blocking the same path, or sitting in the same space, it became a sit-in and in the numbers there was power!

By the time the principal came out of his office the tardy bell had rung. Nobody was moving from the protest against brutality. The student-group demanded to the principal that the two students suffer no suspension. Finally the vice principal came out and said that he wanted to talk, so the whole group walked over to the bleachers to talk. He acknowledged that the manner in which the kids were yanked out of the tree was inappropriate and stated that the two boys would not be punished. He also said that if the sit-in group just returned to class, no one in the group would be in trouble.

We knew the students shouldn't have been smoking on Wilbur property but we also knew that the coach didn't have a right to manhandle students. This was a beginning lesson in non-violent problem-solving and in compromise. It was a step in my journey of non-violent hope and dreams for peaceful change that was to stay with me throughout my life.

Faculty

MRS. MARTHA A. ACEVEDO
Science
MR. NORMAN AIROLDI
Physical Education
MR. HOMER E. ALLISON
Soc. Studies, Reading
MR. ANDREW BALDWIN
Science

MR. CLAUDE A. BARLOW
Science
MISS BOBBIE D. BERRY
Soc. Studies, English
MR. JOHN M. BIGELOW
Soc. Studies, English
MR. FRANKLIN B. BROWN
Curr. Assoc., English

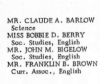

MISS ROSALIA BRUSATI
English, P.E.
MR. DON CAVENDER
Physical Education
MR. THOMAS P. CHAMBERLAIN
Industrial Arts
MR. THOMAS C. CHAPMAN
Soc. Studies, English, Spanish

MRS. PAT G. CHERRINGTON
Soc. Studies, English, Math
MRS. LAURAINE COEN
Music, Science
MISS HARRIET COULSON
Physical Education
MISS GLORIA L. DALENEY
Foreign Language

MR. JOHN J. DALTON
Curr. Assoc., Soc. Studies, English
MRS. ZELDA DAWSON
Soc. Studies, English
MR. MICHAEL DONOVAN
Science
MISS MARJORY DOYLE
Home Economics, Soc. Studies

MRS. ANNE R. DREYFUSS
Science
MRS. SANDRA L. EPSTEIN
Mathematics
MRS. GRETCHEN FANSLOW
Soc. Studies, English
MRS. ULDENA S. FORBUSH
English

4

48

Teacher Shock

I had several teachers in junior high that had life-long impacts on me. One was Mrs. Young; she was short and thin and looked ancient, and her hair must have been set in pin curls every night, because she had a hair-style of many small, tight curls all around her head. I had her for seventh-grade homeroom and for English. Mrs. Young was an expert at making nervous wrecks out of students. I think she shattered at least two yard sticks a week on students' desk.

The class would be absolutely silent. Students would be busily doing their assignments or pretending to do their assignments, no one looking at each other or at her and Mrs. Young would sneak up behind a student and…WHACK! She would slam the wooden yard stick down on their desk so hard that it would break and possibly shatter into many splinters. She did that throughout each class. No one wanted to be called on by her or to look her in the eye. I hated the classes that she taught because she was scary and liked to victimize her students.

For English we were studying Shakespeare and reading aloud the play, *Romeo and Juliet.* Students had to pretend to be one of the characters from *Romeo and Juliet.* Nothing could have been more uncool, more boring, more horrible than to stand up in class and read Shakespeare out loud. The language was difficult to understand and many of the words made no sense. We didn't discuss the words or what they meant; we were just reading it because we were required to. Shakespeare had nothing to do with our lives and was from a long, long time ago. Plus, if Mrs. Young thought that we should read him, well, that pretty much put the final judgment on it, because we all knew that she was crazy. We didn't want to have anything to do with what Mrs. Young thought was good literature.

At that time teenagers in the Bay Area were either "surfers" or "greasers." The greasers were the members of the car clubs who wore black Levis, white T-shirts, black leather jackets and black boots. The car club at the high school was called the "Executors," and its members had cool cars and were the bad boys. Even though we were just in junior high, we all knew about those boys and many of our boyfriends were copying them.

The greasers wore their hair long in the front, sometimes in a "jelly roll," with a lot of hair grease and their hair slicked back except for a long curl that went down their forehead. That was one reason why they were "greasers." They were also called greasers because they liked to work on cars. The greaser girls ratted their hair up in a "beehive" style – tall and smooth on the sides held in place with a whole lot of hair spray and they wore lots of make-up, heavy black eye-liner and black boots. Many of the greasers would hang out at the Fremont Drag Strip on the weekend; that was a drag strip about ten miles from the town of Palo Alto where all types of people would make friends and watch stock car races, drag races and demolition derbys. Drag racing was cool, fast cars were cool, cars that were raised or lowered were cool. Cars were just cool!

Surfers had blonde hair, even if they had to bleach it. Surfers went surfing, hung out at the beach, and listened to surf music. The Santa Cruz Beach and Aptos and New Brighton Beach were places where the surfers hung out. It turns out that the Mavericks Beach near Half Moon Bay along the San Mateo coastline is one of the best places in the world for surfing, but most of my school friends that were surfers couldn't really surf. The waters along the northern California beaches are very cold, the undertows are strong, and a wetsuit and lots of practice are required! But the look was cool!

I tried surfing a few times when I was in junior high, but it was really hard to do, very cold, and I got so disoriented that I was swimming like mad to the surface of the water, but I smashed into the sand at the bottom because I had become very confused in the crashing waves. With a mouth full of sand and lungs depleted of air, sandy scratches all over my body and freezing cold, I decided being a real surfer girl and learning to surf was just not what I was cut out for.

If a person was a surfer, the best car to have was a "Woodie," a station wagon with polished wood paneling on each side. The back window of the station wagon rolled down, so surf boards could not only go on the top of the car, they could go inside the car with the back seat folded down. Surfer guys wore faded plaid shorts made from madras cloth from India, sandals, and T-shirts that were not tucked in. Surfer girls were tan, had straight blonde hair, and hung out with the surfer boys. Surfer girls did not wear beehive hairdos... they had tan legs and arms and wore short dresses to show off their tans. Their relaxed attitude could be a part of what led us all into the hippy and sexual revolution – their feeling that life was a beach and there was more to it than cars and grades and homework and seeing who went steady and who smoked cigarettes.

In Mrs. Young's English class there was one student that was pretty large. He was big and tall, his name was Doug, and he was a greaser. One day, Mrs. Young called on Doug to read part of a scene of *Romeo and Juliet* out loud. Doug was reading and got to a part where there was a line about a hassock. Most people might not say hassock or ottoman, they might just say footstool, but the play said "hassock." Doug stumbled over the word, and ended up saying "hah sock." Mrs. Young became furious, and was yelling at Doug, "Hass-ock, Hass-ock." Doug looked at her and said it again the wrong way. Really loud. On purpose. And then, standing next to his desk he folded his arms and said it again the wrong way. I put my head on my desk and hid my eyes under my folded arms. I didn't want to see what was going to happen. Doug was twice as big as Mrs. Young, and he was challenging her in the same way that she challenged her students. Doug was acting as if he might be able to bully the expert bully, Mrs. Young.

Mrs. Young walked over to Doug's desk and with one blow sent a yardstick shattering into about a hundred splinters. No one dared to even breathe or to move or to look anywhere but straight ahead. Mrs. Young sent Doug to the office, and he was kicked out of our class. The remaining students in Mrs. Young's class were even more nervous than before, hiding our eyes with our heads buried in our arms as we huddled over our desks trying to become invisible.

Mr. Chapman was the opposite of Mrs. Young. I had Mr. Chapman for Spanish and history in eighth grade and he was wonderful. On the first day of school he looked like an old man who wore old-fashioned clothes, with thinning hair and thick glasses, but in a very short time I think all of his students respected and felt great affection for him, and we looked at him fondly. He made us think, treated us respectfully, had a sense of humor, and challenged us. Mr. Chapman inspired his students and motivated us by giving us the tools to succeed.

Mr. Chapman assigned a year-long project for us to research our family tree, and for many, including me, this became a project that lasted much longer than one school year. For our family-tree assignment, he encouraged students to discover the names of elderly relatives and to write to them, asking them to write letters back about their own childhood. Mr. Chapman made history and writing come alive, and his classes always went by too quickly.

And the year-long family tree project? That was an amazing journey for an eighth-grader. I wrote the National Archives requesting war records for soldiers in my family history. All I had to do was enclose a stamped self-addressed envelope and the National Archives would make Xerox copies of whatever they had about that person, and then mail the copies back to me. As my research deepened, it became increasingly interesting to see copies of old, hand-written documents that had been saved, some for hundreds of years. I traced our family on my mother's side to a soldier, Frederick Emert, who had fought with George Washington. There was a lot of information about Frederick because the home of his widow had burned down, and therefore many people in the town had gone to the clerk to testify that the widow was a person of good moral character and that the couple had been married. As the fire had destroyed all the family records, it was the testimony of her neighbors that enabled her to get the Revolutionary War Widow's Pension, because otherwise she had no documentation.

Seeing the beautiful penmanship of these old documents and hand-written checks and realizing that these had been written with a quill pen amazed me. Reading the testimony of words that were more than two-hundred years old astounded me. I received copies of cancelled checks and war records from the war of 1812 and the Civil War and many other documents, most of them hand-written with extraordinarily beautiful penmanship.

I wrote letters to every elderly relative that I could get information about, and then those relatives would write back to me and send me names of other people to contact. An American family story started to form, a story of a young couple from Scotland who crossed the Atlantic Ocean in 1714 and settled in the American wilderness. It was a story of young women who died in childbirth and of husbands remarrying and their next wives either dying in childbirth or having ten or twelve children, and of how many of those young children died before they were five years old. It seemed that if the women lived through the first childbirth, they lived to be very old.

Most of this information was new to my mother and Gramma Gigi. Gramma Gigi had known only about her great-grandmother and no further back in our family history. Grandpa Bob had been born in France, but his family records were all destroyed when the town of Lille was bombarded in both WWI and WWII.

As my interest grew in researching my family tree, the carving out of this country and its history came alive to me. I could, at times, feel in my soul and in my very bones the hard-working pioneers and farmers who toiled in the hot southern and mid-western sun and then worked to stay warm in the cold winters; couples who settled many days' ride away from the nearest neighbor and who were self-sufficient and hopeful and forged their lives and their children's hope in this new country.

I imagined how it must have been to live in Tennessee when it was Indian Country and there were few settlers and how hard their lives must have been. And the letters and the stories and the old documents made history become real.

I read letters about my daddy's grandparents coming to Kansas to farm. All the old people wrote about how good, how honest, and how God-fearing and kind these ancestors of mine were. I read letters about community and relying on neighbors and how important it was to make a good reputation for yourself. These were hard-working people who farmed and grew their livelihood and were at the mercy of the weather and of economic conditions and the politics of the time. Reading about them and receiving letters about them, I felt their integrity and strength and their belief that if a person worked hard, that person could be someone and have a place to live and enough to eat. Theirs was a strong faith that with hard work they could pass on their land to their children so that their children could succeed. I imagined the plowing, the planting, and the building of cabins and homes, and of the self-sufficiency of these people who were my heritage.

I created an inch-thick document that year, typed on a manual typewriter. Auntie Jan had helped Judy and me pick out a typewriter, because in both high school and in junior high, students had to type some of their assignments. My family tree report was hand-typed and included copies of letters and other documents. The following several pages are copies of the family tree book that I created in eighth grade.

I chose these pages because it was interesting to research and find out about ancestors who had left Germany in 1732 to travel by ship to America.

The following information is taken from the publication
"FOOTPRINTS ON THE SANDS OF TIME", by Ruby Catoo, 1964.

"The Library of Congress says the German name would
be properly spelled Emmert. The name Emmett or Emmot is
English or Irish. The early Emert settlers in Tennessee
spoke with a distinct German brogue and had the physical
appearance of what is known as the large "White Dutch",
the real German. Various sources quote the family as
speaking German until the early part of the nineteenth
century.

"The name was spelled Emmett or occasionally Emet on
all old family papers through 1871. In 1882, the next
records found, it is spelled Emert. In a letter written
in 1865, while Frederick Styros Emert was in the Army, he
signed his name as Emert but addresses it to his parents
"Mr. and Mrs. Frederick E. Emmett". Possibly Army records
caused the change in spelling of the name. The 1830 and
1840 census records of Sevier and Blount Counties have the
spelling as Emmitt, Emitt, Emmett, Emet and Emit.

"From Frederick Emmert's Revolutionary War Records
it is definitely established the Emerts were in Pennsylvania
before the Revolution, later moving to Virginia, North
Carolina, and then Tennessee.

"There is said to be a sea chest in the possession of
Mr. Edward Emert of Sevierville, which was brought there by
the original immigrants of this family. It has the following inscription on the side under the look: "Barbara
Aeidfgon, Anne 1772". The chief of the Division of Fine Arts
suggests that the work whom this "Aeidfgon" means "built".
The other words are either the name of the purchaser (Barbara) or of the chest itself, while the other line is the
date, 1772.

While Frederick Emert I is our first definately proven
ancestor, it is believed he is the son of John George Emmert.
John George Emmert was born in 1716 in Germany. He died in
Reading, Burks County, Pennsylvania. He left Leipzig, Germany, in 1732. He settled in Pennsylvania, where, in 1777 he
was a Patriot who signed an oath of Allegiance in Burks Co.

He married Eva Marie Graff in 1742, and they are belived
to be the parents of the following children:

2a

Collecting all the information together in one place where it
made sense was a challenge. Finding out about a relative who
fought with George Washington was pretty amazing!

My parents later visited Emert's Cove in Tennessee and found Frederick Emert's gravestone from 1829.

CHILDREN OF JOHN GEORGE EMERT & EVA MARIE GRAFF:

FREDERICK*   born 10-11-1754, Penn.   died 1-7-1829
                                                 Sevier Co., Tenn.
                    married Barbara Nitish

GEORGE   born 1757 in Virginia   died 1846 in
                                                 Carter Co.,Tenn.
                    married Mary Conley

JACOB   born 1760 or 1770   died Sullivan CO.,
                                                 Tenn.

LEONARD   born 1774, Burks Co.,   died 1804, Wash-
                    Penn.   ington Co., Md.
                    married Catharine Guncle

DANIEL

ELIZABETH   married Henry Harklerood

FREDERICK EMERT

"Frederick Emert, believed to be the son of John George Emmert and Eva Marie Graff, was born 10-11-1754, probably in Pennsylvania. He died 1-7-1829, and is buried in Emert's Cove Cemetery, Sevier County, Tennessee.
"He married, in Pennsylvania, to Barbara Nitish (Knight or Knightish). She was born 5-6-1755, and died 7-7-1842. It is said she is buried beside her husband. The dates of death are from his war records, which state they were listed from tombstones."
The following children are listed as being the children of Frederick and Barbara Emert, according to Ruby Catoo:

BARBARA ANN   born 12-27-1776   died 9-23-1875
POLLY   born 10-21-1778
CATHERINE   born 12-27-1780
MARY   born 11-5-1782   died before 1843*
ELIZABETH   born 11-27-1783, Va.   died 1888
PHILLIP   born 10-17-1786   died 7-23-1821
MARGARET   born 3-9-1788   died 1862
LOUISA   born 2-11-1790   died before 1843*
FREDERICK   born 12-19-1791, Tenn.   died 4-10-1871
DANIEL   born 6-13-1793, Tenn.   died 8-28-1851

2b

57

This page shows my Gramma Gigi, my mother's mother, daughter of James and Carrie, listed as "Audrey." My Gramma Gigi had brothers named Weaver, Lloyd, and Ora Castle and her sisters were Myrle Lee, Erma and Norma.

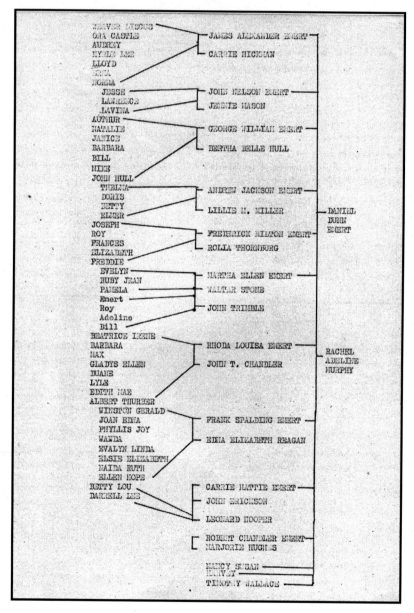

Typing on a typewriter was difficult. The typewriter keys were stiff and had to be pushed down with a lot of pressure to make contact with the ribbon. If the keys were not hit hard enough then the letter of the alphabet or the symbol that was typed would either not show up at all or it would be very light. The only way to fix it was to backspace and type that letter again, and often it did not align properly and wouldn't look right.

Typewriter ribbons were made of inked cloth. The ribbon was inked with one strip of red ink and one of black ink and was reeled between two spools. If a person wanted to type figures in red, they would press a lever down to align the red part of the ribbon. If someone made a mistake typing, then they had to put a correction strip on top of the mistake and type the mistake. The correction strip had white powder on it and would  cover up the mistake, but then the letter or symbol that was supposed to be on that spot was often hard to read, because the ink didn't stick well to the powder.

There was also a special typewriter paper called erasable bond paper, which incorporated a thin layer of material that prevented ink from penetrating the paper. An ordinary soft pencil eraser could be used to erase what was typewritten; however, the erasable paper was expensive and smudged easily.

When a person was typing they had to keep in mind the length of the words as they got near the right-hand margin. This was manual typing and nothing was automatic. Once a person had set the margins for each side of the paper, when they got to the right-hand edge the typewriter would not go beyond that margin unless a release button was pressed. And if they reached the margin, then a little bell would chime. The typist always had to watch and remember to not start a long word when they got near the right-hand margin, because then they would have to extend that sentence out into the margin. If someone misspelled a word they could erase the whole word with a special ink eraser, but it usually made a big mess and tore the paper. The ink eraser was somewhat gritty; it was round and flat with an attached brush to brush away all the eraser and paper crumbs.

Students were required to take a typing class in junior high. I hated hated hated hated that class! Everyone sat at an individual typewriter table with a big, heavy, manual typewriter on it. We had an office chair, and as soon as the classroom tardy bell rang we were supposed to insert a piece of paper into the typewriter rollers and align it with the top of the typewriter. Then a movie would show on a movie screen, a movie of words. Students were supposed to keep their eyes on the screen and touch-type the words as fast as they appeared on the screen.

When I tried touch-typing I always typed garbage because my fingers were never on the right keys. The teacher would walk around and poke a student in the back if they weren't sitting up straight. If the teacher caught someone looking at the keyboard then that student got yelled at. If the teacher caught a student looking at their fingers, the teacher might hit that student's knuckles with a ruler.

Most of the time I would look at the screen, see what was on it, then look at my fingers as sneakily as I could, and then look up again and see more words and look at my fingers again.

The final test for the class had students type while we HEARD the words. And the words were not a story, they were just random words. We had to type fifty words a minute to pass the class, and I failed miserably. Touch-typing was important, and we were all supposed to know how to do it; however, I just couldn't get the hang of it. Girls especially needed to learn to type. After all, both a secretary and a teacher were professions that required typing, as did nursing. Those were the careers that young ladies were expected to pursue, at least until they got married and then their husband would support them

The typing class was a semester long and I was really glad when it was over. Even when I practiced at home trying to do the touch-typing, I still didn't get it right. And, as all I had to do was look at my fingers to type without making mistakes, I didn't see what the big deal was anyway.

Auntie Jan could touch-type more than 90 words per minute without making a mistake. It was amazing to watch her type and know that she got it right every single time! The keys on the typewriters were arranged so that the letter "A" required a person's left-hand pinky finger to strike the key. The intent of this key placement was to slow down the typist, because typewriter keys would jam and get stuck when the typist could type more than 100 words per minute!

Students were required to take art classes in junior high, and I signed up for a painting class. I had already started oil painting on my own, after receiving oil paints for Christmas. Sometimes Gramma Gigi would take me to the beach to paint.

If I was having a stressful day at school, I could call Gramma Gigi from a pay phone, and she would come get me at school and take me to the beach...she loved the beach as much as I did. We wouldn't tell my parents about this when it happened. Gramma Gigi kept paints at her house for me in addition to her own paints and she would bring them when we went painting. I discovered the palette knife, and loved to sit at Pescadero Beach just painting. Pescadero is just west of Palo Alto, about an hour's drive away. On a cloudy day we would listen to the waves, feel the coldness of the mist in the air, and paint oil paintings of the ocean.

Pescadero Beach Oil Painting – Jane, age 14

My eighth-grade art teacher could have ruined art for me forever if I had believed her assessment that I had no talent. She was young and attractive, but she had not taught long and she seemed to have no imagination. She would give us an assignment like, "Paint a boat going under the Golden Gate Bridge," but every student had to produce a painting that was exactly what the teacher had in her head. She routinely rejected what her students created, until everyone's work looked exactly like each other's work, and exactly like what the teacher had in her head. There was no room for creativity in that art class! She also had teacher's pets in each class, and by the end of the year no one but her "pets" could stand her. I didn't believe her evaluations of my talent, but I often wondered how many people had their passion for art or their confidence in their artistic abilities destroyed by that teacher.

When I had begged and begged for oil paints for Christmas, I had not known at the time that my mother had been an artist. In fact, my mother had painted murals on her high school corridors that depicted all sorts of athletics. She painted full-sized divers, runners and gymnasts and she had done that with an intuition and skill that she never ever talked about later in her life. I saw one photo of the mural, but I don't know what happened to it. How sad that things like that get lost.

I was in advanced math at Palo Verde, including SMSG at Stanford University and algebra while in elementary school. SMSG stood for Student Mathematic Study Group, which was also known as "The New Math," and it had been a pilot program in advanced math.

I received a rude awakening in junior high, and my love of math was sorely tested. The advanced math experiment from elementary school did not carry over to junior high. So in seventh grade I was taking the math that I had finished in fourth grade. And to top it of, adding insult to injury, the math teacher that should have been teaching math that year for some reason wasn't there, so the shop teacher was teaching math.

The shop teacher would come into the class looking like he was in a daze. He wore thick glasses and a sports coat with corduroy elbow patches, and when he looked at a student through those thick glasses it was difficult to tell who he was really focused on. Students would be throwing stuff and he couldn't control the class. He was used to controlling boys in small groups, but the math class was beyond what he was accustomed to teaching. We had him for one semester and then the regular math teacher came back. But by then math had become worse than boring; it was not a challenge and I already knew all that was being taught. Sitting in that class for fifty long minutes every day was just horrible. I did, however, become an expert doodler and the outside of my binder was covered with exquisite designs.

MR. CARROLL
E. NICKELS,
Instrumental
Music

MR. LAWRENCE
G. OLINGER,
Math, Social
Studies

MR. JOHN R.
POFF, Math

MR. F. RAY
RAYNER, A.V.,
Science (Curr.
Associate)

MRS. JUDITH
E. RHODES,
Foreign Lang.

MISS SHARON
E. RUSSELL,
Phys. Ed.

MR. PHILLIP C.
SCHNEIDER,
Math

MRS. MICHELE
SHOCKEY,
Foreign Lang.

MRS. BARBARA
SPELLMAN,
Homemaking

MR. WALTER L.
WHITE, Math

MR. CARLTON
WHITEHEAD,
Foreign Lang.
(Curr. Assoc.)

MR. JOHN R.
WILLIAMS, JR.,
Phys. Ed.

MRS. DOROTHY
L. WOLFROM,
Eng, Social Studies

MRS. OLIVIA
C. YOUNG,
Eng, Social
Studies

Dancing Lessons

The Beaudoin's School of Dance was established in Palo Alto in 1932 by Heston M. Beaudoin. Its goal was the same when it started as it was when I took lessons there: "To promote the art and appreciation of dancing, thereby encouraging the love for all the arts, as dancing, music, color, drama and literature are closely related." In the 1950s and 1960s their instruction included etiquette-training for teenagers enrolled in their cotillion and ballroom classes. Boys were taught to escort girls to the car, and girls were instructed to act like young ladies and introduce the young men to their parents.

Well, proper young ladies had to take dancing lessons, as did proper young gentlemen. The trouble was, we were not feeling very proper, and I had a fear of being in the physical spotlight. I also had no confidence that I could dance, at least the rigid and uncool old-fashioned dancing that was taught at Beaudoin's School of Dance.

The dancing they taught was not a free-spirited form of expression; it was far from it. I was enrolled in weekly evening sessions of fox-trot, waltz, line-dancing, Bossa Nova, rumba, and other various methods of torture, which for a basically self-conscious and uncoordinated twelve-year old was pure agony. My hormones were going crazy, which meant that at a moment's notice I would begin to sweat like a pig, except women and girls did not sweat, they perspired, and they only perspired in same-gender company, never in mixed company. "Secret®" antiperspirant was the first brand that offered a product just for women. It was "gentler" said the advertisement, as if young hormone-raging teenaged girls did not have sweat glands that went crazy and that they needed a gentler product. We were in the early 1960s, and young ladies did NOT sweat and were expected to behave properly and be trained in manners and social skills.

I dressed in layers of clothing: a girdle (yes, a girdle!) nylon stockings which had tops that were clipped to the garters that were attached to the bottom of the girdle; uncomfortable but fashionable pointy-toed flats, a nylon slip and a two-layer-nylon-dress-with-a-cummerbund. The thought of going to dancing class made my skin begin to break out and my knees turn to jelly...often I would break out in nervous hives!

Mr. and Mrs. Bedouin would play music on a record player at their Colorado Avenue Studio and they would gracefully walk onto the dance floor and demonstrate the dance that they thought seventh-graders would be overjoyed to learn. I think that they believed if they did a good dance demo that somehow the students would magically learn how to dance...that the ability to move across the floor would somehow be absorbed through the skin by dancing osmosis. The Bedouins had danced as a couple for years. It was their passion and they excelled at it, but that did nothing to inspire me. It only added to my dread and fear of underperforming and of making a fool of myself.

This was co-ed dancing, so it meant that a boy that I didn't know was going to touch me and then make a clumsy and awkward attempt to guide me around a dance floor in an endeavor to replicate what the teachers had demonstrated.

Geeze.

I developed a great hatred of the popular song, *Hit the Road, Jack*, during dance class. Frequently the teachers would select a student to dance with during their demo. For me, the dance-class-icing-on-the-cake came when Mr. Bedouin selected me to be his partner for a demo of the fox trot. Mr. Bedouin positioned me with my arm out straight, his hand at the back of my waist, and my hand on his shoulder. My legs were wooden; my mind was in a panic...everyone was in a circle around us. All the other students were watching the demo of the dance and I felt paralyzed. Everyone's eyes were glued on me and burning holes into me as they stared. I knew that most of them were hugely relieved that they had not been chosen, and that they felt pity that I was chosen. The song *Hit the Road, Jack*, began to play, and Mr. Bedouin started his attempt to dance with me to demonstrate the proper way to do the fox trot. My legs were dragging across the floor as if they did not belong to me, as if they were someone else's legs. Everything seemed in slow motion and I felt like I was going to faint. I wished that a crack in the floor would open up and swallow me.

We finished the dance...the dance that had lasted forever. The music stopped. There was utter and absolute silence, silence of the pin-dropping kind.

"Young lady, I would much prefer to dance with a **piano** than to dance with you. It would be much easier to have tried to move a piano or a hippopotamus around the dance floor than to have tried to teach you to dance." And with that I was summarily dismissed to take my place in the circle of students once again.

Mr. Bedouin then picked a more graceful and eager student to demonstrate his next number.

I was sweaty and I felt like I was going to faint, and I couldn't look anyone in the eye. And dance class was a whole hour long – an hour of torture and waiting for class to be over! I still had to endure forty-five more minutes of dry-mouth, sweaty-armpits, shallow-breathing agony.

A boy came over, took my hand, and asked me to dance. I couldn't even look him in the eye. "I think that you did not move like a piano," he said. "That old Mr. Bedouin is stupid, like we would ever want to dance these old-fashioned stupid dances. Maybe if he taught us the Twist or the Mashed Potatoes then he could see that you really know how to dance! Who wants to do the old Fox Trot anyway?!"

Then he asked me if my parents were making me take the class. He shared with me that his parents were making him take dance and I told him that mine were too. I hated the class and so did he. He went to Jordan Jr. High and I went to Wilbur. At least I had found a friend.

My dad dropped me off and then picked me up for the once-a-week dance class. Each time he picked me up he would want to know what I had learned, and I would tell him the name of a dance and pretend that I liked the class. After all, it wasn't Daddy's fault that I hated the class, and he was paying for it with his hard-earned money with the hopes that I would become a proper young lady with appropriate social skills.

Wilbur held monthly "sock hops" in the school gym during lunch time. They were called sock hops because students were not allowed to wear their street shoes in the gym, so everyone took off their shoes and left them outside the gym and went inside to dance with their socks on! Wearing socks protected the gym floor. Sock hops were really fun; all the grades could attend and students did not need a partner or a ticket. We could just dance like crazy all by ourselves if we wanted to. There was a microphone in front of the record player so that the music was loud, and the audio visual team played records and everyone danced. It was okay for girls to dance with girls in a group. If a boy asked a girl to dance, then he could join in the group, but it wasn't like a real dance where a girl waited and waited for a boy to ask her, standing with a smile on her face like it was glued there and like she was happy when in reality she was praying that someone would to ask her to dance. Sock hops were not like that... no one cared about who danced and who didn't dance.

I had a skirt that was all about the Twist. I had selected the fabric at the Emporium, and my mom had sewed the skirt for me. It was all sorts of bright colors and had words all over it: "Let's Twist," "Twist and Shout," "Twist Again," and it was a very keen skirt. "Keen" was the word. If you were keen or your things were keen, well, then, all was good.

For many of the sock hops I would wear my Twist skirt and go to the gym and dance the Twist. I had learned to dance the Twist by watching *American Bandstand* on TV. We girls would dance with each other, usually in someone's garage while we listened to records and danced and showed each other how to dance until we got it right. Then if we danced at a real dance we knew how to do it.

Dancing with the girls was a little bit like doing each other's hair. We girls were teaching each other how to do the important stuff that we needed to know.

When I was in seventh grade I started getting *American Girl* magazine. *American Girl* was supposed to tell teenagers how to dress and how to act. Then my friends started buying *Cosmopolitan* magazine and *Seventeen* magazine. Gramma Gigi often bought *Cosmopolitan* magazine, so when I went to her house she and I would talk about the articles. *Cosmo* was more about single women and sex advice, so it was pretty interesting! *Seventeen* magazine wrote about make-up and boys and dating. Almost every magazine had a part in the back where people could request free samples. Usually on the weekends when I wasn't at Grandpa Bob and Gramma Gigi's house, my sisters and I would sit around and fill out coupons and mail them so that we would receive the free samples.

We got free sun tan oil, cream rinse, shampoo, eye shadow, lipstick, powder, perfume and makeup. There were so many new products and all a person had to do was fill out a card, mail it, and pretty soon the free samples would arrive in the mail

There was a variety of fan magazines; if you were a fan of a certain singer or a group, then you could buy a fan magazine that had all the latest news about that performer or group and what they liked, and what the latest styles were. Some weekends we girls would sit around and read those magazines and try new hair and makeup styles on each other, often with the new samples that we had received in the mail. Mass marketing to teens was becoming more aggressive, and we were all a part of it!

Just like Carnegie Hall!
...and now for that fresh, clean taste!

American Girl Magazine Ad
1960

Fashion

When I started junior high, girls dressed like each other as much as possible. Dress codes were strictly enforced and did not allow girls to wear pants, slacks, Levis, or shorts to school. Skirts could not be too short, shoes could not have heels or platforms, nor could girls wear patent leather shoes to school. Patent leather shoes were very shiny, and the dean of girls said that boys might see a girl's underwear reflected in the shoes, so we were not allowed patent leather shoes or boots at school! Of course, that made me want to wear patent leather shoes just because they were forbidden.

Girls were required to take home economics, "home ec.," as it was called, in junior high. Home ec. included a semester each of cooking and sewing, and we had to become at least proficient, if not competent, in both of these topics. We were required to sew a complete outfit as part of the sewing semester. The semester of sewing included a required fashion show and session from a woman who ran a charm school. Charm schools taught young ladies how to behave, and were similar to modeling schools and finishing schools. Some of the richer girl's parents would pay for them to attend charm school so they would learn how to be proper young ladies.

The rest of us were taught charm by our home ec. teacher, who was shaped like a heavy overstuffed pillow cinched at the waist with a tight belt. She wore way too much makeup; her lipstick was bright red and she always drew it beyond her real lips, as if she might have looked in the mirror while driving her car and then put on lipstick with shaky hands. Her makeup collected in the many wrinkles of her face, and she would wear bright blue eye shadow and thick black eyeliner. This teacher was our fashion mentor and charm guide, the woman designated to teach us how to dress and act. She looked like a dried-apple doll with hundreds of wrinkles and age spots and a dumpy figure; her legs were mapped with purple veins and her stockings collected in small sags around her ankles. She sounded like she was drunk most of the time, because when she talked her words slurred together and it was difficult to understand what she was saying. I think she had false teeth that didn't fit well so she made slobbery noises and clicked a bit when she instructed us. Many days I watched her in both horror and amazement, fascinated at the variety of her makeup colors, wondering if, and fearing that I would look like that when I got old.

Easter

Jane 12, Jennifer 9, Judy 15

We had to sew an outfit from start to finish, buying as near to the exact amount of fabric as possible, preshrinking it, laying it out, pinning the pattern on the fabric, cutting it out properly, and then sewing it together. We marked the darts with carbon paper, using a tracing wheel; at home we marked them with chalk. The teacher either approved or rejected our choice of pattern ahead of time, and she told us that we could not use any "crazy" fabric, but only conservative colors that were solids or checkered or plaid.

We demonstrated proper sewing techniques, and kept a notebook with samples, which might be hemming techniques, flat felt seams, or how to end a seam, and we wrote their descriptions in our notebook. Fortunately, I had watched my mom make all of our clothes for as long as I could remember, so I already knew how to lay out a pattern, pin it properly, and cut it out just right. I knew how to sew, having been taught by my mom and Gramma Gigi.

My outfit for the fashion show was two-piece with a white top and a black and white checked straight skirt. The top had a collar made from the same material as the skirt and the sleeves were finished in piping, also from the same material. I made a belt from the skirt material too. Our assignment included a requirement to make a belt from a kit that could be bought from the store.

And I had high heels! They were black, and had pointed toes, and short, very spikey, high heels. I was no good at walking in those shoes! I felt like I was going to fall over even though the heel was probably only an inch-and-a-half or two-inches tall. I felt very rocky standing in those shoes, and even more unsteady when I tried walking. How could a shoe make such a difference? I had watched Auntie Jan walk in three-and-a-half or four-inch heels ever since I could remember, and I couldn't even seem to manage my new, quite fashionable shorter high heels! I wanted to walk in those high heels like my Auntie, with her custom-designed clothes and high-fashion style, but my body rebelled. I was growing up and was intrigued at how Auntie Jan could sashay in those tall heels, pivot and twirl so gracefully, as if the shoes were a part of her, just an extension of her slim legs.

In practicing for the fashion show, we had to learn to walk up and down stairs. The stairs were the eight steps on each side of the stage in the cafetorium, and that was plenty of stairs to navigate. We learned to place one hand on our hip, and to hold our head steady, "…as if there is a string fastened to the top of your head, a string that goes up to the ceiling holding your head up…" Then, looking forward and never at our feet, with one hand on our hip and the other hand at our side, relaxed, with our fingers gently pointing.… I can tell you, there was no way to relax when trying to remember all of those instructions while people were watching! How can anyone walk in high heels and not look at their feet?! It was like trying to type without looking at your fingers! I wondered what would happen if I were to fall down the stairs, or trip, or if I had to sneeze, or if something even worse happened, like if I got my period in the middle of the fashion show.

The fashion show was in the evening, and all of the home ec. students were required to participate, and everyone's family was invited, as were their relatives.

Of course, after lying awake at night for weeks, worrying about the fashion show and if I was going to fall down and embarrass myself for the rest of eternity, I managed to swagger and sashay down the auditorium aisle, up the stairs, across the stage, down the stairs, and back down the aisle without dying. I did stumble once, but apparently my outfit was applauded more loudly than anyone else's, so I won first place! I was immensely relieved when the fashion show was over.

The other semester of home ec. was cooking. The home ec. room was set up with six small kitchens. Boys DID NOT take home ec., they took shop, so home ec. was an all-girls class. The girls in home ec. were divided into teams of four, and each team worked together to create the culinary delight of the day. The kitchenettes were so small that the team could not stand together and have any room to maneuver. And of course we had the same teacher for cooking as we had for sewing.

The class was fifty minutes long. Each kitchenette had a wind-up timer. Every day the timer in each kitchenette would go off about five minutes after the class started, as the previous class would have set the timers to ring to disrupt the class which followed theirs. The teacher and the students always jumped as if it was a total surprise. Then the teacher would yell at the class to go turn off the timers, and yell that we better not do the same or we would get marked down in the grade book! And of course, each class did it to the next class. It was tradition.

Our first class was how to make fruit cocktail. Fruit cocktail? You had to be kidding! Fruit cocktail comes from either opening a can or cutting up a bunch of fruit. How complicated could that be?

Well... first of all, we had to be efficient, and learn to save steps. We crammed into the kitchenette together and put everything that was needed onto a tray and then carried it to the other side of the kitchen. However, in reality, we stood in the same place and just handed the tray to the other person and they put it on the counter on the other side of the kitchen. It was silly and ridiculous. We spent a half hour cutting up fruit while the teacher droned on and on. We put the fruit in bowls, put them on the tray, and carried the tray to the eating table that was right outside the kitchen. We then cleaned up the kitchen, wolfed down the fruit salad, washed the bowls and spoons, put them away, and surreptitiously made sure the timers were set to go off in the next class, five minutes after the bell rang.

The making of fruit cocktail and all of our cooking lessons took so long because we were required to keep a cooking notebook. We had to write the recipes in our notebook,  and it was at this point in my education that the words "boredom," "frustration," "incompetence," and "cutting school" began to become part of my speech.

We were instructed in additional topics such as how to change a baby's diaper, and our notebook included a page with handkerchiefs that we had folded in the four different diaper-folding styles and pinned together with safety-pins. The notebook was full of recipes and preparation tips. We included notes on manners and fashion and color coordination and how a proper young lady was expected to behave. We spent time watching the caricature of a charm school teacher tell us how she kept her girlish figure and we dutifully made copious notes.

I had loved school. School and my performance at school helped shape and define who I was. I was the model student…. the overachiever… my expectation was to get straight "A's." I wanted to learn. I had thought learning to cook would be fun. But I was being smothered by some classes, smothered by the shop-teacher-turned-math teacher who could not control his class, smothered by the old and outdated and incompetent home ec. teacher that droned on and on until her voice was like nails on a chalkboard. How could cooking be ruined? I began to dread math and home ec. and art and other classes.

In elementary school, my teachers had been top-notch teachers with a passion and a love for what they were doing. And now I was transitioning to junior high, to where there were teachers who had taught forever and were stagnant. Many of the teachers were old and stale; tenured, just waiting to retire and not putting much effort into teaching but putting the majority of their effort into discipline. At the other end of the spectrum were the teachers who had never taught before but believed that they were the best teachers in the world.

I busted my butt keeping that home ec. notebook current, but when I got mononucleosis towards the end of the school year and missed about six weeks of school, the home ec. teacher gave me an "F" in her grade book for every day I was absent. After all, she said, even though I did all the work at home, and turned in all my assignments, and got an "A+" on the notebook, I failed the class every day that I did not attend. I received my first and only "D" in a class because I was sick and unable to be physically there in class.

I burned with resentment. And I started looking at school a different way, not as an exciting place to learn and to explore, not as a place of discovery but as a prison where those in power held the keys and could make the rules, and we students were powerless to change things...or were we?

"Simplicity" and "McCalls" were some of the companies that made the patterns that we used when sewing our own clothes.

F amily Vacations

The summer that I was thirteen our family went camping at Mount Lassen Volcanic National Park in Northern California. None of us girls wanted to go. Going on vacation with the family was the last thing a teenager felt like doing, especially camping in our pink tent.

Even if all I did during the summer was talk on the phone, listen to my transistor radio, lay out in the sun, walk over to my friend's house or go to the swim club, or play tennis, or take the bus downtown or go to the creek or ride my bike or try to skateboard or try new hairstyles or go to Grandpa Bob and Gramma Gigi's house, or hang out with Auntie Jan, or read, or sew, or draw or paint or sit in a friend's garage and talk about boys....well, those things were way more "boss" that going camping with my parents and my sisters.

Going camping meant a week of preparation. My mom would make lists for each of us of what to pack: Two pairs of shorts, five pairs of socks, two pairs of long pants, two bras, three short-sleeved tops, one jacket, and one pair of gloves. We girls would put the items on our bed in categories, and my mom would come around and check off the stacks of clothes against the list, making sure they were folded and ready to be packed.

I hated folding clothes. I didn't really mind ironing, especially since after we remodeled our house we had an entire room that we called the "sewing room." When we had only three bedrooms, my parents had one room, and I ended up sharing a room with either Judy or Jennifer, but now my parents had a room, we girls each had our own room, and we had a sewing room too.

The sewing machine was in the sewing room. My mom still sewed most of our clothes, and I sewed clothes as well. The ironing board and my mom's yarns and fabrics were there. Buttons…we had many, many buttons; when you purchased buttons, they came on a card with a certain amount of buttons, and we always made sure to buy extra buttons in case we lost one. If you didn't buy an extra button, by the time one fell off that particular button might not be sold any more.

There was a store in downtown Palo Alto called "Irma Schauble's." My parents didn't go to that store; I had discovered it on my own. The old lady, Irma, had a home that she had converted into a store where she sold buttons, ribbons, and fasteners for clothes. She stocked exotic fasteners from all around the world, and Irma's buttons were so beautiful that I could spend hours looking in her store. There were hundreds and hundreds of small drawers, and each drawer had a sample of the content fastened to the outside of the drawer. I liked to go there with my friends and just look and look at the buttons and clasps from all over the world!

In our remodeled house we would iron and sew in the sewing room. Even if we were going camping, we had to iron our clothes! That's just how it was. The one thing that I liked about ironing was sprinkling the clothes. Hardware stores sold stoppers that would fit in the mouth of any regular bottle, like a beer bottle or a soda bottle, and the stopper for sprinkling the clothes was like the end of a watering can: It had a round end with lots of little holes in it. A person would fill up the glass bottle with water, insert the stopper, and then sprinkle the clothes before ironing them. The clothes had to be sprinkled just right, because if the clothes were too wet, it took forever to iron; too dry, then the wrinkles would not come out. However, when we got a steam iron we didn't have to sprinkle the clothes before ironing them.

When my mom did her inspection of my items against her list, she always found something missing, or found something not on the list. Once inspection was over then it was time to pack.

For Christmas I had been given a suitcase set. It was a beautiful red suitcase, with hard sides, a Samsonite suitcase. Samsonite was the best brand of luggage. There was an ad on TV that showed a Samsonite suitcase being dropped from an airplane, and when it landed on the ground it didn't break or open. My set had a big suitcase, a medium suitcase, and a cosmetic case; all red, all with hard sides, and all with a key to lock them!

To pack for camping I put my folded clothes in my suitcase. Because we had to carry our own suitcases, I didn't want mine to be heavy, and I tried to pack judiciously. It was interesting that if we went anywhere for a few days, or for a week, or for two weeks, I needed the same amount of stuff. I would have to pack my hairbrush, shampoo, razors, lotion, suntan lotion, makeup, and bug spray…so much stupid stuff to go on a stupid vacation to a stupid camping place with my stupid family.

I would miss my friends and my boyfriend. What if I finally got an invitation to a beach party when I was away camping in the pink tent? I really wanted to go to a beach party. After all, I was old enough and some of my friends were starting to surf. Why did I have to go camping?! I knew that I would just get a bunch of mosquito bites anyway and have to sit in the car with my family forever. No one else had to go camping. They went to Disneyland. One girl I knew even flew in an airplane some place by herself – no family, just her. But that was because her parents were divorced and she went to visit her father for the summer. Still, people went to Los Angeles, or Disneyland, or all sorts of other places.

Geeze.

My mom packed all the food into our old aluminum ice chest. We packed our sleeping bags that we had gotten by redeeming our S&H Green Stamps. S&H Green Stamps were trading stamps, stamps that people received when they made purchases, and when enough stamps were accumulated, the stamps could be traded for merchandise. Our family's sleeping bags were all from the S&H Green Stamp redemption center.

We left bright and early on a Saturday morning to go to Mount Lassen. The ride was actually interesting and I enjoyed looking out the car window and seeing the sights. We traveled up Highway 5 and went through towns with names like Willows and Red Bluff, and after about four hours we went through Redding. It must have been about one hundred and ten degrees in Redding, and it felt like an oven! In our station wagon it was so hot that I felt like I was going to faint. In Redding, we turned off of Highway 5 and headed east to Mount Lassen.

There were a lot of wildflowers along the highway, and as we drove away from Redding the altitude increased, and finally it began to be cooler. Then comfortable at last, I finally thought that maybe I wasn't going to die from the heat.

When we got to the Mount Lassen campground we found it deserted. The land was almost barren. We had never camped any place quite like Lassen. Shortly after we arrived it started to get chilly, so we hurried to pitch our tent, and then carried our things from the car to the tent.

That night it was so cold that the water in our bucket froze! It was so cold that the S&H Green Stamp sleeping bags felt as thin as old sheets. I woke up in the middle of the night thinking I was freezing, and got my sweatshirt out of my suitcase. I had my flashlight and was trying to be quiet, but then I started worrying that Jennifer might freeze to death. So I went into her suitcase, and pretty soon I had unintentionally awakened everyone. We were all freezing cold and piled on our sweatshirts and jackets. My mom didn't have a sweatshirt. Sweatshirts were a new style and mothers didn't wear them. However, my parents put on their jackets and we all went back to sleep.

In the morning it was difficult to get up. We had our propane stove outside on the picnic table, but the altitude meant it took a long time to boil water, and as the water was frozen solid, breakfast took a long time to cook. My hands were so cold that I had a hard time using them for anything.

When it finally started warming up, the sky was as blue as I had ever seen. The air was crisp and clean and the sun felt the kind of hot that I only ever felt in the Sierra Nevada Mountains – in the high mountains where the sun is close and hot and warms a person to the bone through layers of clothing.

We went on a hike while my mom stayed at the campground. Daddy and we girls all went, and we found a lake that was the clearest lake I had ever seen. There were trout swimming in the lake and I could see straight through to the bottom to these big fish swimming in the cold, cold, clear water. We had never seen any thing like that either. The land was barren and rocky with hardly any plants, and then unexpectedly there was a blue, blue lake that was clean and cold.

We had planned to stay for a week at Mount Lassen. But after three nights we were so cold that we decided to leave sooner. We were so cold that it took us a long time to pack the car. It was as if we moved in slow motion.

We piled into our station wagon wearing coats and jackets and many layers of clothes, and as we drove towards Redding we finally started to warm up. And warm up and warm up. "Daddy, stop the car! I have to take off my jacket!" We kept pulling over to take off more of the clothes we had layered on that morning and by the time we got to Redding we were so hot there that we were whining that we wanted to go back to Mount Lassen where it was cold!

We found a motel that had a vacancy and a swimming pool. All of us but my mom had packed our swimming suits, and we spent the best part of that vacation swimming in the motel swimming pool as the late afternoon turned to evening. The blue water sparkled, and the neon light of the motel reflected in the pool as it grew darker.

We made dinner in our motel room from the food in the aluminum ice chest, opening cans and eating on our metal camping plates. We listened to the sounds of the semi-trucks going down the highway as we finally went to sleep, piled together in the air-conditioned motel room. Ahh...relief and comfort at last!

The car ride home was hot and sticky, but we were all glad to be going home after such a hot-cold-hot trip!

Grandma Ruth Visits

Grandma Ruth came out to visit later that same summer, and we went on more vacations. Grandma Ruth was Daddy's mother; she lived in Kansas and was a retired nurse. Grandma Ruth traveled on the train from Kansas to Oakland, and then stayed with our family for several weeks. And during those weeks we went to Point Lobos on the California coast and to Yosemite National Park in the Sierra Nevada Mountains.

Grandma Ruth and Daddy
Point Lobos

My Parents

Point Lobos in Monterey County
Jennifer, Judy, Grandma Ruth, Jane

Jane and Jennifer at Point Lobos

Point Lobos is south of Monterey and a beautiful place to visit; our family had been there several times before. Each time we would take a picnic lunch and drive south on Highway 101 and then out to the coast and to Monterey. Judy and I used to tease Jennifer and tell her that there was no sand in Monterey; then she would get mad at us for teasing her for when we got there, Jennifer saw the sand. Usually we stopped at Dennis the Menace Park in Monterey and had our lunch. The park had a locomotive that kids could climb upon, along with other unique play equipment. After lunch, we would drive on the 17-Mile Drive, which went past the famous Pebble Beach Golf Course and a lot of mansions. We would see Seal Rock, just off the coast and covered with sea lions and seals.

When we got to Point Lobos it was exciting to see sea otters! The sea otters floated on their backs and balanced oysters on their chests. The otters used rocks, hitting the oysters until the oysters cracked open and the otters ate the oyster's soft insides. That they use the rocks as tools was incredible! There were elephant seals, sea lions, and harbor seals... so many sea mammals to see. We were fortunate to be able to watch these creatures that were only a few-hours drive away from our house.

For some inexplicable reason, we called ground squirrels "buffalo." While eating our picnic lunch, we would say, "Watch out! Here comes a buffalo!" The first time Grandma Ruth heard us say that, she just about jumped out of her skin! But then she got into the swing of things and would chime right in. "Wayne, watch out! There is a buffalo about ready to chew on your shoe laces!"

We took Grandma Ruth to Yosemite National Park that same summer. Yosemite was about a five-hour drive from our house, and I hated and dreaded the last hour-and-a-half of the drive. It was a very scary drive, going down a long, steep, and winding grade to the road that went beside the Merced River at the bottom of a deep canyon. The road hugged the edge of the river for miles, a two-lane road that was bordered by the rock walls that had been built in the 1930s by the federally-funded program, Work Projects Administration (The WPA.) The WPA employed millions of people during the Great Depression when unemployment was widespread and people needed jobs.

The road then climbed up from the canyon bottom on another long and steep grade. We arrived at the park entrance in the early afternoon. We stayed in a camp called "Housekeeping Camp," where there were canvas-sided tent cabins with beds and heaters and picnic tables with fire pits. Each campsite had a place to park, and there were group water faucets and group restrooms. Housekeeping Camp was right next to the Merced River, and by late summer the river was very calm and warm and a perfect place to float on air mattresses. And we didn't have to pitch our pink tent!

It didn't take long to unpack everything and put on our bathing suits. Grandma Ruth sat by the river in a folding chair that Daddy carried there for her. My parents also sat in folding chairs, drinking beer and watching the river slowly flow by in the hot afternoon sun.

Grandma Ruth carried her purse with her wherever she went. She sat in the folding camp chair by the Merced River in the warmth of the sun with her purse on her lap. She had whitish-blue hair and an easy smile and we girls seemed to make her happy. She liked visiting us and we liked her visits. Grandma Ruth wasn't fashionable like Gramma Gigi, but she seemed like a story-book Grandma, with heavy shoes and long skirts, with pin-curled hair covered with a tightly-secured scarf.

Granite walls rose up high all around the Yosemite Valley floor, reflecting the sun and heating the valley. The sky was intensely blue and the river sparkled with little flecks of mica and gold all through the water and on the rocky river bottom. We girls met other teenagers and floated on our air mattresses and went swimming when we got too hot. Because the river was so calm, we barely had to keep an eye on Jennifer. And after a while Daddy went swimming too. It was beautiful and serene and the Bay Area seemed distant and very easy to forget.

And every night at Yosemite during the summer there was a park ranger who conducted a talk. There would be a camp fire and singing and many of the people staying in the valley would come to Camp Curry for the campfire program. People would arrive there as soon as they finished eating, and our family and Grandma Ruth went there too. There was a small amphitheater with an outdoor stage with log benches and the ranger's show would run from eight to nine o'clock in the evening, but what everyone waited for was the end of the talk, because then the Firefall would happen!

For eighty-eight years the Firefall took place in Yosemite, and it was like a waterfall of fire; fire that fell three-thousand feet down the front of Glacier Point. The fire fell down in the dark with thousands and thousands of sparks. At nine o'clock the crowd would be asked to be quiet and the Camp Curry ranger would yell towards the top of Glacier Point, "Hello Glacier!" If the assembled campers were quiet, they could hear the faint reply from the top of Glacier Point, "Hello Camp Curry!" Then the ranger who was leading the campfire program would yell, "Let the fire fall!" And at the top of Glacier Point a bonfire was pushed over the edge of the cliff.

It fell slowly, looking like a waterfall of fire.

While the fire was falling, a person on the stage would sing *The Indian Love Call*. Time stood still while the fire fell in the dark, looking like a sparkly red waterfall. We were silent while we listened to the singing and watched that fire fall. It burned out before it hit the valley floor, disappearing like magic as the embers and sparks vanished.

The audience would start clapping and the sound of the clapping echoed from the high cliffs. Afterwards we turned on our flashlights and walked back to Housekeeping Camp in the dark, the sky above us filled with millions of stars. Often we would see shooting stars and try to name the constellations.

We drove our car through the famous tunneled "Wawona Tree" in the Mariposa Grove of Yosemite Park. We were lucky, because it fell over in a snow storm in 1969, under an estimated two-ton load of snow. The giant sequoia was calculated to have been two-thousand three-hundred years old.

The trees in Yosemite Park and in Sequoia Park were amazing. There were trees that were hundreds of feet tall, dozens of feet around, and trees that were thousands of years old. We went on morning drives to look at the different famous trees and groves of trees, eating picnic lunches in the warm sun and then going back to Housekeeping Camp for an afternoon next to the river.

Not only did we drive through a tree, but there was also a huge fallen tree that cars could drive on. Daddy drove on top of the log but we girls were too scared to try it.

Yosemite had open garbage dumps where the bears would gather in the evening. Park guests drove their cars to the dump or walked to the dump to watch the bears. There were signs posted around the park warning people to not feed the animals, but everyone was really interested in watching the bears and a lot of people fed them despite the warnings.

One evening just before the campfire started a bear came into our family camp ground and picked up Daddy's aluminum ice chest and started to carry it away. The bear was actually walking on its hind legs, and carrying away our ice chest with our food in it! Before we even had time to start screaming, Daddy picked up the cast-iron frying pan, yelling and shouting at the bear! Daddy chased the bear and used the frying pan to hit the huge brown bear! The bear dropped the ice chest and went down on all four paws, running away.

We girls were screaming and Daddy ran over and picked up the aluminum ice chest. "God-damned bear trying to steal my ice chest!" Then Daddy had to apologize to Grandma Ruth for swearing.

Later that evening, after the Firefall, Judy and I went to the restroom, using our flashlights to light the path. I bumped into someone, which was weird because I hadn't seen anyone else on the path. "Excuse me," I said, and I put out my hand. It was then that I realized that I was touching a bear!

Judy and I began running and screaming towards the restroom. We ran inside, slammed the door and stood there screaming. Daddy recognized our screams, and grabbed the frying pan and came running to the restroom. "What in the hell is the matter with you two, get the hell out here now!" Judy and I were screaming about the bear and Daddy and everyone else heard us. Pretty soon there were dozens and dozens of flashlights shining throughout the camp, and crazy teenage boys and their dads were running around looking for the bear!

When we got back to our camp, my mom said that she was going to sleep in the car. She was afraid that a bear might come into our camp again. Daddy fixed up her sleeping bag inside the car, but halfway through the night my mom woke up wondering what the heck she had been thinking, because Daddy had locked up all the food in the car too! If the bear came back looking for food, my mom was locked in the car with all the food! So she came back inside the Housekeeping Camp tent.

One afternoon we hiked to Vernal Falls, and even Grandma Ruth and my mom came along. As usual, Grandma Ruth carried her purse with her. The mist from the waterfall helped cool us off, and staring at the water as it cascaded down from the top of the falls was hypnotic. I think we could have stayed there for hours in the cool mist watching the water tumbling down and down, listening to the sound of the water roaring as it crashed on the rocks below.

Many people hiked the trail that afternoon, and some of the teenage boys would tease us as they passed by: "Oh, a bear! Oh, look out, there is a bear!" They mimicked us in high falsetto voices, because it seemed that everyone in camp had heard us screaming and running from the bear!

That evening there was a teenaged boy from one of the other camps that came over and gave us six fishes that he had caught. He said that he caught so many fish that afternoon that he couldn't eat them all. Daddy kicked a boulder repeatedly after the boy left; Daddy had tried fishing that same afternoon and hadn't caught anything!

Jane, Judy, Grandma Ruth & Jennifer
Vernal Falls

When we drove home from Yosemite, we drove again on the same steep and winding road, then back through Mariposa, Merced, and Los Banos in the Central Valley. We drove past acres and acres of cotton and tomatoes and figs. The roads were congested with big trucks brimming with tomatoes on their way to canneries.

After Los Banos we headed to Gilroy, passing acres of garlic all around the town and the big garlic-processing factory. We drove up Highway 101, which was peppered with mom-and-pop fruit stands from Gilroy to San Jose. We stopped and bought fresh produce, including cases of juicy strawberries to take home for making jam and for dessert that night.

At the end of Grandma Ruth's visit, we drove her to the Oakland train station and she went back to Kansas. And soon it was time to plan for the beginning of the school year, which always started in mid-September.

My family went shopping at the Emporium at Stanford Shopping Center, and I bought material for a new school outfit, and I also got additional material to make hip-hugger bell-bottom pants and a crop-top. I went to Gramma Gigi's house and used her sewing machine, making the pants from fabric striped with narrow red and green vertical lines and the top from red material with green dots scattered over it in a random design.

When I finished the sewing, I put on my new outfit and took a long walk through the streets of San Carlos, wearing my below-the-belly-button flashy pants and my skimpy crop-top!

Green hair

In the 1960s, advertisements for Lady Clairol hair coloring asked, "Is it true blondes have more fun?" We listened to those ads on radio, watched them on TV, and read them in magazines; my friends and I concluded that blondes must have more fun. Everyone wanted to be blonde. The surfer-girl look was popular, and blonde was the "in" look, especially in California. California girls were stereotyped as blonde, and surfer dudes, beach bunnies, and beach movies were all the rage: *Gidget, How to Stuff a Wild Bikini, Beach Blanket Bingo, Where the Boys Are, A Summer Place, Pajama Party,* and *Gidget Goes Hawaiian* were popular movies that set the California-girl standards.

However, California was like two states, a northern state and a southern state, because in Northern California, where we lived, it was often cold at the beach. Santa Cruz was the only beach near us where people would splash around and perhaps try swimming in the ocean. But these beach movies really spread the blonde beach-bunny stereotype!

Hair dye was now sold over-the-counter. Women had previously gone to beauty shops to get their hair set weekly and dyed monthly, but now women could dye their own hair in the privacy of their homes! "Cover Girl" make-up was sold in grocery stores and targeted to teens. Mascara and powder were newly available at grocery stores and at dime stores. When we were little, there was a make-up section at Fremont Pharmacy that featured cosmetics such as powder and lipstick. Now there were more types of products with more variety and brands. Cosmetics and hair dye were available at stores other than pharmacies, and we could buy them at Bergman's Department Store at Midtown in Palo Alto.

I decided that I wanted to dye my hair bright red. I had already bleached my hair with hydrogen peroxide, resulting in what Gramma Gigi called "coyote-colored" hair. I had poured peroxide on my hair every day with no visible changes, and then suddenly my hair became a whole lot blonder! I had done this mostly because Gramma Gigi said that hydrogen peroxide would NOT bleach hair, and I wanted to see if it really would. I decided that I wanted red hair, redder than my brownish, blondish, reddish hair, so I went to Bergman's and bought capsules for dyeing hair. The package showed bright red hair, but when I mixed the powder that was in the capsules with hot water, which was what the directions said to do, the liquid turned purple.

The directions said to ignore the color of the liquid because it would turn the hair whatever color it was advertised to be. The trick was to put it on your hair immediately and leave it on your hair for the right amount of time. And it stunk to high heaven! I was trying to be sneaky about dyeing my hair, and I figured that I would just proceed and see what happened.

Well, when I rinsed the dye out of my hair and finally looked into the mirror I did not have red hair. I did not have purple hair. What I had was green hair. Green hair that was a multitude of different colors of green... like seaweed green and

Kelly green and grey-green and colors of green that you can't even imagine and that I had never seen before, but there they were in streaks in my hair. If I had been a mermaid or some sort of exotic undersea creature my hair would have been perfect.

I stood in the bathroom looking at my hair. I washed the sink and cleaned up the mess, and was sitting on the toilet lid looking at the box of hair coloring when I noticed that it said "wash-out coloring." I read the fine print again and it said that the coloring would wash out in six weeks. It turned out that this wasn't true at all, but for the moment it gave me hope. I reasoned that if I lived in the shower for a day and just washed and washed my hair that I would revert back to coyote-colored hair instead of green hair.

My daddy is red-green color blind. So is Daddy's brother, Uncle Jack. Grandma Ruth always said that her boys were never color-blind until they got married, but everybody just secretly smiled when she said that. Red-green color blindness means that those two colors look the same. Whenever we went on a ride in the country and there was a row of red roses, all of us but my daddy would be saying, "….Oh, how beautiful, look at the roses," but for Daddy to see the roses we would have to stop the car. Then he could see the shape of the roses in front of the shape of the leaves. The roses and the leaves looked the same color to Daddy. I think they looked grayish, but who knows? How can a color-blind person describe colors to someone else and how can a person who is not color-blind describe the colors that they see?

When I sat down at the dinner table I think that my mom was still at the stove because she didn't even notice my hair. Daddy looked at me, then he looked at Judy, then he looked at Jennifer and with a rather baffled look on his face, he pointed first at Jennifer and then at Judy and said, "Did you two girls do something to your hair?!" Because I was sitting between my sisters Daddy could tell that there was something different about our hair, but he couldn't tell what it was. So his guess was that Judy and Jennifer had done something with THEIR hair!

My sisters just shook their heads, "No!" Daddy looked at all three of us, made a puzzled face, and started eating his dinner. I couldn't even look at my sisters; I was afraid that I would start laughing! How could I have gotten off so easily?

By the time my mom came to the table, I was done eating. It was the fastest meal I had ever eaten! I excused myself and let out my breath. My sisters weren't going to tell on me, my daddy hadn't figured it out, and my mom hadn't noticed!

I had green hair for the next two months. It slowly faded. No one at Wilbur Jr. High had ever had green hair before. Girls were busy with ratted hair, hair spray, bows in the front of their hairdos, bleaching their hair blonde and trying to look like surfer girls. Green hair was about the weirdest thing that could happen. But I decided that I liked it in a rebellious sort of way. And another weird thing that happened was that all my mom did was look at me, shake her head, swear a lot, and that was the end of it. Nothing more.

In one year I had gone from super ratted and sprayed hair, to really curly hair all out of place, to really straight hair, to blondish hair, and then to green hair.

My daddy never saw that I had green hair. It was actually pretty funny.

C amp Campbell

Camp Campbell is a YMCA camp located in the Santa Cruz Mountains along Highway 9. When I was fourteen there was a church-sponsored weekend at Camp Campbell, and teenagers from all over the Bay Area were invited to attend. It was supposed to be a spiritual retreat, but I guess it depends on your interpretation of spiritual whether or not the retreat met the goals of the sponsors.

At the last minute several of the chaperones that were going with our group from Palo Alto cancelled, so our group had fewer adults than required. As the event had been planned for months, the decision was made to attend and not back out from it due to limited supervision. After all, it was a church event. And, coincidentally, whatever ailment our chaperones suffered from was striking chaperones of other Bay Area groups. The end result was that Friday evening there were more than two-hundred teenagers in the little cabins in the woods with very few adults to supervise them.

Judy and I had both signed up to go, and ended up in different areas of the camp. When I got to my cabin, a cabin that had two bunk beds designed to hold four people in one cabin…well, I met my weekend roommate.

Her name was Vanette. She was from East San Jose. She had already told the other two roommates to take a hike and find someplace else to sleep, because she planned to have some fun and didn't want to share her cabin with a bunch of squares.

Vanette had the tallest, blondest, smoothest, most perfect beehive hairdo that I had ever seen in my entire life. She looked like a model. Her makeup was perfect with her ultra black mascara and eyeliner and powder blue eye shadow. She had perfect skin, and wore pale pink lipstick that was pearly iridescent. Vanette had the tightest pants I had ever seen, and she had a perfect figure. Her arms were tan, and her sleeveless blouse was so low-cut that if it had been any lower, well, she just might as well have had on nothing at all!

Vanette. Why had my parents named me "Jane" instead of "Vanette?" Vanette was a name that sounded sexy and exotic. And there I stood in front of Vanette, holding my S&H Green Stamps sleeping bag and my pillow, while she looked me up and down. "Okay, you can share the cabin with me. What's your name?"

Dinner was held in the beautiful, rustic, redwood dining hall and many people pitched in to help prepare the meal. After dinner there was a presentation, but the teenagers began sneaking out and pretty soon there was a mass exodus from the hall. I wanted to go for a walk, to go to the cabin, and to walk in the woods with all the other teenagers, so I left too.

Having Vanette as a roommate was a bit more educational than I had bargained for. There were already several boys in the cabin when I got there, and they were smoking cigarettes and pot, while passing around a bottle of sloe gin. I had a few sips of the gin and decided that I didn't like the way the boys were leering at me. There were several more lurking outside and I thought it was best to leave them all to Vanette. I was way out of my league!

About that time the loud dinner chime began to ring…not for dinner, but for the people to assemble at the dining area for another presentation. But no one was going there. Instead, teenagers were running wild, going from one cabin to another, meeting new people, smoking and drinking. Record players magically appeared in many of the cabins and people began to dance outside the cabins' open doors. There was a full moon, and teenagers were dancing in the moonlight.

I needed a break. I had had too many drinks from too many different bottles, visiting too many different cabins, and I wasn't even sure what most of the drinks were. I just knew they were alcohol and some of them tasted the way that gasoline smelled. My head was spinning and I headed towards the stream that ran through the camp. I found a little trail that was going downhill, and in the moonlight I could see pretty well; pretty well for a fairly-drunk wandering teenage girl!

I sat down at the stream on a boulder and cooled my hands and face with the stream's water. I felt pretty uncoordinated, like I was washing my face but missing it half of the time, and that I was splashing water all over by mistake. And then I saw that I was not alone, that there was an older boy sitting nearby, a handsome boy that I had seen earlier.

He came over and sat on the boulder in the moonlight next to me. He was eighteen and tall and was a senior in high school. And when I got cold, he put his shirt around me, and then we started kissing in the moonlight. The sound of water was soothing, and in the distance we could hear laughter and music; sometimes we could hear the sounds of people running.

We kissed on that boulder in the moonlight in the redwood trees in the Santa Cruz Mountains, and then we did a whole lot more. So it was really a spiritual occasion for some of us that attended. And I wasn't sure if the stars that I saw were in the sky or in his eyes or in our hearts, but it was an absolutely perfect religious retreat!

Later, I did not want to go back to the cabin that I shared with Vanette. I knew that she would look at me and be able to tell that there was something different about me. I didn't want those boys in the cabin to look at me with their leers.

So my friend and I snuck into his cabin and shared his sleeping bag in the bottom bunk bed. And all through camp there were teenagers sharing sleeping bags and dancing and kissing, and the few chaperones that were there had no control. How would they have even known where to start?

The next morning at breakfast there were a lot of starry-eyed teens. Judy asked me where I had been the night before because she couldn't find me. Then she realized that I was in line with this handsome boy, and saw that we were holding hands and kissing. I figured I was in big trouble, because Judy would either tell on me or hold it over my head as blackmail.

After breakfast my friend and I went off into the woods.

Saturday night an ambulance came into the camp because there was something wrong with one of the girls and she was being taken to the hospital in Santa Cruz. And then someone yelled my name: I was asked to call my father, because the person in the ambulance was my sister Judy.

They took Judy to the hospital but released her the next morning. They could not figure out why she had been in so much pain, as she didn't have appendicitis or anything else they could find.

My daddy had picked me up at Camp Campbell on the way to the hospital, and he and I spent the night at the hospital in Santa Cruz. Sunday morning he drove Judy and me back to get our things from Camp Campbell. I went to the cabin to get my S&H Green Stamp sleeping bag and my pillow, and a very tired Vanette waved good-bye to me with a smile, barely picking her head off the pillow. Empty liquor bottles were scattered all through the cabin and I didn't want my daddy to see the mess, so I hurried as fast as I could!

I left without saying good-bye to the handsome, tall eighteen-year old with the charming smile. I never saw him again. But I always remembered him with my own smile, a happy, secret smile.

First Real Boyfriend

When I was in eighth grade, the Congregational Church at the corner of Louis and Embarcadero Roads was a great place to meet other teenagers from all around town. There was a strong and vibrant youth group and many opportunities to volunteer; through the church, from within the community, throughout the United States, and internationally. The church was a great place to meet boys, because everyone's parents encouraged them to go to church.

One evening there was a family potluck followed by movies and games. The church had a movie projector and screen and could somehow rent movies and then project them just like a real movie theatre.

I was helping clear off the food tables when seemingly out of nowhere a motorcycle-booted foot stuck its toe under the hem of my skirt and lifted my skirt up as I walked by!

Humph! It was a student from Paly (Palo Alto High School) who was much older and had a really bad reputation. He was a junior and had a car and a job and hung out at the Fremont Drag Strip. Everyone knew to stay away from him because he was really wild; he seldom came to church, but there he was with a devilish grin, wearing a leather jacket and winking at me! And he was breathtakingly cute!

"How come you wear your skirt so long? I think you would look a lot better showing off your legs... I'm sure you have great looking legs..." He was grinning at me and winking and making me feel really uncomfortable. I hoped that no one else had seen him flirting with me. But throughout the evening he followed me around and kept trying to talk to me. He was older and roguish and I didn't know why he was bothering to talk to me, but he sure made my heart pound!

When he found out I was in junior high he started laughing. He had thought that I was older and in high school. And before I knew what was happening, he had scouted out my parents, who were still eating at one of the tables, and he was talking to them!

I kept clearing off tables and pretty soon he came back over to where I was and started to help. Most of the other teenagers gave him a wide berth. A lot of the boys were afraid of him and most of the girls had heard about him being wild, so they wanted nothing to do with him. But as he started talking to me, I became more interested in him and it was as if the rest of the world didn't exist, as if he and I were the only two people in the entire universe. We were locking our eyes and time stood still. I looked at him and I could hardly breathe.

His name was John, and not only was he a junior at Palo Alto High, but he was assistant manager at the Varsity Theatre on University Avenue in downtown Palo Alto. He loved cars and loved racing cars. He asked me if I would go out on a date with him the next Friday night. I told him I didn't think my parents would let me, but he said that he was sure that they would. He took my phone number and said he would call me.

Whew! An older boy with a bad rep from the rival high school. Wilbur Jr. High fed into Cubberley High School, so Paly High was our rival. I was so conflicted inside, because I really liked him and wanted to go out with him, but I wasn't sure about the whole thing. What if he wanted to do something that I didn't want to do? What if he really didn't like me after we were on a date? What if ...what if.....what if....? My mind was racing around over the whole thing. But I liked his sleepy eyes and his confidence and his swagger.

On Monday afternoon his car was in front of Wilbur Jr. High, and he was leaning on it, looking like a movie star. He asked me if I wanted a ride home. And how could a girl say "No" to a question like that?! I got into the front seat and sat self-consciously next to the passenger door, without words and nervous as could be. He dropped me off at my house and said he would see me the next day! After that, he was there every afternoon, picking me up at school.

John became my boyfriend for the next year. We could talk about anything and everything and spent hours and hours in his car. Most Friday nights we went to the drag strip in Fremont and watched the races. The bleachers were always full and there were teenagers and families from all over Northern California. And I had a boyfriend who sometimes raced his car in the drag races there!

He had two cars and loved to work on cars. His station wagon was the car that we would drive to the drive-in movies on Colorado Avenue in Palo Alto. The first time we went to the drive-in, he jumped into the back of the car, folded down the back seat and was lying down. I was in the front seat not knowing what to do. All of the stories I had heard about him were racing through my head, including the rumors that he had gotten his girlfriend at Paly pregnant.

I stayed in the front seat while he kept on asking me to get in the back seat. I was so afraid that if I didn't go in the back seat and do it with him that he wouldn't like me any more, but I also didn't want to be in the back seat of his car. Everyone in town knew his car and would probably be walking by it to see what was going on! After a little while he started laughing and told me that he had never seen such a ridiculously stubborn girl. He came back to the front seat and we spent the rest of that movie steaming up the car windows, drinking sloe gin and sharing passion and excitement!

Other times John and I would just sit in his car in my driveway. If it was summer time and I was wearing shorts and barefoot, then he and I would tickle each other with our toes and he would run his hands and feet up and down my legs. John was the one who took me to the free clinic in East Palo Alto to get birth control; he said that someone didn't really love me if they wouldn't talk to me about birth control!

To get birth control I had to have an East Palo Alto address. There was one address that all the teenaged girls used and it was the same address but no one at the clinic seemed to care. And I had to lie about my age and say that I was eighteen. There was only one kind of birth control pill, Ortho Novo. It was very strong and made me feel sick to my stomach many mornings, but I was lucky to have that pill. I had birth control pills in my purse, and hoped that my mother did not do one of her random purse inspections and find them.

Some evenings John and I would drive to the beach at Pescadero and watch the sun set; then we would neck and steam up the windows in the car. As long as I was home by midnight, everything was okay. If I was out after midnight and hadn't told my parents ahead of time that I would be late, I had to find a phone booth and call home and tell my parents where I was and when I would be back. As there were no answering machines I would be talking to one of my parents in person, and that was stressful so I tried to be home on time.

There were other nights when we might go out to the Palo Alto Yacht Harbor and park and watch the moonlight sparkle on San Francisco Bay. There was always so much to talk about. We talked about school and our hopes and what we wanted to do with our lives. We talked about politics and about the war, about our families, our spirituality, and our friends. John had such a bad reputation, but he treated me so special and so nice, and was always pristinely kind to me.

Of course, we didn't just talk. We loved to kiss and hug and test our boundaries, to explore what we were comfortable with and where we wanted to set our limits. But it was all so new, all so exciting. I had confusing feelings along with lust and morality and conventions and wanting to throw away what had been good enough for the past for something that was more suited to NOW. Our parent's generation and those who came before them had been confined by the same Puritan ethics and sexual repression that we had been brought up with. Now women were starting to have some choices. Girls could actually plan to protect themselves from pregnancy and anticipate that they might sleep with someone and have some control about making that choice. And girls could say "yes" or "no" or even initiate sex. Having birth control as an option revolutionized our choices!

Times were changing in many other ways. There was a war in Vietnam that worried many of the older boys. John wanted to go to college and to make something of himself. He wanted to have a life that included a career and a family and a way to blend his passion for fast cars and mechanics and racing and women all into a life that he looked forward to. Now there was the draft and he was anxious that he might be drafted.

I was developing strong anti-war feelings. And the more we talked about the war, and what being an American meant and what war meant and who should sacrifice themselves and why, the more we began to refine our thoughts. John began teasing me that I was turning into a hippy. He would run his magical hands up and down my legs with his laughing eyes and tease me, asking me if I was going to be one of those crazy hippy chicks who quit shaving their legs and started going on peace marches. He would smile his sweet smile and my heart would melt.

He and I could talk and talk and had that precious window in time when our love protected us from the harshness of reality. He would envelope me in his arms and the world was safe and war was forgotten and there was just the two of us with everything we wanted right there in each others eyes.

I kept a journal during most of my teenaged years. Below is an excerpt from my journal written when I was fifteen, copied exactly as written:

"There were about a million and one things I was going to write this weekend…the main reason for this is because I have been broke and busy for the last week, so I couldn't buy canvasses to paint it out; besides, I hardly had enough time. But I'll be out tonight, so I am trying to rest for a while, so I'm gonna take some time to write before.

I was really mad a while ago, because of the things my boyfriend's parents expect from him. What would you do if you were just turned eighteen, going to Foothill, living with your parents and owed $700? I'll tell you what type of schedule John's parents expect him to maintain: He goes to school from around 8:00 to 5:00…then he eats dinner from around 5:15 to 5:45, if he has time. He goes to work from 6:00 to 1:00 in the A.M. Then he has homework to do from 1:00-3:00 or 3:30…And then he goes to sleep from 4:00 to around 7:00….3 hours of sleep a night. On weekends he sleeps 'til noon, then works 12 hours. He's lost weight and is back to chain-smoking again. That makes me so mad when parents take advantage of their kids.

And he isn't a stupid guy. Graduated from Paly with a B+--A- average. And yet his parents are just pushing him. I'm sure he'll live through it and all that, but couldn't they be conscious of his health, at least?!"

I still spent some weekends at my grandparent's house, although with less frequency than when I was little, and Auntie Jan always came over to our house several times a month. We would have so much fun when Auntie Jan came over. She had her sports car and I loved to go out riding in her car with her!

One of the best things about Auntie Jan was that she had boyfriends and I could talk to her about boys. She never got too serious, but sometimes she and I would "go to the store" together, which really meant that we would take a drive and park some place and talk. We smoked cigarettes together while we talked and she explained so many things to me! Auntie Jan was funny and beautiful and laughed a lot and had traveled all over the world. I loved Gramma Gigi and could talk with her, but not in the same way that I could talk to Auntie Jan.

I would even get clothes from Auntie Jan on occasion, and when I got some skin-tight golden stretch pants my mom couldn't really say any thing about it because they were pants that Auntie Jan had worn and then handed down to me, as tight as skin and not sewn at home!

Auntie Jan tried giving me the best advice she knew how, but she also told me that a lot of times people followed their hearts and their bodies instead of doing the things that their intellect told them was right. She would smile her brilliant smile at me and explain that since the beginning of time men and women yearned for passion and closeness and we were just made that way. I loved my Auntie for understanding and for accepting me.

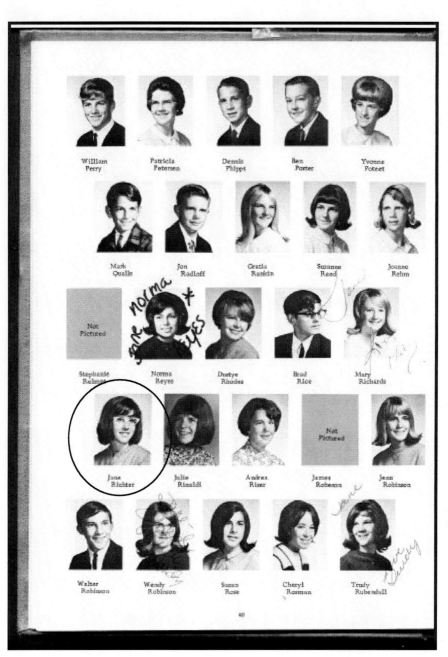

"My" page from my junior high school yearbook

Mono

I got sick with mono towards the end of eighth grade. Mono's real name was mononucleosis, but people most often called it "mono," or the kissing disease. People thought that promiscuity caused mono, so having mono gave a person a bad reputation.

I missed several months of school, and did my homework at home in order to pass the school year. I had a major assignment in music-appreciation class that was due towards the end of the year. My music appreciation teacher was the dreaded Mrs. Young. I hated music appreciation class because most of it was spent listening to short pieces of classical music or jazz, and then students were expected to memorize the composer, the name of the piece, and the date it was written.

I have no musical memory. I can hear a song many times and each time it is as if I never heard it before; therefore that class was extremely frustrating for me. But when I was at home with mono I became interested in Beethoven. I studied about him and found his life fascinating. I wrote and researched, and wrote some more. School reports in those days were either written long-hand in ink or typed on the typewriter. There was always a rough copy and then a final copy, and the final copy was what was turned in. Teachers would sometimes ask for the rough copy if they thought that a student had copied someone else's work. We were required to keep our rough copy until our final copy was graded in case the teacher wanted to see our original work with all of our notes.

I spent entire days when I was sick with mono reading about Beethoven. I read and wrote and read and wrote, and when I returned back to school I submitted my report to Mrs. Young along with other projects to other teachers that I had done while I had been sick.

When Mrs. Young returned the report to me, I opened it up and saw that she had written "F" in red ink over the entire front page, an "F" that was about four inches tall and was circled in deep red. I had NEVER received an "F" on any written assignment before and I felt my face turning red and I had to sit down. Her written comments were in red ink below the "F:"

"No student could have the ability to write a report of this caliber, and it is obvious that you plagiarized someone else's work. Do not insult my intelligence by attempting to claim another's brilliant writing as your own. Because you plagiarized, no make-up or corrections will be allowed on this assignment, and this is your final grade."

I talked to her and pleaded with her to let me turn in my rough copy; that way she would see that it was really my work! Mrs. Young said that even if I had a rough copy she was not interested in seeing it, because she believed that I would have just created a rough copy from someone else's work.

I had not respected Mrs. Young in the first place because of how she had treated us in seventh grade, always crashing her yardsticks down on our desks with her violent temperament. If it had been possible for me to respect her less than I already did, her actions certainly warranted it! The following year when I had Mrs. Young for ninth grade science I didn't do any of the work because I felt there was no point; Mrs. Young wouldn't believe it if I did good work. I started cutting science class in ninth grade and going to the restroom and smoking instead. However, Mrs. Young quit teaching part way through ninth grade. The rumor was that she had experienced a nervous breakdown. I hoped that she was never coming back.

The summer vacation following eighth grade was a real drag. We went on a family vacation drive-to-Kansas-like-a-bat-out-of-hell-trip, which included numerous horrible and boring stops at stupid places that I didn't want to go to, like the Grand Canyon and Mesa Verde and the Garden of the Gods.

Having mono meant that my spleen (having a spleen sounded really disgusting) could burst if I experienced a sudden change in temperature. The vacation was like this: Drive and drive in a really hot car. With no air conditioning we all would be sitting in pools of sweat, and it would be at least as hot inside the car as outside, and our first day of travel always included the roasting-hot Mojave Desert with its hypnotic rolling road that repeatedly reflected mirages just over the next hill.

The end of our first day would be spent at a motel...a motel in Barstow, a motel with a blue swimming pool full of cool water, water reflecting the hot sun in a thousand prisms, and families splashing and diving and cooling off and having fun. I would be roasting hot but I was not allowed to go swimming! "Remember, the doctor said no swimming because the sudden temperature change could burst your spleen!"

One other symptom of mono was that I was so tired I could barely move most of the time. Just getting out of the car was a lot of work. I was so hot and tired, my throat hurt constantly, and all I got to do was ride in the hot car and then go into the motel and lie down. It felt like my feet were made of lead and that I was slow inside and out.

My sisters would finally come inside after playing and cooling off in the pool, wrapped up in their wet towels and smelling of chlorine, all cooled off and relaxed and tired. I would still be in my sweaty and stinky clothes, too tired to get off the motel bedspread.

Every place we went it was difficult and painful for me to get out of the car, and once out I would sit down immediately. Sitting by the edge of the Grand Canyon in the hot sun or sitting at the top of Mesa Verde in the hot sun…well, I just wanted the summer to be over.

When we got to Kansas our cousins had grown and looked older. We still liked watching the home movies that Uncle Jack had taken previous summers, but now we listened to the Beach Boys with our Kansas cousins.

One of our cousin's friends asked Judy and me if we carried razor blades in our hair! He had heard that girls in California hid razor blades in their hair; that we ratted up hair to hide razor blades there! When Judy and I protested, the boys then asked if we wanted to go "…shuck some corn down in the crick." I yearned for the simpler days when we had played in the dark and the Kansas sky was full of stars and lightening bugs were like flying jewels. … "shuck corn?!" Geeze.

I could not wait to get home! I missed John, missed talking to him on the phone every day and seeing him in the evenings. I worried that he might forget me while I was on vacation. At home I was allowed to use the phone for one-half hour each night, but on vacation I couldn't phone John. It cost way too much money to call long-distance, so I had to wait until I got home to see him.

When we got back from vacation he had not forgotten me. He was going to start his senior year at Paly, and I was going to be in ninth grade at Wilbur Jr. High.

Eichler Swim Club

There was a neighborhood swim club right down the street from us on Louis Road. When my parents first moved to Palo Alto, Louis Road had been a dirt road. Palo Verde School had not yet been built, but even after Palo Verde was built there was no bridge across the creek and Louis Road dead-ended right beyond Palo Verde School.

But once a bridge was constructed and Louis Road continued over the creek, there were new Eichler homes built throughout our neighborhood. This included a large Eichler development between my parent's house and Highway 101. And with the Eichler homes came community Swim and Tennis Clubs. Joseph Eichler was a developer who included parks and swim clubs in his building plans as part of his goals to construct planned communities. He also was ahead of his time in offering homes for sale to anyone of any religion or race. The Eichler homes were different from our house and from the homes we were used to, with their glass walls, open floor plans and indoor atriums and skylights. Eichler homes also had radiant heat, not like our house with its cold asphalt tiles and area rugs.

Because my parents were in the neighborhood, our family joined the club, even though we did not live in an Eichler. The swim club was at first open to the entire neighborhood; there were not enough Eichler owners to support the club and therefore neighborhood homeowners were needed to insure the success of the Eichler Swim and Tennis Club. Later, when more Eichlers were built, the swim and tennis club enrolled only Eichler homeowners, but the original members were not terminated because of non-Eichler home ownership.

This meant that during the summer I got to walk down the street to spend hours and hours at the swim club.

Two-piece bathing suits had become socially acceptable. However, it was still considered risqué to have your belly-button show and certainly no part of one's bottom could peak out and the display of cleavage was discouraged. Conservative and modest two-piece suits were tolerated and even the bikini was starting to be seen on occasion.

Auntie Jan got a bikini, and when she wore her bikini it was almost as if she was naked! Her belly-button showed and you could almost see her whole body. Sometimes Auntie Jan would go to the swim club with us. She had moved to an apartment in Palo Alto on Alma Street, so she was much nearer than when she had lived in San Carlos. There was a pool at her apartment complex, but we girls would occasionally talk her into coming with us to the swim club. Her skin was very, very fair and was so thin that all of the bumps on her spine showed through her translucent, fair skin. She had a big chest like Marilyn Monroe used to have, but the rest of Auntie Jan was pale and tiny.

At the swim club, Auntie Jan always wore a hat with a wide brim along with her sunglasses, and would sit under a large umbrella on the deck next to the pool. There was no sun screen in those days, just sun tan lotion, so people would sit in the shade to protect their skin from burning. It was normal for people to put baby oil on their skin and then sit in the sun, frying their skin! Auntie Jan said that sitting in the sun aged her skin, so she was very careful to protect herself from direct sun.

The summer between seventh and eighth grade a new style of swimsuit shocked our neighborhood. It was a swimsuit that had a fishnet see-through top, and there were also "topless" swimsuits!

A few houses down from the swim club there lived a lady who must have been around thirty-five years old. One day when she took off her bathing suit cover, which was like a very short bathrobe made from sheer fabric...well...the whole pool deck became silent. That woman was wearing a one-piece suit with a fishnet top so that you could see all of her breasts! All of them. Both breasts. Right through the fishnet top. She casually and slowly put her bathing suit cover over the back of a chair, adjusted her sunglasses, and lay down on her back on a poolside chaise lounge!

Well. Well. Well.

People were looking at each other. We teenaged girls started to giggle and the teenaged boys all jumped into the pool and pretended that they did not notice. But the boys kept swimming closer and closer to the risqué lady, and then they would get out of the pool and walk past her on the way to the snack booth. And then they would do it again. And again. I suspect the snack booth probably sold out that day for the first and only time!

Most of the women who came to the pool and lay in the sun did not look very appealing. They were lumpy and saggy and middle-aged, with veins that looked like stringy highways in their legs and a lot of thickness around their middles. They would come to the swim club and swim a few laps during adult swim and then lay in the sun, relaxing for an hour before they went home. They seemed only to want to swim and relax and make sure that the swim club was worth paying their monthly dues. My mom had never come to the swim club...I wasn't even sure if she could swim or if she even owned a bathing suit.

But the woman in the see-through top had a nicely-shaped tan body, and the other women were suddenly busy covering themselves up, looking for their sons and daughters, and then leaving. I think that they had compared their crepe-like necks, jiggling thighs and upper arms to the younger woman, and did not feel happy with the result of the comparison. Up until then the ladies that spent time at the pool every day had been comfortable in their own bodies and had enjoyed their bit of time to relax.

The fishnet-topped suit became a neighborhood outrage. Everyone was talking about the woman and her swim suit – or lack of swim suit! There had been an article in *Life Magazine* about the new style of topless suits, and now we had a neighbor publicly wearing one! There was no rule about what kind of suits people could wear at the swim club. No one needed any rules except to wear flip-flops or beach-walkers on the deck; people knew how to dress and how to behave (except for boys who did cannonballs off of the high dive.) And now we had this...this....this SCANDAL!

As the summer flew by, my girlfriends and I became accustomed to the lady and her swimsuit, and our routine was no longer disrupted by "that woman."

My girlfriends and I liked to sit at the pool and talk about boys. We thought the lifeguard was cute and we flirted with him. He was a nineteen-year-old college student. One time he asked my friend and me if we wanted to go to his apartment some time in the evening. Did we ever! We were so flattered; we felt special because he was a college student asking us to go to his apartment. So when he got off work, we piled into his car and went over to his apartment complex at Del Medio, near the Sears Shopping Center on San Antonio Road. When it started to cool off we all went swimming in the pool at his complex. He shared an apartment with other college students and after we were done swimming, we drank beer and laughed and went swimming some more. They drove us back to my friend's house and I walked home in my bathing suit and my skimpy cover-up. It was a warm summer evening, almost dark, and as I walked past the house where the lady with the see-through top lived, I wondered what it would be like to be so brave to just go out in public in a bathing suit like that!

Jane 13, Jennifer 10, and Judy 16
Tanning in the backyard on a warm spring day
We were getting ready for summer!

Jane and Judy washing Judy's Chevy Nova in our driveway
A bathing-suit fashion show!

Segregation

When I was growing there were no legally segregated facilities in Palo Alto. Legally, everyone could eat at the same lunch counter and ride in the same bus. There were parts of East Palo Alto, parts of San Francisco, and parts of Oakland where few white people lived; there were places like Los Altos and Los Altos Hills where few Negroes lived. But in the Bay Area we did not have signs like in the south, such as "Whites Only," or "Colored Only." Nationally, sports were becoming integrated in the United States, but still largely only on the playing fields. Negro sports players traveled separately from the white players, ate separately, and stayed in separate accommodations. Entertainment was becoming integrated, but in parts of America legal segregation was still normal and accepted.

We saw the evening TV news about protests in the south against integrated schools. We couldn't imagine people living where the schools were segregated, and that organized groups were against integration. And we were appalled at the governor of Alabama, George Wallace. George Wallace was elected governor of Alabama in November 1962, and took office on January 14, 1963, standing on the gold star marking the spot where, one hundred and two years prior, Jefferson Davis was sworn in as President of the Confederate States of America.

In his inaugural speech, George Wallace used the line for which he is best known: *"In the name of the greatest people that have ever trod this earth, I draw the line in the dust and toss the gauntlet before the feet of tyranny, and I say segregation now, segregation tomorrow, segregation forever."*

To stop desegregation, Governor Wallace stood in front of Foster Auditorium at the University of Alabama on June 11, 1963. This became known as the "Stand in the Schoolhouse Door." And of course we watched this on TV News. My mother said that George Wallace was a fucking idiot, a phrase she used rather judiciously with scorn and contempt.

Racial hatred was foreign to us. I couldn't understand how these people on TV, people who looked like regular people, could open their mouths and spout out this racial bigotry. It made me embarrassed to be a white person. And the Negroes that I had known all my life were becoming angry and conversations that we could have had in the past were no longer possible because of anger. Instead of being friends, people were now separating along lines of color.

I hadn't kept slaves. My family hadn't kept slaves. Why were all my Negro friends so angry? Judy's best friend, Sylvia, was a Negro and we never thought anything about it. But now, groups that had worked together were separating. I had volunteered in a reading program in East Palo Alto, tutoring elementary students, but Gertrude Wilkes, the head of the program, told me that she was tired of rich white girls coming over to her town and she didn't want me volunteering any more. And when I watched George Wallace on TV, I could understand some of the feelings – there was so much to be angry about!

George Wallace again attempted to stop Negro students from enrolling in four separate elementary schools in September 1963. After intervention by a federal court in Birmingham, the children were allowed to enter on September 9th, becoming the first children to integrate a primary or secondary school in Alabama. I lived in America, and those four children lived in America, but it sure didn't sound like the same America.

We had grown up singing about the land of the free and the home of the brave, but it didn't sound like these little girls in Alabama lived in the land of the free. Nor did George Wallace sound as if he was one of the brave. It was absolutely shocking to come to the realization that this government official, this elected governor, was doing everything he could to prevent elementary-school integration. It was shameful!

It sounded like two different Americas. One America for whites and one America for Negroes. It was embarrassing that George Wallace seemed so proud of himself. Wallace disapproved vehemently of the desegregation of the state of Alabama and wanted for his state to remain segregated. In his own words: *"The President (John F. Kennedy) wants us to surrender this state to Martin Luther King and his group of pro-Communists who have instituted these demonstrations."*

The John Birch Society was another organization that promoted fear and racism. We didn't buy any Welch's products, because the John Birch Society founder who created the candy "Sugar Daddy," had possible ties to Welch's. The John Birch Society opposed the 1964 Civil Rights Act, saying it was in violation of the Tenth Amendment to the United States Constitution and that it overstepped the rights of individual states to enact laws regarding civil rights.

We read about these groups in our newspaper and watched on TV adults trying to keep children from going to school because of their skin color. I couldn't understand it. It was as baffling to me as if people thought black dogs could only play with black dogs or that white cats could only live in homes with white cats. We wanted segregation to end so that this would indeed be one America with Liberty and Justice for All.

This photo, printed in Life Magazine, was seen worldwide.

What people saw on the news and read in the press about Birmingham, Alabama, was frightening and disturbing. The Birmingham police and fire departments' actions were captured on film, including the above photo of high school students being blasted by a high-pressure water jet. The pressure was set hard enough to tear the bark off a tree, and we were horrified to see the students pushed down the street by the water while the police stood by watching.

"The Birmingham Campaign," as well as George Wallace's refusal to admit Negro students to the University of Alabama, convinced President Kennedy to address the issues between black and white citizens in the South. President Kennedy said, "The events in Birmingham and elsewhere have so increased cries for equality that no city or state or legislative body can prudently choose to ignore them."

Birmingham's public schools were integrated in September 1963. Governor Wallace sent National Guard troops to keep Negro students out, but President Kennedy reversed Wallace's mandate by ordering the troops to stand down. President Kennedy's administration drew up the Civil Rights Act bill, and it was passed into law in 1964.

Slumber Parties

In elementary school we had sleepovers. A friend or two would sleep at my house or I would sleep at a friend's house, but we didn't have slumber parties.

When I started junior high, this changed. Girls would have slumber parties...it was the new thing. If a girl was never invited to a slumber party, well, that girl just had no friends or wasn't popular or there was something wrong with her. Being invited to a slumber party meant you were cool.

Slumber parties were talked about during the week before the party, then the party happened, and afterwards everyone talked about the party during the entire following week. It was more of an event than a sleepover had ever been.

My first slumber party experience was pretty tame; there were about fifteen girls attending, and the mom fed us non-stop and made a special drink that was milk and root beer mixed together. Then we had as much ice cream as we could eat, sitting in the back yard and eating ice cream and talking and looking at magazines. We stayed up giggling and gossiping and eating until we couldn't keep our eyes open. In the morning we all slept in, and then the mom made a humongous breakfast of pancakes, eggs, sausages and eggnog. We feasted and talked; the best part was finding out that during the night some boys had rung the doorbell and the father had to chase them away. The party was truly a success!

My most memorable slumber party was at my new best friend's house. Sharon was the tiniest teenager I knew, and was the cutest girl at school. When I went to her house, there was a short, overweight woman who looked more like a man than a woman. I thought that maybe it was a housecleaner or cook; especially since my friend lived in a huge house and the way she barked commands and was quite rude to the woman.

However, every time I went to my friend's house, the same woman was there. When I finally asked Sharon who the person was, she looked at me like I was an idiot. It was her mother! I was astounded…how could this tiny, beautiful teenager come from this dowdy, sullen, overweight woman, and why did Sharon's mom act more like a servant than a mother? It was really weird.

When Sharon's birthday came around, she had a slumber party! I was accustomed to her mother by then and her mother had started talking to me. They were from a foreign country where women were expected to act like servants, and through conversation and observation I was learning about their culture, customs and their traditions.

The day of the slumber party came and eight of us girls arrived at Sharon's house on Saturday after lunch, ready to go to the matinee at a movie theatre on University Avenue in Palo Alto. We all piled into their family station wagon to get dropped off at the theatre, but on the way we stopped by Bergman's Department Store to buy wax lips; all of us had glossy red wax lips made from sweet wax and shaped like oversized smiling lips.

We put the lips on while we were waiting in line to get our tickets, looking at each other and trying not to laugh.

The movie was a double-feature and the second movie was the one we really wanted to see. It was *The Raven*, and starred Vincent Price, Peter Lorre, and Boris Karloff as rival sorcerers and Jack Nicholson as Rexford Bedlo. We purchased our tickets, and inside the theatre the usherette used her flashlight to find a row where we could all sit together. The theatres in those days were dark when you entered prior to the show, and an usherette in a uniform that looked like an ice-skating skirt and blouse would safely direct the theatre-goer to a seat. Once we were seated, we took off our wax lips and started eating popcorn, ready to be scared out of our wits.

The first movie of the double-feature started. Movie ratings had not yet been established, so we had no way of knowing anything about the movie that was showing before *The Raven* on that Saturday afternoon.

As the black and white movie unfolded, we girls began to hunker down in our seats. The movie, *Peeping Tom*, was about a young photographer who used a modified portable movie camera to murder women. He would trick young women into thinking they were going to do a modeling job, but when the filming started, a stiletto would extend out from his camera, and he would film the women as he pierced their throats or their chests... all while the girls and women where backing up, terrified and trying to escape once they realized that the camera was a weapon. Then the killer would develop the film himself, and he would watch the murder on film over and over again. At the end of the movie he recorded his own death, leaving the camera running as he impaled himself.

Whew. We were horrified, and I felt like the air-conditioning had been turned up all the way and that I wanted to keep my eyes closed and not be at that movie!

None of us girls were looking at each other. This was Sharon's birthday slumber party. She was one of the most popular girls, and we were there at the theatre watching an incredibly weird and disturbing movie and we didn't know what

to do. Her dad wasn't going to be back for hours to pick us up, and we were numb with disbelief while we watched that movie of an insane man photographing murder. The movie was not exactly teenaged-girl birthday fun and not what we had been anticipating.

When the lights in the theatre came on for the intermission, it was as if we all had been in a stupor. We shook our heads and looked at each other speechlessly. I felt like I was going to throw up after watching that nightmare-producing movie. We all went to the lobby and then to the restroom; the elegant movie theatre restroom with carpet and marble wash basins and linen hand towels.

Walking around gave us the opportunity to get our needed balance back. What we had watched was horrible, but we didn't know it was going to be horrible until we were in the middle of it!

We stayed at the theatre and watched *The Raven*. It was funny and silly-scary. We all ended up eating our wax lips, after sharing tubs of buttered popcorn and paper cups of Coca Cola.

Sharon's dad picked us up outside the theatre, and we all piled into the station wagon. When he asked how the movie was, we talked about *The Raven* and how much we had liked it. No one said anything about the other movie.

We had a huge dinner at Sharon's house, which her mom cooked and served, and we gave Sharon the presents we had bought for her. Later we headed to the living room in preparation for the slumber party. No one wanted to go to sleep, because one of the girls there had promised to play a trick on the first person who fell asleep. So we told jokes and scary stories, and put on our pajamas and spread out our sleeping bags. I had my S&H Green Stamp sleeping bag. Some of the girls had brought only blankets because they didn't have sleeping bags. As the night wore on, we realized that one of us had, indeed, fallen asleep.

One girl then said that if you put someone's hand in a warm bowl of water that the person would wet their bed. Another girl said that she had planned something better. She said that she would pretend to perform an appendectomy on the sleeping girl, and that when the girl woke up she would think that she had really had the operation to remove her appendix! Having described her plan, she then lifted up the girl's pajama top, displaying her tummy. "You are at the hospital, you came here in an ambulance, and now we have to remove your appendix. I know it really hurts, but we will make it better!" Then she took a damp cloth and rubbed the girl's stomach with it, as if she was putting iodine on the girl.

We were all watching. It had been a creepy day and now this was getting creepier. We were looking at each other behind the girl's back. "Now I will have to operate on you, so you might feel something," and then she took out a ball point pen and drew a line right on the girl's stomach, and the sleeping girl began to whimper and squirm. Then we all erupted, "Stop, stop! This is not funny!" We had to make the girl who was pretending to operate stop, and the girl that was sleeping was crying and squirming and trying to get away.

We woke her up and she was panicking. The other girl was mad because we had stopped her. Then Sharon's dad came in and yelled at us that it was late and that some boys had just rung the doorbell looking for the slumber party, and that he had chased the boys away.

We were all glad to switch the topic to boys. We could talk about boys for hours. Boys were stupid, boys were cute, boys were stupid. And then it finally felt like we were actually having the slumber party that we had all been waiting for.

When I look back on that party, the movie is what I remember most. That horrible movie stuck in my head, and I couldn't understand why someone would make a movie like that, or how it was that a group of thirteen and fourteen-year-old girls had gone to watch it as part of a birthday party. None of us had said a word about that movie; we had gushed over *The Raven* and wouldn't stop talking about *The Raven*. *The Raven* was creepy, but we all knew the story from Edgar Alan Poe ahead of time, because we had studied it in school. The other movie was truly the horror movie because the murderer filmed murders of young women and girls, and I think we all had that horrible, "….what if?" inside our heads.

It was a slumber party to remember, wax lips and all.

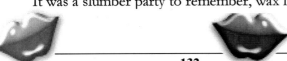

Assassination

On November 22, 1963, I was sitting in Mr. Chapman's social studies class when one of my classmates, Darwin, came running into the room, white-faced and shaking and shouting that President Kennedy had been shot. Darwin was the audio visual monitor for the classroom and had gone to the office to get a movie projector. He ran all the way back to the classroom without the projector, in shock because of what he heard in the school office.

We first thought that Darwin was joking, but then we realized that Darwin didn't act like he was joking. It was apparent that he thought it was real. Mr. Chapman said for us to wait a minute, he would find out what had happened. He pulled the metal chain on the P.A. system to call the office, but there was no response, so Mr. Chapman turned on the black-and-white television that we had in the classroom. We started to see that it might be true, and that the President had indeed been shot. We watched and listened as the scheduled TV show was interrupted by a local newscaster who read:

"Here is a bulletin from CBS News. In Dallas, Texas, three shots were fired at President Kennedy's motorcade in downtown Dallas. The first reports say that President Kennedy has been seriously wounded by this shooting.

"More details just arrived. These details are about the same as previously, President Kennedy shot today just as his motorcade left downtown Dallas. Mrs. Kennedy jumped up and grabbed Mr. Kennedy, she called "Oh no!" the motorcade sped on. United Press [International] says that the wounds for President Kennedy perhaps could be fatal. Repeating, a bulletin from CBS News, President Kennedy has been shot by a would-be assassin in Dallas, Texas. Stay tuned to CBS News for further details.

"Further details on an assassination attempt against President Kennedy in Dallas, Texas. President Kennedy was shot as he drove from Dallas Airport to downtown Dallas; Governor Connally of Texas, in the car with him, was also shot. It is reported that three bullets rang out. The President, cradled in the arms of his wife, Mrs. Kennedy, was carried to an ambulance and the car rushed to Parkland Hospital outside Dallas. The President was taken to an emergency room in the hospital. We will keep you advised as more details come in, stay tuned to CBS News for further details."

The local news switched to the national news, where we saw the famous newscaster, Walter Cronkite. He appeared on-air in his shirt and tie but without his suit coat, which showed the viewers the unprecedented nature of the broadcast. For Mr. Cronkite to not have the time to prepare to be on-camera added intensity; this was real, live, spoken-from-the-heart and unrehearsed:

"This is Walter Cronkite in our newsroom in New York. There has been an attempt, as perhaps you know now, on the life of President Kennedy. He was wounded in an automobile driving from Dallas Airport into downtown Dallas, along with Governor Connally of Texas. They have been taken to Parkland Hospital there, where their conditions are as yet unknown."

This was impossible. This was the President of the United States, the greatest country in the world, the country where the President had asked people to "…ask not what your country can do for you but what you can do for your country."

How could this be real? Students started crying, and Mr. Chapman took off his glasses and wiped his eyes with his handkerchief. No one knew what to do.

Then the school principal came on the public address system for the entire school and announced that the President of the United States had been shot, and that school was closing so that students could go home to their families.

I was walking home, but it wasn't right, because this should have been a normal day. It should have been a day where boys teased girls and teachers paid attention to details and discipline, and students tried to get away with things, just like any other day. But instead I was walking home by myself, joined momentarily by others who then separated to go their ways, people almost wandering, almost staggering. There were no cell phones in those days, no way to connect with others, and I walked the two-and-a-half miles from school to home, and all along the way there were people hugging each other and crying. Cars stopped, and both friends and strangers asked if I wanted or needed a ride.

A man who had been admired and respected and half of a couple who had loved each other were now possibly lost to the world in a way that hurt so much that no words could explain it. There was no way to erase the swollen eyes or remove the lump in my throat, no way to explain the fear that made me swallow too often and my throat close up and want to be alone and yet to be with others at the same time. Nothing would fix it or wipe away the tears or erase the pain and shock, because a father, a husband, a president, and a good man had been shot, and if he wasn't safe then no one was ever safe again.

When I got home my mom and my sisters were already there with the TV on. Every Palo Alto school had closed and sent students home at the announcement that the President of the United States had been shot. I wasn't sure how I was supposed to feel, because the concept that people could admire a person while disliking that person's belief was beyond my understanding. I didn't know if the fact that Kennedy the person, who was a Democrat that my parents disliked, and the shooting of Kennedy the President, would be a good thing or a bad thing. I don't think older people ever understood how this experience was seen through the eyes of an innocent. I didn't know a person could hate a political party or an ideology but still want the person who represented that party to live and exist and have happiness. I had a grasp of democracy, but not an understanding that people had power to vote for more than a person, and that a person could be greatly admired even if what that person believed in was not. Integrity and politics were still very far away from the understandings of a young person.

We sat together the kitchen table in front of the TV, and listened to the frequent, often-repeated news bulletins. Then Walter Cronkite was handed a bulletin and he stopped speaking for a moment, put on his glasses, looked at the bulletin, then took off his eyeglasses, and we listened to what he had to say:

"From Dallas, Texas, the flash, apparently official: President Kennedy died at 1 p.m. Central Standard Time, 2 o'clock Eastern Standard Time, some 38 minutes ago."

My throat closed up. We sat in the kitchen, stunned. Tears filled my eyes, and it was suddenly very difficult to breathe. After making that announcement, Cronkite paused, put his glasses back on and then read the next sentence of the news report:

"Vice President Johnson has left the hospital in Dallas, but we do not know to where he has proceeded. Presumably, he will be taking the oath of office shortly and become the 36th president of the United States."

How does a story continue after the president of your country has been killed? The country seemed to be spinning and spiraling backwards. The tale goes on, but in a different way, in a way that is a little bit like going from the dream to going back to what is old and comfortable and familiar. It was going from the hope and the glamour and the passion around excitement and change, back to a routine and steadfast humdrum of slowly continuing without fanfare and with ordinariness and steadiness. Back to the commonness that looked backwards instead of the fast-paced high road that we had been walking with hope and enthusiasm.

It was as if there was a pain that would never go away.

What followed was non-stop TV and radio news-coverage of the assassination and of the ceremonies which followed. Black-and-white live coverage of people throughout the country lining the streets, some sobbing, others hugging one another, men and women wiping their eyes with their cloth handkerchiefs. Regular people lined the streets, not knowing what to do or how to act now that such a horrible thing had happened. We watched the same live coverage as people throughout America, and heard the reporters with the same questions that we all had. Our questions yet had no answers, and live news coverage let us commonly share and experience that all Americans felt the sorrow and loss and the inability to understand how to behave from that point onward.

There was no model for us to look to, no example of how to behave when your president has been shot and killed. The body of President Kennedy was brought back to Washington, D.C. and placed in the East Room of the White House for twenty-four hours. On Sunday afternoon, about 300,000 people watched a horse-drawn caisson carry Kennedy's flag-covered casket down the White House drive, past soldiers bearing flags, then along Pennsylvania Avenue to the Capitol Rotunda to lie in state.

Schools were closed for several days. On Saturday, the day after the assassination, the new president, Lyndon Johnson, declared Monday to be a national day of mourning.

In the only public viewing, hundreds of thousands people lined up in near-freezing temperatures to view the President's casket. We watched this on live TV, feeling like we were a part of the mourning as we shared the viewing. There was a lot of weeping at our house, frequent taking off of eyeglasses and wiping of eyes. One of us would start to cry and then the others would too. My throat felt as if it would never stop burning, and my nose felt as if it would never stop running.

But what happened next is that the country did get a role model, did see the standard set for us for how to react and how to behave in this crisis and sorrow. Thirty-four-year old Jacqueline Kennedy wore a black veil and held the hands of her

children. John Jr. celebrated his third birthday on the day of his father's funeral. Little Caroline behaved with strength and character. Caroline was less than a week from her sixth birthday. Looking at that young family made all of us feel devastated. We watched Mrs. Kennedy, dressed in black, bravely walking behind her husband's casket. The casket was covered with an American flag, and the

Kennedy family walked with the casket for blocks and blocks, behind and with the horse-drawn wagon that carried the body of the President. In the background we could see the Capitol of the United States, and streets lined with crowds of people. These were respectful people in tears, men removing their hats in respect, and children saluting as the casket passed them by.

We cried for days and days until we could cry no more. Seeing the young Kennedy children and their mother react with such dignity gave us reassurance that if Jacqueline Kennedy could somehow get through this horrible time, then perhaps we also would make it through. I think that if we had seen her sobbing or reacting with hate or anger, then we all would have lost hope completely.

The television replayed scenes, including Mrs. Kennedy at the airport still wearing her blood-stained suit. It was the blood of her husband, the blood of the President, and even with our black-and-white TV we recognized it for what it was. And it was real, and she wore it as if to share the tragedy. Even though I was not verbalizing this at the time, I had not only a sense of the pivotal point in our history, but of also the importance of the news coverage and how we were a witness to a window of sharing these very intimate moments of this sorrowful time.

And then, as if the assassination story was not enough, another story began to unfold about the suspect in the shooting.

About two o'clock in the afternoon on the day of the assassination, Lee Harvey Oswald was arrested on suspicion of killing Dallas police officer J. D. Tippit and soon connected to the assassination of President Kennedy. Oswald denied any responsibility for the murders. We were glued to the television in disbelief, listening about this man named Lee Harvey Oswald. Why would he shoot the President of the United States?

Two days later, before he could be brought to trial, this suspected murderer, Lee Harvey Oswald, was shot by a man named Jack Ruby on live television. We watched that murder. Sitting in our kitchen and not being able to believe the enormity of what we had seen and heard in less than a week, we saw and experienced second-hand the pandemonium. It was yet another moment of disbelief that one more shooting had happened and that we had witnessed it. We saw it happen on TV…it was real… uncensored…how could that be? What was happening to our country? How and why did all these people have guns?

Jack Ruby was a Dallas nightclub operator, and he shot Lee Harvey Oswald right before our eyes…we heard the gun go off and watched Oswald curl up a bit. Oswald was handcuffed to another man so he couldn't fall all the way to the ground right after he was shot. The fact that Oswald wasn't on the ground added confusion as to what had happened.

Unconscious, Oswald was put into an ambulance and rushed to the same hospital where President Kennedy had died two days earlier. Forty eight hours and seven minutes after the President's death, Oswald was pronounced dead at seven minutes past one in the afternoon.

Our lives had changed so much in the span of just a few days. Up until that time in my life, presidents and other important people drove through towns and cities in convertibles, stood on the back of trains, and walked in public believing that the United States was a safe place. Up to that point there was confidence that all people were protected and that anyone could go where they wanted to go without fear.

These historic events had changed our thinking and attitudes. There were more and more guns being made, and many, many kinds of guns. Guns were very easy for people to get, people like Lee Harvey Oswald and Jack Ruby. And these dangerous guns were easily available to dangerous people.

We went back to school after a few days. Daddy and Grandpa Bob and Auntie Jan went back to their jobs, my mother and Gramma Gigi went back to their housekeeping. Daddy had only stayed home one day because of laws that controlled how long banks could stay closed. People needed an open bank to access their money, as there were yet no ATMs or debit cards, so Daddy had to be at work. Banks were nervous that the assassination might cause a rash of withdrawals, and wanted the trusted managers there to reassure their depositors.

News reporters continued to analyze and attempted to make sense of what had happened, disclosing new facts, and theories as they came to light.

We learned all about Oswald's story, and his wife's story, and about Jack Ruby. We saw diagrams and aerial photography and phrases like "the grassy knoll" and the "book repository" became commonplace. People didn't know how to talk about their feelings of what had happened. We all talked about everything but how we felt; people became experts on the facts of the assassination.

For months we heard more detailed information about Lee Harvey Oswald, about his life, his history, his wife, and there was ongoing speculation about why he assassinated the President. Lee Harvey Oswald was twenty-four years old when he shot President Kennedy and when he, in turn, was shot by Jack Ruby.

We were a nation in grieving. And when I lay in bed at night and wondered about the future, I had bigger fears than before; fears that would grab me from inside and squeeze tightly around my heart.

I returned to school after the assassination feeling like a changed person. My classmates and I, along with Mr. Chapman, shared an event that we would continue sharing for the rest of our lives. We would never forget exactly where we had been and what we had been doing the moment we heard the news about President Kennedy. It was a snapshot in my mind that could be pulled up in an instant.

The Beatles

Summer was almost over and there was a big dance planned for the teenagers at the Congregational Church. I made a new dress out of a blue, scratchy material, a "shirtwaist" dress, with a tight waist and a belt. The dress buttoned down the front from the neck to the waist, and then had a full skirt that flared out from the gathered waist.

The day of the dance, my sisters and I lay for hours in the backyard in our bathing suits, slathered with baby oil and turning from one side to the other to get an even tan. Daddy and my sisters tan easily, and in the summer Daddy looked like an Indian and Judy looked Hawaiian and Jennifer sported a beautiful tan. I was the one who should not have been lying out there in the backyard all oiled up, cooking my skin. But we wanted to be tan.

By the time the dance started that night, I knew that I was in trouble with very bad sunburn. I was blistering and my skin was hot and red, but I wanted to go the dance! So I went, wearing my scratchy new shirtwaist dress, which rubbed painfully on my sunburn.

It was crowded in the auditorium of the church, and there was an actual DJ playing records. The Beach Boys were the popular music group, but that night at the church I heard my first Beatle song. Someone brought in an album by a group called the Beatles who were from England. Suddenly we were dancing to the song *I Wanna' Hold Your Hand*, and the Beach Boys were no longer as cool as they had been. There was a new group with a new sound. The Beatles had long hair and black boots and cute British accents! I danced in spite of my severe sun burn and suffered, excited about this new music group!

Almost immediately, people began to change how they dressed, depending on if they liked the Beatles, or if they liked the Rolling Stones, or if they liked the Beach Boys. The surfer look was still popular, with bleached blonde hair and madras shorts or mini skirts and tan, tan skin. The Rolling Stones were dirty, sexy and sleazy. The Beatles were long-haired and shook their heads when they sang. Everyone had a favorite Beatle. I wasn't Beatle-crazy, but if I had to say which Beatle was my favorite, it was George. I liked George because he wasn't cute like Paul, and he didn't try to attract attention like Ringo, and he wasn't the star like John. George seemed to be the underdog of the group, and beside that, he had crooked teeth which made him appear to be a bit more humble than the others.

In the 1960s, the Cabana Hotel was the most glamorous hotel in Palo Alto. We would drive past the Cabana just to look at the fancy hotel with all the fountains out front. Only rich people could afford to stay there, and it was rumored to have connections with the Mafia. However, it was perfect for the touring Beatles, and they stayed there twice after concerts at the Cow Palace in Daly City.

When the word spread that the Beatles would be staying in Palo Alto at the Cabana there was so much excitement! Many people thought that it was a rumor, but the night of the first concert there were about three-thousand fans crowded into the parking lot, a parking lot that was not designed or intended for crowds of people. Fans stretched across the street, and crowded into the parking lot of Ricky's, which was the restaurant and motel across the street from the Cabana.

Judy's best friend, Sylvia, was almost successful in her attempt to get inside the Beatles' room on the eighth floor. Sylvia dressed like a maid, and the security guards didn't notice her right away. They just thought that she worked there, and she was able to go right up to the eighth floor! But Sylvia got caught at the room door and was kicked out, having gotten closer to the Beatles' room than anyone else we knew. A few brave and crazy girls actually slipped past the outdoor security guards and began to climb the outer grating of the hotel!

The arrival and departure of the Beatles was like their movie, *A Hard Day's Night*. Fans climbed onto the Beatles' limousine, rocking the car and denting the roof when the Beatles arrived at night. The next morning the Beatles made a crazy getaway, with two decoy limos and a truck. As the truck was leaving the Cabana the driver realized he had left Ringo behind and had to slam on the brakes to let Ringo in.

Room 810 has been named the "Beatles Room" with walls decorated with images of the band posing in the lobby.

Judy, Jennifer, and Daddy went to the Beatles' final concert, held at Candlestick Park in San Francisco. I wouldn't go; I didn't want to do what everyone else was doing. While they were at the concert, I cut some Beatles' photos out of a fan magazine and taped the photos inside the toilet seat lid. Then when someone went to use the toilet, they would see the picture of the Beatles. It wasn't that I didn't like the Beatles; I was just getting tired of hearing about them all the time.

When Judy, Jennifer, and Daddy got home after the concert, Daddy was upset because he lost his Navy blanket. He had an old, green woolen blanket from when he had been in the Navy, but with the pushing and shoving and trying to keep Jennifer from being trampled in the crowd, Daddy's blanket was mislaid. For many years, Daddy would get irritated whenever he thought about losing his blanket. Poor Daddy! He was so patient to take my sisters to the concert and it was unfortunate that a piece of his personal history was gone forever.

After their final Candlestick Park performance on August 29th, 1966, the Beatles would never tour again. But because of the Beatles and the "British Invasion" of music groups, our clothes, our way of thinking, and our music had changed. Until the Beatles came onto the musical scene, we assumed that surfing music was the best. We seldom thought about international music or teenagers, or what types of music that they might like. The Beatles showed us that the world was bigger and had more commonality than we realized. Fashion and music and the psychedelic culture started to feel global, as if nationalism might recede because young people had more similarities than differences. Perhaps we would grow to celebrate both diversity and sameness.

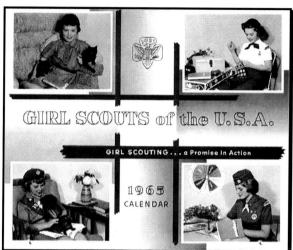

GIRL SCOUTS of the U.S.A.

GIRL SCOUTING... a Promise In Action

1965
CALENDAR

Girl Scouts

The social unrest of the 1960s was reflected in Girl Scout program changes, and their National Board went on record as strongly supporting civil rights. Senior Girl Scout Speakout conferences were held around the country and the "ACTION 70" project was launched in 1969 as a nationwide Girl Scout initiative to overcome prejudice.

I was in Girl Scouts in junior high, but it was really uncool. Most Girls Scouts would never, ever, wear a Scout uniform to school because that would be the absolute kiss of death as far as popularity or credibility of being at all groovy. A girl could be cool, wear nylons, smoke, have the right hair-do and make-up and go steady; however, wearing a Scout uniform to school labeled a person as a goody-goody who was doomed to be a social outcast.

The troop that I was in had many girls that I had not known before joining, and there was one girl that I became really good friends with, Carin. Carin lived about six blocks away from me and was in high school. Girl Scouts was a mixture of ages and grades, with girls from junior high and high school in the same troop.

Carin had a driver's license and was permitted to drive her parent's station wagon. And of course families would let their Scouts go to Scout activities in the car. And twice a month we had our meeting at the Girl Scout House in Palo Alto.

The Girl Scout House was old and sturdy with wooden floors, a large kitchen, and the feeling of well-built and well-worn wood. In 1926 Palo Alto had granted a piece of land for a Girl Scout House, which was built adjacent to what is now the Palo Alto Junior Museum, the museum where I had displayed my insect collections when I went to Palo Verde. Lou Henry Hoover, the wife of President Herbert Hoover, donated five-hundred dollars in 1926 to build the Girl Scout House, along with two other donors.

Stonemasons built the Scout House's fireplace from the sandstone of the fallen arch over Stanford's Palm Drive. The arch had been destroyed in the 1906 San Francisco earthquake; in the 1920s the building of Scout House became a community affair where local builders, architects, painters, and many others gave their time and their money to complete the project. Today, the Lou Henry Hoover Girl Scout House is the oldest Scout meeting house remaining in continuous use in the United States.

When I was a teenager, our troop would bring TV dinners to the Girl Scout House to eat during the bi-monthly meetings, and that was really fun! I would walk over to Carin's house and we would bake TV dinners in her oven and then take them with us to Scouts.

TV dinners were an absolute luxury, and to us they were a real treat. The dinner came in an aluminum tray that was divided into three or four parts: one part for the vegetable, one for the entrée, one for the starch, and one for the dessert. The whole thing was covered with heavy-duty foil, and all a person had to do to prepare a TV dinner was to put the frozen dinner into the oven and bake it for about thirty five or forty minutes!

I would walk over to Carin's, carrying my frozen TV dinner and we would bake hers and mine together at her house. Then, when they were cooked, we would wrap them in dish towels to keep them hot. The TV dinners would still be hot when we got to Scouts, and we could put them in the oven there if it was going to be a while before we ate.

We felt so modern with our convenience food! The tray was what you ate from, so you didn't even have to bring a plate, just utensils. And when we were done we saved the trays, because there were so many different uses for them. We even realized that we could make our own TV dinners if there were leftovers at home from a meal; just put them in the tray and into the freezer, like the store-bought ones. When we had remodeled our house we bought a big refrigerator that had a freezer on the bottom, so we had plenty of space to store TV dinners and other frozen foods.

When Carin and I drove together to Scouts, I would put my feet up on the dashboard, open the window, and smoke my cigarette. It was impossible for me to get into her car and not smoke. I was addicted to smoking, and like most smokers there were certain activities that triggered the desire for that cigarette. For me, being a passenger in any car prompted me to put my feet on the dashboard, roll down the window, and light that cigarette! Carin would have the driver's window wide open and we would turn on radio station KYA and crank up the volume dial as far as it would go. We listened to the music and laughed and joked around, and I would blow my smoke out the passenger window because Carin didn't like the smell of it.

We did many service projects with senior citizens and visited the elderly at convalescent homes and volunteered babysitting for young families who could not afford it. We also went camping together as a troop.

One of our Scout camping trips took place at the beach. Our leaders drove us to a beach near Capitola, just south of Santa Cruz, to camp Friday and Saturday night. After we pitched our tents and everything was set up in the camp, I was bored… bored with that itchy teenaged feeling like I just needed to be some place else doing something else. It was still afternoon and I tried to talk Carin into hitchhiking to the town of Capitola with me, but she didn't want to. So I went by myself.

There I was, in my bathing suit, hitchhiking to Capitola, when I got picked up by a woodie station wagon full of surfers. It turned out they lived in Capitola and had their own apartment, so we all went there, one block from the beach in an apartment that was almost under the old train trestle.

I spent a few hours at their apartment, having fun, drinking, smoking pot and hanging around. And when I told them I had better get back to my campsite and that I was camping with my Girl Scout troop, the guys all decided that they would drive me back to the campsite because they wanted to meet the rest of the scouts! We got in the woodie and drove back to the campground.

Carin was pretty surprised to see me with the surfer boys… she hadn't even realized that I had left. She really chewed me out for being so stupid, but the boys offered to come and get us the next day and take us surfing, so Carin calmed down and agreed to go too.

The boys came the next day and we sneaked off to Capitola with them. And I became friends with those boys. For the next several years they would come to Palo Alto every now and then and pick me up and take me to the beach. Or they would stay over at the Glass Slipper Hotel on El Camino Real and my friends and I would party with them.

That was a surprising outcome of Girl Scouts!

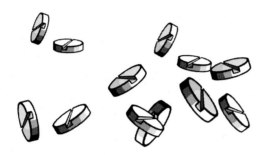

LSD

I frequently went to the Palo Alto Library to do my homework. As a child, I went to the Children's Library every week, but now I went to the new Palo Alto Library at Embarcadero and Newell Roads. Sometimes it actually was to do homework; other times it was to get lost in the books, exploring poetry and new authors. I liked being a part of the muted-voices and whispering in the library, and the musty smell of the library. I craved quiet time to study and do research and to discover books new to me.

After a while, I realized that some other students were on the same schedule as I was. Taking my smoking breaks outside the library gave me the opportunity to become casual friends with quite a few Stanford students.

One evening some students invited me to a party at Stanford, and after I accepted one of them jokingly asked me if I was over eighteen. Because they were going to be taking LSD, they did not want anyone under eighteen at the party when they were "tripping."

Oh woops. I told them I was fourteen, and they all moved away from me as if I was a leper, and said, "Never mind," that they weren't really serious about the party. On my bike-ride home, I tried to remember what the name of the drug was and what it was that they had said. LDS? No, that was the Mormon Church…was there a drug named after the Mormon Church? If it wasn't LDS, then it must have been LSD.

The next day I asked some of my friends if they had heard of a drug called LDS or LSD and if they knew what the phrase "tripping" meant. It didn't take too long to learn that there were rumors about a street drug that people were taking that caused hallucinations. People were tripping on LSD.

The next time I was at the library I visited with some different Stanford students that I had chatted with previously. When they offered to take me out to Stanford to party…well, I had suddenly aged four years and was over eighteen. I had my first introduction to LSD out at Stanford and tripped on acid. After all, this was the sixties and things were changing and LSD was legal. Until October of 1966, LSD was a legal experimental psychiatric drug. However, LSD was also being manufactured illegally at the same time.

From my Journal:

"Met the most unusual person at the library today. She is a girl, nineteen, and after being asked to leave San Jose State, is attending Foothill. Apparently her roommate at San Jose was a homosexual, and things got so bad that Laurie didn't want to go back to her dorm…consequently, she didn't…at first she slept in other girl's rooms, said is was such a tough situation. She ended up crying most of the time…so in the end she was living a pretty wild life…not even going to the dorm at all. She is a really likable person, petite, slightly Mexican looking, very pretty. We were sitting with another girl who was a freshman at Foothill. We all got started discussing the use of LSD — that sounds like a pretty interesting experience —might even

"take a trip" sometime — could make me pretty philosophical. (LSD is a drug which is legal for professional use, and separates the mind from body —makes the mind react so fast that when under the effects one can think in three minutes what it would normally take three hours to think...it also makes everything seem so beautiful...makes every leaf, every blade of grass, seem like an individual wonder...can also make E.S.P. come through in small thoughts. After 12 hours, when the drug wears off, you can't remember all the good things you saw...just that there were good things.) Anyway, we discussed drugs, medicine, curfews, homosexuals, booze, and about 20 billion other things. And the funny thing is, none of us (Laurie, Suzi or I) had ever come to the library on a Saturday afternoon, at least not for a long time...and we all met there on one afternoon. Laurie and I could be pretty good friends; it's amazing how things in life turn out...she just thought I went to Foothill, we started talking, and when she found out that I was 14 she didn't believe it...and she seemed to quickly forget anyway....and pretty soon we were talking like we had known each other for years. Sooo....someday I'll just have to go out to lunch and do sumpin..."

LSD was distributed underground not for profit, but because those who made it believed that the psychedelic experience could do good for humanity, expand the mind and bring understanding and love. Augustus Owsley Stanley III, known as "Owsley," set up a LSD lab in San Francisco and supplied LSD at parties held by Ken Kesey. Owsley led other events such as the "Gathering of the Tribes" in San Francisco in January 1967. Ken Kesey was a name that we all considered synonymous with the mountain town of La Honda, with San Francisco, and with the hippy-acid free-love parties of the times. Eventually many of us teenagers, including me, partied in the mountain town of La Honda with Ken and his buddies. Kesey was the author of *One Flew Over the Cuckoo's Nest*, which was inspired by Ken's work on the night shift at the Menlo Park Veterans' Hospital, right next to the Palo Alto border. Published in 1962, the book was an immediate success.

Ken Kesey and his Merry Pranksters had a hippy bus that was painted with psychedelic drawings, and soon home-built campers, converted school buses and VW buses became common sights all around the Bay Area. It was an exciting time, the air was sparkling and full of energy, and "free-love" was the new attitude.

Owsley was the name we trusted in LSD. My friends and I could get Owsley acid in little tabs that actually had the "O" for Owsley stamped on them, and we trusted those tabs as pure and safe to take. I knew that if I took Owsley acid that I would not be poisoned by someone who did not understand how to manufacture LSD properly, or someone who cheated by dyeing little artificial sweetener tablets and selling them for a buck just to make money.

When Owsley's lab was raided by police in February of 1965, he beat the charges and successfully sued for the return of his equipment. The police were looking for methamphetamine, but found only LSD and LSD wasn't illegal at the time.

"Tripping on acid," meant that for a few hours of my life I had a brain full of images over which I had little or no control. However, I could control the way I reacted to the images, and whether or not I would let them control me. I took acid for sixty or seventy times before I ever had a "bad trip," and once I had a few bad trips I quit taking acid for several decades. But the good trips I experienced were magical and sparkling – my head full of flowers blooming and sunshine and love and peace.

When I finally experienced bad trips, they were visually frightening. There was one trip when I was riding on the back of my friend's motorcycle, and as the acid kicked in I turned my head to look behind me. It was getting dark and because I was tripping I saw the street behind me full of creepy-looking little naked alien creatures, creatures that looked like two-foot-tall, gray, hairless androgynous bipeds. They were all grinning and had razor-sharp teeth. And not only was the street behind me full of the creatures as far as I could see, but they were also climbing houses, buildings and phone poles, and getting nearer and nearer to the back of the motorcycle.

I urged my friend to go faster and faster because I was afraid the creatures would catch up with us and start attacking me. By the time we got to my house, Louis Road was overflowing with the horrible and terrifying things, and I ran into my room and shut the door.

I then could hear them crawling all over my house. They had sticky hands and clung to the house, and made hissing noises. I had to tell myself over and over again that LSD was water-soluble, that my mind was playing a trick on me, and that soon it would be over.

It is impossible to go to sleep during a bad trip. You can't close your eyes and make the scenes disappear, because with your eyes either opened or closed you see the same hallucinations.

The second bad trip was when I was driving with some friends. We all had taken acid and we were all tripping, but we kept getting lost. We attempted to go to Antioch, a town in the east bay, to pick up a friend. As we drove, every overpass we came to was on fire, the on-ramps were on fire and I was terrified that we would burn up. So we kept avoiding on-ramps and got increasingly farther away from our original goal.

Hours later when we all started to crash, to come down from the hallucinations, we discovered that we were only about thirty miles away from where we had started. We had been driving around in circles to avoid the burning freeway on-ramps that were only on fire in our minds.

One time I was at a "happening" in Golden Gate Park in San Francisco. The air was crisp and the sky very blue. Hippies were sitting on the grass, blowing bubbles, laughing, smoking pot and sharing stories. I didn't need to know any of these people to visit and laugh and was there to meet other people. We were young and life was exciting and everyone shared. I went up to an apartment in the Haight-Ashbury district and someone warmed pastries in an oven and slathered them with butter and we listened to music and talked and smoked pot and for that very moment, for that exquisitely beautiful moment, time stood still and I was a part of the collective love of humankind and life was one big smile, one big grin, one big happy and joyous experience where gender, age, status, race, anything that might normally put inhibitions or barriers between people just dropped. We were one race, we were one mind, we were the essence of life and of humanity and I wanted to live and to love and to learn everything about the entire world.

Music sounded different on LSD – each note was its own experience and I would find myself mesmerized by music, by rhythm. The abundance of new and talented musicians and sounds made LSD the perfect avenue for me to actually hear music; the way my childhood hearing loss affected me, I normally didn't appreciate music. Music was something I could give or take, but listening to albums or live music on LSD changed all of that. It was as if those moments on LSD were the first time I had ever experienced music and heard the sounds, and I felt that I understood to a very small degree how the deaf

Beethoven had been able to hear music in his head and transfer it onto paper without having functioning ears.

When Owsley was busted in 1966, *The San Francisco Chronicle* newspaper announced: "LSD Millionaire Arrested." His bust inspired the Grateful Dead song, *Alice D. Millionaire.* Owsley had close connections to the music groups of the Grateful Dead, Jefferson Airplane and Big Brother and the Holding Company. Owsley's nickname was "Bear," and the Grateful Dead's dancing bear logo was created by Owsley. All of those concerts that people attended and all of those dancing bear artworks and stickers helped spread the word about acid. There were blotter sheets that had small dancing bears printed all over them, and each printed bear was a hit of acid. And so the acid-hippy-drug and San Francisco scene grew and expanded in a very short time.

The music that had themes about getting high or using drugs was everywhere, and often we would see the Grateful Dead or Neil Young or other incredible groups just playing in the parks or on the streets or at people's apartments.

When Owsley was arrested again in 1967, people were still able to get Owsley acid, but after a while the supply dried up. Without Owsley, sometimes we would get tabs that had no drug at all. Other times, some of us might be tripping, while some of us weren't even getting high, because acid on the street from a stranger was not guaranteed as to its quality.

There were parties where sugar cubes were handed out, and each sugar cube had a drop of LSD on it. The guests at the party would watch light shows and dance, having psychedelic experiences. The light shows were simple: someone would have an overhead projector, and put clear oil, perhaps baby oil or vegetable oil, on the glass plate of the projector, and then add some drops of food coloring to the oil. They would stir it around a bit, and project the results on a wall. The oil and the water-based coloring would start swirling by themselves from the heat of the light bulb in the projector, and droplets would join each other, new colors would form, and it looked amazing. If we went to the Fillmore or to the Avalon Ballroom we were guaranteed to have a new experience and listen to some music that no one else had ever heard before, or would ever hear again.

And guess what? There I was in Palo Alto, able to get great LSD and listen to songs of drugs and love by Jerry Garcia of the Grateful Dead. The Dead made the rounds of St. Michael's Alley, Stanford's Tresidder Union, the Tangent Coffeehouse on University Avenue and other local places, including Ken Kesey's house in La Honda.

During the "Summer of Love" I would hitchhike to San Francisco as often as I could, sometimes everyday after school and always on the weekends. Going to the Haight and to Golden Gate Park was one big LSD party. I could go to San Francisco and end up in an apartment listening to music, taking acid, talking and eating and connecting with all sorts of new friends from all over the world. LSD and the hippies and the hope and love and peace filled my life and the life of my friends. It was as if we were on the very edge of making great changes in society, and taking LSD was an incredible tool to help understand the psychedelic messages in life and beautiful patterns and harmony that were all around us... all around me and the universe.

The times were changing so quickly that every day was a new happening, a new kind of music, a new music group. Teenagers and young adults were this new exciting way of life.

Owsley also produced a new psychedelic called STP. And this was hilarious, because there was a car-oil additive named STP, so there were already STP stickers made to advertise STP. Teenagers everywhere were suddenly sporting STP stickers on their binders and on their lockers. But many of the people who took STP acted crazy; it didn't have the same positive mind-expanding effects as LSD, and quickly developed a deservedly bad reputation.

Most police, teachers, and parents had little knowledge about either LSD or marijuana. One time I was hitchhiking with a friend and we had a paper grocery-store bag full of small plastic baggies of pot, and when a cop car came around the corner we scrambled to get back on the sidewalk. In the process, we spilled out our entire bag's contents – dozens of plastic bags full of pot! The police officers pulled up next to us and asked if we needed help with anything, and when we said "No, thank you," they just drove off!

Those cops were only offering to help us and when we said that we were okay, they drove off. My friend and I finished picking up the pot and continued hitching to where we were going. At the time we had not heard of much police corruption, evidence planting, random beatings or other types of behavior that later seemed representative of cops.

However, in those days the cops would take in young girls they caught hitchhiking and charge them with soliciting prostitution, even if a girl's big toe was the only thing in the gutter. So when girls were hitching rides we had to always be on the lookout for cops, because it was a real drag to get hauled in on those bogus charges. The law stated that a female that was hitchhiking was soliciting for payment for sex. How ridiculous that girls could not hitchhike but that boys could!

Drugs were exploding into the consciousness of everyone, everywhere. And "generation gap" was becoming part of the vocabulary. Things were changing culturally very quickly, and drugs were a big part of it. Teenagers still respected their parents and their teachers and the other adults in their lives, but part of that respect included an urgent need for change, a change away from complacency and conformity, a change that included women being in charge of their own bodies and people being able to legally marry someone of any race. It included the radical idea that there might be more to life for women than marriage and motherhood. Some young adults were even living together although not married!

Drugs fit into all of this because they united us and we formed a community – a community that would sing together, protest together and march together and dance and dream together. It was an exciting hopeful feeling, a feeling that anything was possible and there were no limits, because together we were going to undo and get rid of all limits. We would be the generation to fix the wrongs, stop the wars, stop the phony piece of paper that was somehow needed if you loved someone and wanted to live with them. We were going to form tight communities of equality and hope and love and peace, and the sparkling freeing of our minds and tripping with each other was a joyous way to share and hope and dream of making this all come true.

F riends Outside

Rosemary Goodenough, an Englishwoman living in California, began the work in 1955 that was to become "Friends Outside." 1955 was the middle of the repressive McCarthy Era, yet Rosemary defied conventions of the times and spoke out for incarcerated people, for their families, and for their children. In that spirit of change, as a teenager in the '60s, I wanted to carry on her effort to help families that were struggling to raise children while one parent was incarcerated.

Lou Riley was the assistant minister at the Congregational Church in Palo Alto, and he worked devotedly on many social causes. He and his wife, Skip, inspired many of us teenagers to do good works. And the irony of the times was that teenagers like me were volunteering hundreds and hundreds of hours each year to help out less fortunate people or people that had mental problems, while at the same time we were often looked upon as a privileged middle class, even though I didn't feel that way. Our family never ate at restaurants, never flew places, my mom made most of our clothes or they were hand-me-downs; we grew much of our food and canned much of what we ate, but because we had a Palo Alto address people automatically assumed that we were economically privileged.

With the support of Reverend Riley, monthly Friends
Outside Day Camps were started in the winter of 1960, followed
the next year by weekly day camps during summer vacation.
And as a young teen, I became part of the staff. Rosemary
believed in empowering the community teenagers: "We let
them, not adults, run the Day Camps," was her belief, and it
worked. Rosemary had only one adult day camp director and
the rest of the camp's staff were teen volunteers.

This built the relationship of "Big Kids playing with
Little Kids." I became very involved with Friends Outside. I
spent many, many hours volunteering, including running a
summer day camp at the Congregational Church for the children
of parents who were doing time in jail, and organizing both an
Easter event and a Christmas event.

For the Easter event we had about one-hundred and fifty
children who attended our egg-dyeing afternoon, and Olivera
Eggs in San Jose was generous enough to donate one-hundred-
and-sixty dozen eggs so that each of the kids could dye twelve
eggs and take them home. Olivera Eggs even delivered the eggs
to the church for us! I had called many companies and
distributors trying to get eggs donated before Olivera make their
offer. I never knew if Olivera Eggs realized the impact that they
had on the life of those kids – each kid was so happy to be able
to have those eggs to decorate!

I was in charge of getting those eggs ready for the kids to
dye. The Congregational Church had a large kitchen with a
multi-burner gas stovetop. I organized other
teenagers to spend the afternoon at the church
boiling the eggs. We had pots and pans full of
boiling water and eggs, and about half way
through the boiling, I lost track of how long each
pot had been boiling. We ended up cracking

open one egg from each pot. Pretty soon we had thirty or forty hard-boiled eggs, and as we didn't want to be wasteful, we ended up making egg-salad. For many years the smell of boiling eggs or egg salad was enough to make me feel sick. Boiling more than eighteen-hundred eggs in several hours took its toll!

I got to know many of the kids who attended our camp and, again they called me "maestra," teacher. Taking children for a day or a morning meant that wives had time to go visit their husbands in jail without taking their children with them. It also was a way for the women, many of whom didn't speak English, to develop a trust in an agency that was really looking out for them and their children. I think that if the camps had been held anywhere other than a church, women would not have brought their children there. Holding the camps at a church meant that the moms could trust leaving their children.

For our Christmas event, I canvassed Palo Alto, going to stores asking for donations. We received enough donations that we wrapped one-hundred and fifty gifts, and each child got a present. We had a tall and beautiful tree that was donated, and, again, I relied on my teenaged friends to help me decorate it and to wrap the one-hundred and fifty presents.

These were many of the same friends that I was dropping acid with and smoking pot with, and we were passionate about change and wanting things to be better. We knew that it all started with one person and that if we made a difference in the life of one family or of one child, well, then it was all worth it.

The children were so happy! The moms usually got transportation from volunteers, and when the moms and the children came into the church auditorium and saw the big tree, the plates of Christmas cookies, the decorations and the presents, well, it was a very thankful day for everyone.

Friends Outside empowered us. We were given responsibility and enormous tasks to complete, and I learned that many times all I had to do was ask someone to help, ask someone to donate, and that people were generous and kind and wanted to do the right thing.

In 1967, Fairchild Semiconductor Charities Committee donated a brand new cream-colored Ford bus to Friends Outside, helping to expand the youth department's programs.

The Missing Chapters

I knew the time would come when, in the writing of this book, I would have to make the decision about including or omitting certain life events.

So I will tell the reader now that there are some missing chapters, only because writing them might cause pain or betrayal to people who are still living. My choices were to write those chapters anyway, or to wait several decades to write this 60/70 Sparkling as a complete story, or to write as much as my heart and my personal responsibility would allow.

Those of you who are near and dear to me will know that parts of my story are omitted...and the rest of my dear readers? Perhaps there will be an entire volume written some years down the road about my first trip to Mexico and about other stories and tales and joys, loves and sorrows that just cannot be part of this particular book.

Please continue reading, sharing, and journeying with me. There is still a lot to tell even without the missing chapters.

High School

There was no way to predict how explosive, exciting, energizing and despairing high school would turn out to be. There was the sense that the future was near, that all I had to do was reach out and I could be an artist, or a traveler or whatever I wanted; there were no boundaries. The very next minute there was a feeling that the Vietnam War would kill everyone I knew, that the civil rights movement would never solve anything, and that there was so much happening all at once that I could not begin to understand it.

The President had been shot and there was great social unrest. I was working hard with Friends Outside to fight for social justice and children's rights. I volunteered at the Veterans Hospital in Palo Alto, and had been to Mexico, teaching at a very small impoverished school.

There were riots all throughout the country, frequent peace marches, student unions were forming, cops were now "pigs" and everyone wanted to come to San Francisco for the Summer of Love. LSD was available legally in the United States as an experimental psychiatric drug. Prior to LSD becoming illegal, it was some of the magic that teenagers used to blow our minds. We tripped while listening to music, while talking with friends, when we were trying to solve the problems of the world and the problems of our state and the problems of our own families and schools.

As students we were incredibly empowered. Students smoked cigarettes or pot in the middle of the playing field, and often the smell of pot scented every corridor and restroom at the campus. The feel of the very air was electric, charged with an energy and hope that promised us that if we worked hard at a cause and believed that it was the right cause, we could do anything to change the world and make it a peaceful, loving, generous, compassionate, warless and free-love place … a place were the best of all people became evident and strong, and where making love solved all the problems of the world, and the peace sign reigned.

We spent days and weeks on drugs, sharing our drug-induced trips and explorations with each other, traveling from deep within to far across many universes and back again. And the innocence of the times allowed us to have the incredible hope and joy that I felt all the time. We were going to beat the Establishment; we were going to go from war to peace. We were going to go to love, joy, peace, happiness, and feel the very essence of the best part of humankind.

Hitchhiking was the norm. Getting into a vehicle the first thing I would be asked was, "Are you holding?" That meant "Do you have any drugs?" Of course, everyone who was hitchhiking was holding so that we could share our stash of drugs with whoever picked us up.

We sat in our high school classrooms eating oranges that had been injected with vodka, smoked pot during lunch, and took acid with great abandon. The pot names were based on the location of origin, like Acapulco Gold, Tijuana Tops, Maui

Wowie and Panama Red. Acid might be orange tabs – as simple as a drop on a tablet of coffee sweetener, the little white artificial-sweetener tablets that were popular in the '60s and made a perfect platform for that minute drop of LSD.

Combining this with the somewhat liberal slant of Palo Alto made high school a big experiment. There was one time when I was on acid for forty days straight without a break. I went to school, went out with friends, did my homework, did everything that would get done anyway, but the music, the food, the classrooms, the teachers and all that was happening shimmered and glittered with the intensity of the water-soluble drug that coursed through my body. It was a bit like the forty days and forty nights with Noah and the Ark; doing everyday functions while also looking at the world with a hugely different perspective. We were tripping and expanding our minds and some of us blew our minds and never came back. It was all part of the sparkling times where every day was full of questions and great hopes that the problems of the world not only could be solved but that they could be solved my me.

We had a high-school school newspaper, *The Catamount*, which was the platform for our opinions of how we felt and what was important. The next few pages share some of the topics, and what gave them their importance. We had a public address system at school for daily announcements, but there was no Internet or cell phones and therefore the articles in the school paper were vital in uniting the students and the teachers and in transmitting our thoughts and concerns. We stayed connected through our printed media.

Fund sale plans made

In response to the overwhelming student body approval to sponsor the construction of a school under the Peace Corps Partnership Program, a chocolate sale will be held, beginning February 9 at a kick-off assembly.

To raise the $1,000 needed to build the school, chocolate covered almonds, boxed by World's Finest, will be sold.

Promoting enthusiasm, the art department is constructing a large poster on which is a school wall with empty spaces for 200 "bricks." As the campaign progresses, sellers will receive cardboard bricks according to the amount of chocolate sold, and their signatured "bricks" will build the wall until enough money is raised. Of the money garnered, $150 will be spent in prizes for the top salesmen.

The assembly on February 9 will be highlighted by guest speakers Mr. Paul Dorrah of the Peace Corps, and Mr. Forbs of World's Finest Chocolate.

Members of the fund committee include the class presidents, members of the activities board, and other interested students, with Student Activities Commissioner Mickey Suen heading the Committee.

Student Acitivities Commissioner Mickey Suen displays the Peace Corps school banner that promotes the chocolate sale.
Photo: FISHER

On March 1, 1961, President Kennedy signed an Executive Order that officially started the Peace Corps. The Peace Corps' purpose was, "To promote world peace and friendship through a Peace Corps, which shall make available to interested countries and areas men and women of the United States qualified for service abroad and willing to serve, under conditions of hardship if necessary, to help the peoples of such countries and areas in meeting their needs for trained manpower." And several years later the idea of a Peace Corps fit in with our idealistic views, like those of Kennedy, of "…asking not what our country could do for us, but what we could do for our country…" or even more for people all around the world.

Cubberley students showed their support of the Peace Corps by raising $1,000 to build an overseas school.

The articles in *The Catamount* reflect the political involvement of the students in the 1960s. We were passionate about free speech, civil rights, and about defining and challenging limits. We interacted with organizations such as the ACLU (American Civil Liberties Union) and the USM (United Student Movement.) Yet we were also battling with dress code issues and if girls would be allowed to wear slacks, or shorts or jeans to school!

Below is an ad from *The Catamount.* Many local businesses supported the school paper through advertisements. Notice that no area codes or zip codes were used at the time.

There was an exciting energy and synergy around *The Catamount*.
We put our hearts into the articles, using *The Catamount* as the
venue where everyone could get their ideas included.

April 26, 1968   CUBBERLEY SENIOR HIGH SCHOOL   Vol. 12, No. 17

Board defines club policy

By MIKE MACOVSKI

For the purpose of defining and carrying out the much-debated School Board policy on student organizations, a sheet setting administrative proceedures has been drafted by representatives from Cubberley, Paly and Gunn and will go up for general discussion at the Board meeting on Monday, May 6th, before the five members vote on its acceptance.

Presently, the Board of Education policy, revised last January, states that "Student organizations shall not be permitted to engage in political advocacy or activities of a partisan political nature" but that "critical examination and balanced presentation of controversial issues have positive educational values and are encouraged."

In the procedures drafted to implement this policy, "political advocacy," as applied to school organizations, means "intent to indoctrinate" and "partisan , political nature" is defined as "a consistent point of view which does not allow for consideration of other points of view."

Associate Superintendent Dr. Andrew Stevens, a member of the committee that drew up the administrative procedures, commented, "The committee

that drafted the sheet defining and carrying out Board policy interprets it as guaranteeing that any individual can speak but an organization is not permitted to form for the purpose of giving out propaganda. An organization cannot prevent people from giving the other side."

Before the May 6th vote, the proposed implementing sheet will go up for general discussion and comments. If passed, Cubberley will follow the nine rules and three definitions as school organization policy.

Strictly following the School Board policy, the administrative procedures sheet directs that "School clubs are permitted to engage in contro-

versial issues but are not permitted to engage in political advocacy or activities of a partisan political nature. No publication of a sectarian, partisan, or denominational nature may be distributed by school clubs."

Mr. Ron Jones, who has withdrawn his sponsorship of the USM(United Student Movement), has been trying to get a wide variety of organizations and individuals to discuss the Board policy at the meeting. One of the groups he called, who has since "questioned the constitutionality of the policy," is the American Civil Liberties Union (ACLU).

In a letter to the School Board, the ACLU stated, "The essence of dynamic American democracy lies in the involvement of citizens in partisan political debate, persuasion, and political advocacy. It's the Board's(of ACLU directors) position that the only legitimate need for placing limits on student political activities arises when such activities interfere with education."

Mr. Jones expects the ACLU to present their opinion at the general discussion at the School Board meeting on May 6th. After this presentation and any comments by students, teachers and others, the Board may postpone their vote to a later date.

USM put on probation

For failing to secure the approval of club sponsor, Mr. Ron Jones, before distributing a controversial leaflet, the United Student Movement has been placed on one semester probation by Dr. Scott Thomson.

Following the initial probation, Dr. Thomson asked USM leader Chris Menchine to sign a document outlining specific limits for USM operations at Cubberley. The USM countered with a request that any limitations be made uniform for all school clubs.

The following restrictions have now been placed upon all Cubberley clubs: 1) Within a three-day period, speakers on both sides of an issue must be presented; 2) all club publications must be approved by the sponsor before distribution, and 3) clubs may sell or distribute books, but not newspapers, pamphlets or circulars, unless these materials are published by the Cubberley school club or bear solely the Cubberley address. Exceptions to this are documents which the club advisor considers as noninflammatory.

This article is pretty typical of what was going on at Cubberley. Students wanted a say in what was happening. We wanted our rights, we wanted to make decisions and provide input into what was going on, not just be puppets led by other puppets.

The world was changing quickly; there was a war going on, and many of us did not want to follow along blindly and do the same things that had always been done. We wanted change and we wanted change NOW!

We were part of the United Student Movement. When the principal placed the USM on probation for one semester, the USM countered with a request that if the USM have restrictions, then all the school clubs have the same restrictions. Students were challenging authority at every level, and our school administrators had to make quick changes.

Ron Jones was the teacher who sponsored the USM. From Mr. Jones we learned a lot about passive non-violence and how to change our world. He was an amazing teacher!

Dress poll reveals opinion differences

In the last issue of the CATAMOUNT, the statistics of the dress code questionnaire were "exposed." Now for a "peek behind the scenes." What did you put in the way of comments? Did you play sheep and follow the crowd? Or break away and non-conform, adding your "two cents" about the subject?

Perhaps you identify with the member of the gentler sex, who wrote, "Girls shood be able to wear bermudas. It's to cold wearing skurts." (The spelling has been left in its pure form to protect the CATAMOUNT!) She continued to describe her winter ensemble of "tea-shirts and tights."

As to solid comfort, we present the girl who commented, "I think the girls should be able to wear pants because they should be comfortable, they would probably do better work when their comfortable." (Conclusion: pants stimulate the brain.)

Aside from comfort, the next big issue on the student body mind was appearance. Topmost in the male mind of girl-watching was how certain clothes would brighten the daily drudgery of the school humdrum. As one confused connoisseur regurgatated, "..short pants on some girls would add a nice tuch to the school." Short pants on other girls....

On the other hand, the comments pertaining to the dress codes as a whole seemed slightly less gentile. And we quote, "Are you kidding? Who the h _ _ _ gives you the right to tell me or anybody else what to do." Followed by a Dylan quote to pardon this language, "Obscenity who really cares,

propaganda all is phony." Progressively violent, a young fascist in his own right subtly screamed, "Long hair, untidy dress,-you'd think we ran pig sty here...Nor are we running a hang-out for latent homosexuals."

Half-cocked minds also produced astounding results. One boy made an attempt to speak logically, but ended up saying, "People should be aloud to wear anything they want that they can be picked up for." (If he really has a strong desire to see the inside of a police station, how about trying nudism?)

Another great literary mind of our time, "Boys on the football, baseball, basketball, swiming should not have long

hair or beards not real long and no beards(?)"

A long one on hair sadly commented, "I think its just awful about the boys hair and girls and boys dirty close. I think we should dress the way if we were going to work. Who ever is responsible for letting people dress they want to is very wrong. Are they afraid!!? What is class??" (Pretty interesting, huh?)

Not all the remarks were "winners," some people actually tried to give their honest opinions legibly. It would then follow, in true fairy tale form, to say that the misfits were in the minority.

PILGRIMS UNITE!

Charleston Shopping Center

This article was a follow-up article about the school dress code. Girls could wear mini-skirts but not shorts; we always had to be careful about how we sat. We always were confined to dresses or skirts. We wanted change!

When I started junior high the only kids who rode bikes to school were the complete nerds. No one would have been caught dead on a bike! Yet in a very short time, bikes were back in style and high-schoolers were having fun commuting places together on bicycles.

I rode my blue three-speed Schwinn bike to school and all around town, even to Menlo Park and sometimes to the top of Page Mill Road and back down again! My bike had a bright yellow seat; it was kind of like the pink family tent, in that I could always spot my bike in a sea of parked bicycles because I had the only blue bike with a bright yellow seat. Palo Alto still issued bike licenses at the fire stations, and the licenses were a little screw-on plate that fastened to the bike. Most of us were pretty good about getting our licenses renewed at the fire station each year.

Twice a week I rode my bike after school to the Palo Alto Veteran's Hospital, where I volunteered. The hospital was near the Alta Mesa Cemetery in the foothills; it was a long uphill ride from school to the hospital. However, the ride home was fun because it was downhill for most of the way.

My bike was stolen from school one day. I went out to get my bike to ride to the hospital, but I couldn't find the blue bike with the yellow seat. My friends and I looked everywhere. Sometimes kids would borrow bikes and leave them on another part of campus, but after searching and searching I finally had to conclude that my bike was gone. My bike. Gone. Who would do such a thing? No one locked their bikes... we all just parked them in a huddle.

A friend drove me out to the hospital so I could volunteer. The director that I volunteered with was concerned that I was late and relieved when I arrived. I got along well with him and enjoyed the office work and research that I was doing with him. Much of his research was with non-English speaking veterans, specifically those who spoke only Spanish. Sometimes I was allowed to interview these patients in Spanish, as the staff at the hospital often had no Spanish translator on duty. The director offered me a ride home the day my bike was stolen, which I gladly accepted.

Daddy and I went to the police station and reported my bike stolen. We had enough bikes at home that I borrowed a bike to ride when I needed or wanted to, but it wasn't the same; my bike had two side baskets in the back and my special yellow seat and I was accustomed to it.

About a week later the police called. My bike had been found in the creek and they had it at the police station! Daddy and I took the station wagon to the police station, not knowing if I would be able to ride my bike or not…it might have been vandalized or damaged or stripped.

When we got there we found that my bike was filthy but undamaged! We stopped at the hardware store on the way home and bought a chain lock and Daddy made me promise to lock my bike.

The following *Catamount* article writes about how bicycles were overtaking the Cubberley campus. Riding a bike to school had gone from being a kiss-of-death on the popularity scale to being what everyone was doing.

Photo: WALLACE

'Velocipedes' swarm to Cubberley

By KAREN HASIN

"Once upon a time in the land of Londra, a Stephan cree dismissed the angry shouts of his havoc-ridden mother, and, disregarding the ancient warning which stated that no boy over a certain age rode a velocipede, DID ride his bike to school. Since laughs and foul remarks did not fall upon his ears from peers, and since it was certainly a convenient mode of travel, Stephan rode it again..."

And AGAIN and AGAIN.

Whispers behind his back began, little mumblings, "If he can do it, so can I." He was joined by a few more courageous ones, equipped with paint, wax and cleaning oil. New tires were bought. Finally, a whole new generation began galloping to school on their Schwinn's and Hercules'.

Thus, Stephan's one-man crusade against "being dropped off by Mommie and having to kiss her goodbye" has spread to Cubberley. Bicycle numbers have quadrupled over last year. What was once "out" -- the riding of bicycles to anything after junior high school -- is now "in."

More bikes increase the problem in "stashing" them. More racks have been added, but the vehicles cluster under trees, fall against each other in gossipy groups. During the recent rainy season, they have begun huddling against the wing walls, in fear of the inevitable rust.

If the influx continues, there may be as many bikes as students. More facilities will be

We had an interesting mix of teachers at Cubberley, including a new science teacher from India, Malti Prasad. Mrs. Prasad had taught in Canada before coming to Cubberley. It was the first time that I had seen a teacher from India, who came to school dressed in her sari.

Mr. Fleming was our history teacher and he was black. We were starting to say "black" instead of "Negro," and Mr. Fleming was impatient and at the same time very long-suffering with his idealistic students. He wanted the same good, Palo Alto life for himself and his family as did everyone in the suburbs, and he ended up building a fancy new house on Middlefield Road near Cubberley. All the students knew where he lived because his son was a student at Cubberley. Mr. Fleming wore his sports coat with corduroy elbow patches and tried to be tolerant with students who seemed to be wasting their lives getting stoned all the time.

Cubberley had a great art program. Mr. Adams taught the clay class that was part of the art program at Cubberley. It was rumored that he slept with some of his female students, but still people considered him a great teacher. The clay room had electric potter wheels and also foot-pedaled wheels, and when a student walked into that room, they felt as if nothing was impossible, that anyone could be a clay artist! It was such an opportunity to have a clay studio and kiln at our school and to see students with splatters of clay on their clothes and watch as they formed their creations.

I was not a clay person. I would visit the clay studio because it was so interesting to watch students take lumps of featureless clay and throw them and massage them and create an object from the clay. I liked to play with the clay, to push it around and squish it and have it slide back and forth in my hands, but I seldom connected with the clay in a way that the clay artists did.

Mrs. Johnson and Mr. Schink were our drawing and painting teachers. Mr. Schink was a professional oil painter who lived in San Francisco, and it was inspiring to have him as our teacher. Sometimes on weekends we students would meet him at his mother's home in old Palo Alto to make sketches, and a few times we had nude models pose for us. We couldn't have nude models at school, but we could have them off-campus. It was exciting to be taught by an artist who was passionate and skilled and loved to teach! One model came from San Francisco to pose for us, and she kept talking about how beautiful Palo Alto was with all its trees, and how San Francisco didn't have street trees. And on my bike ride after I left the drawing session I really started to look at those beautiful old trees and realized what she had meant.

Sometimes when I cut school, Mr. Schink would write a note to excuse me. When I was a junior, my friend Sandy and I took over one of the boy's restrooms and made it into our own art studio, and Mr. Schink supported us. It was really simple. We put an "Out of Order" sign on the restroom door and moved our easels, paints, brushes and rolls of canvas and the wood for frames into the restroom. We spent hours in there painting, sometimes together and other times by ourselves. It was cool and quiet and had a high ceiling that dissipated the smell of the oil paint. When I just couldn't leave painting to go to my next class, Mr. Schink would write me an excuse for my classes that day.

I created a four-panel self-portrait that ended up being sixteen feet tall with a bottom panel that was six-feet wide and a top panel that was three-foot square. I built the canvas frames and stretched the canvasses, and when all four pieces were done they hinged together. It took seven months from start to finish, and I sat in the bathroom studio unaware of the passage of time, painting, and pursuing my passion for creating art.

My painting was on display for several months at Tresidder Hall at Stanford University as part of a student art exhibit. It was a self-portrait of souls, love, shadows, self-destruction, hope, drugs and of growing up.

Faculty exhibit artwork

Two of Cubberley's art teachers -- Mr. Chris Schink and Mr. Art Adams -- have been active recently in their professional fields.

A painting by Mr. Schink is on exhibit at the Annual Society of Western Artists Show at the De Young Museum in San Fran-cisco. He will also display watercolors at the California National Water Color Society at the Otis Art Institute in Los Angeles beginning November 9.

Ceramic sculptures by Mr. Adams has been on exhibit at Palo Alto's Los Robles Gallery during the month of October.

A *Catamount* article about the teachers' exhibition and a student-drawn ad for the Charleston Pharmacy

Journal Entry:

"I am sitting here thinking and I'm wondering. Why am I doing this? Why can't I be at the beach painting? Why is it that I have to go to school and do what I don't want to do? This is a selfish attitude, but I am tired of being generous. I only have one life, as far as I know, and there is one person with whom I'd like to share it. Go ahead and laugh, I just don't care any more. There is another thing I am wondering about. I wasn't born to make my parents or my teachers or anyone but myself proud of me. I don't see why there are laws regulating the fact that you have to go out and have a stupid little man with a white collar and a black drape say a few words to you and a very special person before you may live with him. For the guys, it's even harder. They can be drafted because they are not old enough to be married and have kids legally without their parent's permission. You're not old enough to drink. Marry, do this, do that, you have to go to college, or you're no one. But you're old enough to be in high school. And there, there is no goofing around. Work, Work, Work. Every teacher knows that their class is the Most Important. And what freedom? Your boyfriend is in an even worse grind, only at college level. Foothill [Junior College] tolerates no messing around. I know you can't expect something for nothing, but what is everyone working for? Say you live 70-80 years. School for the first 20 years, then work; work for what? So you can grow old and ugly and die? ..... No one is living — they all exist like a bunch of ... toys wound up with a key. What are we here for and what is our purpose?"

Journal Entry

"All I have to do is get a pallet knife in my hand and I can be a different person. Put on an old shirt with 20 billion layers of paint on it already. Get a big big canvas and put the wet one already on the easel against something...

Then let loose. It's a marvelous way to get rid of tension. If you're mad, take it out one that canvas. Just paint it out! And no matter how you feel, if you paint, you will feel a lot better. For a while anyway, you can forget anything that is bothering you. So if you spend sixteen dollars a week on canvas and paints and liquid fiberglass (for a table top I am making) and then starve at lunch the next month…so what!"

Below is the "Principal's Message" from the Cubberley Yearbook, 1967. The message exemplifies how students were encouraged to pursue uniqueness while at the same time being obligated to the general welfare.

The Cubberley ethos encourages an ideal, that of the egalitarian individual, a free man among equals. Students do find at Cubberley the opportunity to become unique human beings, to be thinking individuals not greater or lesser than other human beings. Reciprocity, a respect for other faces and unfamiliar thoughts is encouraged. Egocentrism, the obsession with self to the exclusion of others, is discouraged.

Thus, "The Many Faces of Cubberley" is a most appropriate theme for our yearbook. This theme suggests a large group of young people, our student body, with unique faces rising above the crowd and yet obligated to its general welfare.

Scott D. Thomson
Principal

Boycott Grapes

The Delano grape strike began on September 8, 1965, and lasted more than five years. It was ironic that this date was my parent's nineteenth wedding anniversary. It had been several years since my sisters and I had secretly prepared my parents' anniversary cake, including the mystery fly that landed in the frosting and that we had never found. We had jumped out from behind the couch singing the Fred Flintstone version of "Happy Anniversary" as they returned from one of their few dinners away from home. Even now when my parents felt more comfortable going out to dinner several times a year, politics and human rights were still our standard dinner-table discussions most evenings at home. Not only was the country changing, which drove changes in our dinnertime discussions, but it seemed that the San Francisco Bay Area was a Mecca for change, a focal point for eliminating much of the long-standing sexist, racist, and unfair double-standards that were the fabric and basis of more than just a few people's lives.

Even though the Bay Area did not have official segregation, many parts of the United States were still legally segregated. And in California, where we grew and processed much of the nation's produce, we had grower/picker/producer/consumer segregation that had developed over more than a century of agricultural practices. The Central Valley and Santa Clara Valley possessed unbelievably rich soil with climates that enabled the high-quality fruits, nuts, and vegetables that fed California and much of the rest of the nation. Cheap labor was traditional and a part of the valleys' agricultural processes.

In Santa Clara Valley there were many canneries. High-school and college students could expect summer jobs in the canneries, and for many women the cannery jobs were one of the few options for employment outside of their homes. The cannery work was hot and back-breaking, but it was nothing compared to the hard job of harvesting California's crops. That job went to the migrant workers.

Many migrant workers spoke only Spanish. They either came to California from Mexico, or were American-born in Spanish-speaking communities. There were other migrant workers as well, the families who had come to California during the dust-bowl era from places like Oklahoma. These were second and third-generation farm workers. These workers toiled under back-breaking, heart-breaking conditions and the civil rights movement of the sixties gave birth to the right conditions for the examination of how our foods were harvested. The *Harvest of Shame* documentary by news reporter, Dan Rather, brought to the forefront the shame and scandal associated with our bountiful, abundant crops and how they were harvested. This documentary originally aired in 1960, on November 24th, the day after Thanksgiving. And it resulted in a shift in thought, so that by 1965 the times were ripe for a worker's strike, something unheard of in both its scope and support.

The Delano grape strike began when the Agricultural Workers Organizing Committee, mostly Filipino farm workers in Delano, California, walked off the farms of the local grape growers. One week after the strike began, the predominantly Mexican-American National Farm Workers Association, led by César Chávez and Dolores Huerta, joined the strike. Eventually the two groups merged, forming the United Farm Workers of America. Reverend Lou Riley, our assistant minister, went to Fresno to meet with César Chávez and later went on to march to the California State Capitol side-by-side with the Farm Workers in a march protesting low wages and horrible work conditions. This march was an attempt to bring justice to a very unjust way of life, drawing attention to the migrant workers and to our "Harvest of Shame."

At the Congregational Church we felt a responsibility to help these workers. They lived and worked hundreds of miles away from us, but we ate the table grapes at an affordable price; grapes that were at the expense of the workers' quality of life. At our house we supported the grape boycott, which meant that we made a commitment to not buy green table grapes. Once the strike started, there were strikebreakers brought in to pick the grapes; "scabs" they were called, so grapes were available even though there was a strike going on.

As long as grapes were picked and grapes were available at the stores, the regular consumer was not impacted. That was the hope of the growers and was why scabs came in to pick the grapes and to break the strike. If people could no longer buy grapes because grapes were unavailable, then the consumer might examine what was happening. But if grapes were still at fruit stands and grocery stores, the strike was not effective.

This was a time for social change and to do what was right. I was not a farm worker, but I did have the power to talk to people, to influence purchasing, and to go on marches. The grape boycott gained national attention regarding the plight of migrant workers. The previous year the Bracero program had ended, but that end did not end the exploitation of farm workers or of newly-arriving immigrants from Mexico or South America. Braceros was a program started by the United States in the 1940s to bring cheap, seasonal and legal labor to the United States from Mexico. The Braceros legally worked at the jobs that no one else would do or wanted. Still, there was a perception that the Braceros took away jobs from Americans, and there was a lot of prejudice, fear, and disdain for these workers from Mexico. The end of the Bracero program did not end the plight of families that struggled and worked hard but could barely eke out a living. Instead, the low-paid migrant workers were bearing the brunt of our demand for high-quality, low-cost produce.

And how did we know about the Bracero program? Trips to San Bernadino to visit our relatives showed me one great difference between the Bay Area and Southern California. My relatives in Southern California talked about the "wet backs" and the Braceros with scorn and fear. They said that these people were taking away jobs from Americans, even though the Braceros were doing legal work that no one else would do.

Through music and protest songs these civil rights issues entered into my heart. There were many protest songs, and many protest singers. I would hear the songs and they would go into my soul and I knew that things needed to change, things that were not fair or right. Even though I was hearing about César Chávez on the radio and seeing him on the evening news, it was the protest song by Phil Ochs, *Bracero*, which really touched me:

"Come bring your hungry bodies to the golden fields of plenty; from a peso to a penny, Bracero

"Oh, Welcome to California, come labor for your mother, your father and your brother, for your sister and your lover, Bracero

"Come pick the fruit of yellow, break the flower from the berry, purple grapes will fill your belly, Bracero

"And the sun will bite your body, as the dust will draw you thirsty, while your muscles beg for mercy, Bracero

"In the shade of your sombrero, drop your sweat upon the soil, like the fruit your youth can spoil, Bracero

"When the weary night embraces, sleep in shacks that could be cages...They will take it from your wages, Bracero"

When my family drove down Highway 5 through the Central Valley of California to visit our relatives and we were roasting hot in our car, I would look out our car window through the heat haze to the hot, dusty fields, and I would see the stooped-over people in the fields picking all types of produce. These people toiled in the long rows of food, rows that disappeared to the horizon and made straight rhythmic patterns as we drove down the highway, a hypnotic pattern of straight rows stretching to the horizon in the haze. There was no shade and only a few outhouses. I wondered how the workers could stand to work like that.

Because, as the song said, "...*there are others who are willing, Bracero.*"

The activist and folk singer, Woody Guthrie, wrote a song about a real plane crash which happened in 1948 and resulted in the deaths of four Americans and twenty-eight illegal immigrant farm-workers who were being deported from California back to Mexico.

At the time of the crash the radio and newspaper coverage of the event did not give the victims' names, but referred to them merely as "deportees." In contrast, the flight crew and the security guard were all named in the *New York Times* story. The Mexican victims of the accident were placed in a mass grave at Holy Cross Cemetery in Fresno, California. There were twenty-seven men and one woman, and only twelve were ever identified. Listening to that song, I wondered about that woman, what her dreams had been and how old she had been when she died. I imagined how terrifying her last moments must have been.

By now my friends and I were playing the guitar, and singing this song with friends made me incredibly sad and also very angry; angry that people struggled to come to this country, struggled to work at jobs that no one else wanted, and that when they died in something as horrible as a fiery plane crash…well, their names were not even important:

The crops are all in and the peaches are rotting,
The oranges piled in their creosote dumps;
They're flying 'em back to the Mexican border
To pay all their money to wade back again.

Goodbye to my Juan, goodbye, Rosalita,
Adios mis amigos, Jesus y Maria;
You won't have your names when you ride the big airplane,
All they will call you will be "deportees."

My father's own father, he waded that river,
They took all the money he made in his life;
My brothers and sisters come working the fruit trees,
And they rode the truck till they took down and died.

Some of us are illegal, and some are not wanted,
Our work contract's out and we have to move on;
Six hundred miles to that Mexican border,
They chase us like outlaws, like rustlers, like thieves.

We died in your hills, we died in your deserts,
We died in your valleys and died on your plains.
We died 'neath your trees and we died in your bushes,
Both sides of the river, we died just the same.

The sky plane caught fire over Los Gatos Canyon,
A fireball of lightning, and shook all our hills,
Who are all these friends, all scattered like dry leaves?
The radio says, "They are just deportees"

Is this the best way we can grow our big orchards?
Is this the best way we can grow our good fruit?
To fall like dry leaves to rot on my topsoil
And be called by no name except "deportees"?

Well, that was just not right. My family started paying more attention to where our food came from, how the food was grown, and how we could use our protest rights and purchasing power to make things change for the better. Knowledge was powerful; marches were powerful, letter-writing was powerful, and the pocketbook was powerful.

It was not only food that I began to scrutinize, but other products as well. I used my purchasing power to quit taking the antihistamine, Novahistine, the green liquid that Daddy and I had taken each morning since I was a little girl. We sneezed our heads off because of our allergies and Novahistine was a very effective drug against those allergy symptoms.

But Novahistine was manufactured by the Dow Jones Chemical Company. Dow was also the manufacturer of Napalm. So how, in good conscience, could I use their allergy drug and add money to their coffers, when that money went to making Napalm? Napalm was the horrific gelled gasoline-like product that was dropped on Vietnam and would stick to people's skin and burn them. So we quit buying Novahistine, and we quit buying Saran Wrap, and we quit buying anything else that Dow manufactured. Supporting a company that made such a heinous product was not right. I wrote letters to Dow, explaining why I wasn't buying their products and that I was urging my friends to do the same economic boycott.

We practiced non-violent support or non-support of products and the ideals they supported with our money. It was an effective way to try to change how companies operated. One person boycotting – well that didn't matter, or so it seemed, but when thousands were united, it began to make a difference! It was called, "Power to the People!"

We would see cropdusters when we drove to southern California on Highway 5. We had seen the cropdusters on all of our trips through the Central Valley. When we were little it was so exciting! The small planes, usually bi-planes, would fly so near to the ground that if one flew over our car it sounded like it was going to crash right on top of us! And we would watch how the pilot guided that plane straight over those long rows, and we would see the dusty powder come out of the plane and land on the crops below. We knew that the cropdusters had to do their chore when there was no wind, otherwise their powders might not land on the crops, but instead might blow away and land somewhere else.

But what we were starting to hear about was that some of these dusts and powders were very poisonous and dangerous. It was the beginning of the battle between big agricultural businesses and small, unknown people. Rachel Carson was one of those people. Her 1962 book, *Silent Spring*, was about DDT and pesticides that were being used with very little controls. Birds' eggs were becoming paper-thin due to their exposure to the pesticide, DDT. There was information and speculation about how pesticides were not safe and of how DDT stayed in the ground and would damage wildlife for years. People began to wonder what these pesticides would do to humans.

Rachel Carson was a woman who took on the Establishment by writing a book. Eventually, because of Rachel Carson, there was a reversal in national pesticide policy and a nationwide ban on DDT and some other pesticides. The grassroots environmental movement inspired the creation of the Environmental Protection Agency (EPA) on December 2nd, 1970; however, when I was growing up there was no federal agency to protect people from environmental hazards. As we made those trips through California and passed those migrant workers, and watched cropdusters dispensing their poison, I knew that there must be a way for me to make a change. I wanted to help prevent the unfair things from happening.

The article on the next page was from *The Catamount*. Cubberley students started a food drive to benefit the farm laborers. The teenagers who spearheaded the food drive were members of the car club, the Executors. Radio station KFRC was asked to contribute to the food drive, and donated one-hundred dollars. Students wanted to make a change!

Nun inspires Delano Christmas drive

Inspired by a speech given at Cubberley on December 8th by Sister Mary Margaret of Presentation High School, exposing the poverty conditions in California and the plight of the poor in general, seniors Tom Tamplin, Joe Alvidres and Richard Alldis launched an energetic campaign to aid the Delano migrant workers.

Shortly afterward, the boys stationed collection boxes in the student center and cafeteria area. During the drive, which ended yesterday, students generously donated clothing, bedding and canned goods.

Money was also collected and will be used to purchase bulk food products such as flour and rice. All contributions will be presented to the farm laborers in the name of Cubberley High School.

Earning sub-standard wages in the Delano vineyards near Bakersfield, the Mexican and other migrant workers compose one of California's worst "poverty pockets," according to Sister Mary Margaret. Dependent upon seasonal employment, deficient diet and unsanitary living conditions have led to widespread sickness and disease in the area.

A petition has been circulated and submitted to radio station KFRC requesting $100.00 for the Delano workers as Cubberley's "Christmas Wish."

More Family Outings

One of the benefits of living in the Bay Area is that it is only a short drive to the beach or to redwood trees or to San Francisco. There are hills and a coastal range on one side of the Bay and more hills on the other side of the Bay, and interesting, historical places north and south of the Bay. As a teenager this meant that my family would plan trips that were not vacation trips, but one-day car trips.

I dreaded going on these trips. I wanted to do teenager things, not sit in the car with my sisters and fight car-sickness, go some place, walk around, and then drive back home again. But if Grandpa Bob and Gramma Gigi or Auntie Jan came with us, then the trip took on a whole different feeling and was actually fun…or at least it didn't feel like the same old car trip.

When I was fifteen we went to Pinnacles National Monument for a day trip. It was only about a two-hour drive. We took a picnic lunch and Auntie Jan came with us. Pinnacles is extremely hot in the summer, but we liked going there because there were caves to explore and rocks to climb, and the hot, barren rock formations were different from any other place.

Auntie Jan wore tennis shoes and slacks and that was when I realized that she and I were the same height. Auntie Jan usually wore high heels but without those tall heels I realized that she and I actually were the same height! Judy was taller, and Jennifer was only eleven, but at fourteen it was fun for me to see that my Auntie and I were the same height; almost five foot, four inches tall. I had been the same height since I was ten, but had not realized Auntie Jan's height until she was wearing flats!

We spent the entire day at Pinnacles, laughing, hiking and picnicking, and then just being lazy in the picnic area. It would have been about a two-hour drive home, but we stopped at a fruit stand on Highway 101 near Gilroy and bought strawberries and other fresh fruits, just taking our time and not rushing. At home we grew apricots, plums, peaches, boysenberries and cherries, so we didn't buy those, but we always liked to buy flats of strawberries to eat and to use for making jam.

The weekend after ninth grade was over, my family plus Auntie Jan and Grandpa Bob and Grandma Gigi went to Rio del Mar Beach for the day. Rio del Mar is a beach south of Santa Cruz. The parking lot is on the top of a cliff and when I was a teenager there was a long, long wooden staircase going from the top of the cliff down to the beach.

My mom packed a picnic into the old aluminum ice chest. We took towels and blankets and a transistor radio and Auntie Jan brought a beach umbrella. We brought our folding chairs so Grandpa Bob and Gramma Gigi could sit comfortably and we wore our swimsuits under our regular clothes and everyone wore sunglasses. In those days people were permitted to build a fire on the beach or take their barbeque with them; we had a picnic packed and didn't need to barbeque on the beach.

We lugged our stuff down the stairs, making slapping sounds with our flip-flop shoes as we balanced all the items we had brought, successfully navigating the stairs and then walking through the warm sand to stake out a place where we would spend the day.

It was a beautiful day. The fog had burned off, the sky was so blue that it almost sparkled, and the water was calm enough that we all went wading. My parents had forgotten the church key, the bottle opener to open their beer, so Judy and I borrowed one from some boys so that my parents, grandparents and Auntie Jan could open up their beer. We were beginning to see "pop tops" on some brands of soft drinks, but people still needed a church key to open canned beer. And the problem with the pop tops was that they were not fastened to the cans, so people would just toss them away. Littering pop tops was like throwing razor blades in the sand. It therefore became dangerous to walk barefoot in the sand because the pop tops were razor-sharp. The sand would cover up a pop top and a person wouldn't know it was there until they stepped on it or even kneeled on one, which could result in a very bad cut.

We built sandcastles, and then Judy and Auntie Jan and I walked down the beach, picking up sand dollars and shells and pieces of driftwood. We talked about boys and what we wanted to do during the summer. We were excited because Auntie Jan was engaged to be married! She had been married twice before, but her first marriage ended in annulment and her second in divorce. Now Auntie Jan was happily engaged again.

Part of me was glad but the other part was jealous because I didn't want Auntie Jan to move somewhere else and I didn't want to have to share her with her new husband. Now that Judy had a driver's license and a car, Judy often drove us to Auntie Jan's apartment. In the fourteen months since Auntie Jan moved from San Carlos to Palo Alto, we girls had spent a lot of time at her apartment. Sometimes I even traded clothes with her! We loved sitting in her oriental-decorated apartment with the lacquered desk and her temple rubbings from when she had visited the Tiger Balm Gardens in Thailand.

After our walk on the beach, we sat on towels and blankets and ate, and talked and laughed and I made a sand sculpture. There were some people barbecuing near us and it reminded Grandpa Bob of a story about his brother, our Uncle Ernie, an event that happened during World War II. Here is the story that Grandpa Bob told us about our Uncle Ernie:

Uncle Ernie lived with his wife, our Aunt Maude. They lived near Redondo Beach in Southern California. A lot of my mom's cousins and other uncles and aunts lived near there, too. During World War II there was rationing of many items, including cigarettes, meat, nylon stockings, fresh fruit, and produce. All these items were hard to get because they went to the soldiers before private citizens could get them.

Living at Redondo Beach, Uncle Ernie and Aunt Maude went to the wharves every evening and strolled down the beach. They dug in the sand for long-necked clams and found mussels along the wharf. Often they would eat the seafood raw, right then and there the very moment they dug it up. If they got full they would dig for more to take home for their lunch the next day. They got tired of eating clams and fresh seafood day after day, but there was no meat to eat and finding their own food was something many people were doing.

One day a friend of theirs showed up at their house with a piece of beef and some green onions! Uncle Ernie and Aunt Maude were so excited because even though they knew it was black-market meat that had been obtained illegally, it had been a long time since they had eaten beef and they couldn't wait to fix it.

Uncle Ernie, Aunt Maude and some of their friends and relatives decided to go to the beach and stew the beef over an open fire. It was a tough and stringy cut of beef, but they figured if they made a stew and everyone contributed to it, then all of them would have a chance to have some of the beef and some of the onions.

Maude and Ernie took their big stew pot to the beach, and as the sun set over the ocean they sat there with their friends, talking and smelling the wonderful stew as it simmered over the fire. At last the beef was tender, and Uncle Ernie served some stew for everyone on their plates. Everyone waited until all those there were served so they would take their first bite at the same time.

They took their first bite of delicious-smelling stew at the same moment – the smell had been driving them crazy with anticipation and most of them didn't even care if they burnt their mouth…it had been so long since they had tasted beef!

But the stew was inedible. Uncle Ernie's friend had started the fire with kerosene. The kerosene fumes had made the stew taste exactly like kerosene. Everyone took their first bite of the stew and then they spit their stew out. All they could do was smell it and try not to blame the friend who had been so eager to start the fire that he had used valuable kerosene as a fire-starter. Grandpa Bob said when Uncle Ernie told the story he just shook his head in disgust… that was all the explanation that was needed. Sometimes he would even get tears in his eyes.

Uncle Ernie took the stew and buried it in an empty field. They had all looked forward to that beef, but at least they still had clams and sea urchins to eat.

Grandpa Bob was not much of a talker. Listening to him tell the story of his brother and that stew was mesmerizing. My parents and Auntie Jan and Gramma Gigi had all heard the story many times before; everyone ended up adding more to the story as Grandpa Bob told it. It was difficult for me to imagine those times when food was rationed. Gramma Gigi often told us girls stories of how it had been in Oakland with the food rationing, but Grandpa Bob's story had every one of us laughing and then almost crying, we were so glad he shared that part of his family history with us.

As the sun set, sinking brightly into the Pacific Ocean, we went back up the long set of stairs, carrying the ice chest, blankets, towels, umbrella and chairs. Gramma Gigi walked slowly because her heart condition made climbing all those stairs difficult. She had suffered her first heart attack when she was forty-two, and she always had to carry nitroglycerin with her to put under her tongue if she experienced chest pains.

We had enjoyed a memorable day at the beach in the sun, talking and laughing and walking together. I loved to hear the stories of how it had been for my family a long time ago.

Excerpts from My Journal

"I started to think: I am so many different persons, all of them me, but all of them a different me. And I realize that I must seem like a very studious person to the kids at school. I guess I am, because to me, school and the rest of my life are completely different. You may wonder "why am I so against school?" I can't find an exact tangible reason, except that I don't like dong anything I <u>have</u> to, and I also feel that I could be spending my time much better elsewhere. But that isn't what I started to say. You see, I don't understand the enthusiasm kids my age have about school. In fact, I don't understand kids my age, really. In my non-school life, I spend it with people much older, usually men, people who I can understand. These aren't kids gossiping about so-and-so's bleached hair, or la-de-dah's cute outfit, or Coral's new boyfriend. These are people who are <u>real</u>. When I said older, I meant anywhere for 18 to 21, 21 to 27. It's people that are this age who are young enough to have fun with, but old enough to break away from the crowd, and say what they want and to hell-with-everyone else.

"I also notice that I seem to sound so serious. When I'm in this mood, which is about this time, before I have a plan for the

evening, I guess that I am serious. However, most of my friends say that I am the most carefree and extroverted person they know. I guess that's because being with guys makes me happy; that and painting is how I spend my time. I have one girlfriend, and she is absolutely serious. Yikes! So she thinks at times that I'm absolutely horrid; especially 'cause if a guy drops her, or moves, she mourns for him, practically. She just attaches herself to people. Not so with me. I figure that with all the guys I know (by "guys" I refer to people of the male gender) I can't be hurt. They are a lot of fun...we go out to escape, and to forget, and even if I go out with 6 different guys in a week, and pledge my heart to them all, that is certainly no reason to feel guilty. I can't understand her reasoning.

"Guys were invented for fun, and that's what I use them for. I don't think that I could be true, but right now there is a certain guy who believes in free love; we match eye-to-eye on that, and I've been dating him steadily for almost seven months — since I was 14 and he an old 17. And he is serious and had a lot of problems, I think a guy like that needs a girl like me — if a guy has a problem he need someone to make him laugh, someone to cry, someone to be serious for him. I can do the first easily, but the second and third ones come hard.

"I don't know what I've accomplished in this. I just write what I feel like."

"During Easter vacation my Gramma Gigi — yes my grandmother — and I went to Calistoga, in the Napa Wine Country. Visited wineries, and she got her car stuck on the railroad tracks by the winery and some men pushed it off the tracks for us. We went by way of Inverness, had breakfast there, up by the Russian River — thousands of apple and peach trees in bloom. We went to Lake Berryessa; I met some guys from El Cerrito who had a two-seater speedboat and one of the boys, Dave, and I went out on it. They asked me if my friend wanted to go too! "That's my grandmother, not my friend," I told them. I went on the boat and got to drive it.

"I also took a mud bath – Gramma Gigi was buying a bathing suit at the time and she looks okay in it! The mud bath was okay too. Our motel had a mineral swimming pool, like bath water – neat. There was a boy staying there from Sunnyvale, 17 years old, cute – his mother is really nice – they lived in Washington until last year when her husband left her with two kids in college and two other potential college kids – so to forget that she came to California knowing nothing about it.

"I also met a guy named Bob. I was swimming in the late afternoon in my new indecently decent bathing suit when I saw a cute guy so I started to talk to him; got out of the pool – he is 19, lived in L.A., hated it, moved to St. Helena (lovely town) a construction worker – tan, curly hair, sideburns – cool – and my ex-boyfriend Rick knows him! I found that out Saturday when I got home and Rick phoned me! Yikes!"

"About guys and me and their problems. October 4 was a special day. It was the birthday of a guy who I went around with who shot himself. He was the only guy my parents didn't approve of, and I went out secretly with him. Steve wasn't stupid. He ran away from North Carolina when he was a kid. His parents followed him, and they all lived together in Fremont, California...through Steve's high school. When he was in high school he and his best friend made their girlfriends pregnant, only Steve's girlfriend didn't have her baby...it is a complicated story, Steve's parents were not living together, they were Catholics, and Steve had eight younger sisters and his mother was working, so Steve and his best friend, Jamie, came here to Mountain View, and Steve was in a lot of trouble with the police. When I met him I was 14, and he was just about 20, and I thought he was a good-looking normal guy. But I sorta realized – through Jamie and Steve – what the score was. I didn't try to find Steve with problems, he just needed someone to talk to, then someone to yell at, then someone to talk to – someone who might understand...and how can I write my deep feelings on paper?

Such Sadness to Break my Heart

Auntie Jan had gone to Yosemite for a few weeks with Grandpa Bob, just for the fun of it. She took vacation from her job at Hewlett-Packard, and Grandpa Bob and Auntie Jan went horseback riding and stayed in a cabin together, enjoying the beauty of such a majestic place, plus that special love that a daddy and his daughter have that let them be just themselves... safe and special with each other. Because Auntie Jan was engaged to be married this trip was bittersweet. Once Auntie Jan was married, she and Grandpa Bob would probably never again go on trips with just the two of them.

Later Grandpa Bob would say that he noticed how Auntie Jan relied on her prescription sleeping pills to go to sleep, but he knew that she got them from her doctor and that without those pills she would lay awake, tossing and turning all night.

On a summer morning a few months after the trip to Yosemite, Auntie Jan's work called our house. Auntie Jan had not come to her job and she had not called in. Her manager was really worried about her, because Auntie Jan always came to work on time, and if she was ever sick she would call, so he didn't know what to think. He wondered if my mom knew any reason why Auntie Jan would not be at work.

School was out, so my mom and we three girls were at home. My mom got off the phone and said that something must be wrong, that Jan hadn't called in sick and she wasn't at work. She called Auntie Jan on the phone, and there was no answer. Then she called Gramma Gigi, and asked her if she had talked to Jan that morning. Gramma Gigi had talked Auntie Jan the night before, and everything was all right then. We didn't know what to think, except that something was horribly wrong.

My mom, Jennifer, and I got in Judy's car, and Judy drove over to Auntie Jan's apartment.

Auntie Jan's car was in the car port, her white Triumph Spitfire...there was no way of confusing her car with anyone else's car. We went up the elevator to her second-story apartment and banged on her door. There was no answer. My mom couldn't find the key to Auntie Jan's apartment, maybe because my mom was so upset. It seemed like time was going in slow motion and that whatever was happening shouldn't be happening and that we needed some help.

We broke into the apartment...we couldn't wait to get help to get in. And we found Auntie Jan in her bed, but she wouldn't wake up. Auntie Jan was like a rag doll, all warm and floppy and when we shook her and tried to get her to sit up she just fell over. We didn't know what the matter was, and then my mom told Judy to call for an ambulance. Judy dialed "O" for the operator, and told the operator that we needed an ambulance.

I looked at the bed stand next to Auntie Jan's bed. There were two prescription pill bottles from a pharmacy. One bottle was dated three days earlier for fifty pills, and the other bottle was dated two days earlier, also for fifty pills. One was empty and the other one less than half full. They were Auntie Jan's sleeping pills.

I looked at those bottles and my mind was racing. It looked like Auntie Jan had taken about seventy-five sleeping pills in just a few days! How could that be; I didn't understand. We couldn't wake her up. We kept trying and trying, but she never opened her eyes and wouldn't wake up.

My mom told me to go wait out front by the street for the ambulance. On my way to the elevator, a man came running up the stairs, and I thought he might be the doctor, so I ran to him and asked him if he was a doctor. I started to cry. He said he wasn't, but could he help, and I told him that my Auntie wouldn't wake up and that we had called the ambulance. He knew who my Auntie was, and he went downstairs with me and waited with me by the street until the ambulance came.

They took my Auntie Jan away in the ambulance. The ambulance driver and the technicians couldn't wake her up. I showed them the pill bottles and they took those with them. My mom called Gramma Gigi and Daddy and told them what had happened, and then my sisters and my mom and I got into Judy's car and Judy drove to Stanford Hospital. The ambulance had taken Auntie Jan to Hoover Pavilion at Stanford, the same hospital where my sister, Jennifer, had been born.

My beautiful Auntie Jan was in the hospital for two weeks. My Auntie who had worn the highest of high heels, who had her clothes made in exotic foreign countries, and whose laughter lit up entire rooms. And now no one could wake her up. She was in a coma from taking too many sleeping pills. It turned out that what they called the fatal dose of those pills was thirty pills, and her doctor had prescribed one hundred pills in just three days. Auntie Jan had taken seventy five pills in one night. She never came out of the coma, never got to hug us or laugh or listen to us tell her how much we loved her. After two weeks Gramma Gigi signed the papers to take Auntie Jan off of life support and then Auntie Jan died. She was thirty-four years old and my heart broke into a million jillion trillion sharp pieces.

We went to Roller and Hapgoods Funeral Home on Middlefield Road for the funeral. My Auntie was dead in a casket, dressed in a tight hot-pink satin dress, her hair fixed perfect and hot-pink lipstick on her lips. But she looked like she was made of wax, and for the first time in my life I knew what hot tears were, knew how hot tears felt, because hot tears poured out of my eyes and burned and burned and my throat ached with the burning sorrow of my Auntie being dead. I saw her in the casket and then I knew she was really dead and that I would not hear her laughing ever again, and those tears did not feel like they could come fast enough or cool enough and my heart broke with the sadness and the pain and the sorrow.

Gramma Gigi's heart broke, and so did all of our hearts, us girls and Daddy and my mom and Grandpa Bob.

Hewlett Packard had Auntie Jan's photo in their magazine in two places, with one special page for a memorial about her. Many, many people came to her funeral. The day after her funeral I went to my summer book study, and a few days after that I went to Mexico. How would the world ever feel the same without my Auntie there? It wouldn't feel the same. It never did. Gramma Gigi started to drink too much and Grandpa Bob spoke even less than he had before. And the weekends that we had looked forward to because Auntie Jan would be there were gone. She left her clothes, her bikini, her car, and her cats, her Oriental table and desk and paintings. Her smile is still in my heart and her laugh is still in my heart too. My throat burned and burned and ached and ached from the pain of my Auntie being gone.

We wondered why the doctor had given her so many pills all at once. In those days people didn't sue at the drop of a hat like they do today; we never even thought of suing the doctor, but we did think he had been negligent in checking on why Auntie Jan needed so many pills at the same time.

Grandpa Bob felt guilty for the rest of his life. He had noticed when they went to Yosemite that Auntie Jan woke up in the night and would grab pills and take them without even knowing that she was doing it. In the morning she would wonder why so many pills were gone. Grandpa Bob felt that he should have told the doctor that Auntie Jan was addicted to those pills, but Grandpa Bob knew how much trouble Auntie Jan had going to sleep without the pills.

Now she was asleep forever.

Pills blamed ✓
in Palo Alto JUL 4 1966
woman's death

Janet Gail Houplin, 34, of Palo Alto, died Saturday at the Palo Alto-Stanford Hospital of the effects of an overdose of tranquilizer pills, police said.

Miss Houplin was found unconscious in her apartment at 3375 Alma St. on June 22. Police said the death probably was accidental. They said she had been taking tranquilizers for the past four or five years because of a nervous condition.

Miss Houplin was a secretary at Hewlett-Packard Co. in Palo Alto. She was a graduate of San Leandro High School and attended San Jose State College, where she was a member of Alpha Phi sorority. She also was a member of Job's Daughters. She had lived in Palo Alto for 16 months.

She is survived by her parents, Mr. and Mrs. Robert Houplin of San Carlos; a sister, Mrs. Louise Richter of Palo Alto; and three nieces.

Funeral services will be at 2 p.m. Tuesday at the chapel of Roller and Hapgood, 980 Middlefield Road, Palo Alto. Inurnment will be private

JANET GAIL
1932-1966

Mexico

I went to Mexico a few days after Auntie Jan died. I had been to Guadalajara, Mexico, the previous summer, teaching school, and I yearned to go back. I had taught art at Centro Culturo Jasmin, and I would be doing the same job again for the second time.

I flew from the San Jose Airport to Los Angeles International Airport and my ticket to Los Angeles cost thirteen dollars. The previous summer had been the first time I had ever been on an airplane. At both San Jose and LAX Airports the passengers walked from the terminal onto the runways and boarded the plane on portable stairs that went from the runway to the door of the plane. From LAX we flew in a four-propeller plane to La Paz, the capital of Mexico's Baja California Sur. Looking out the window at the crystal-clear turquoise water along the coast was amazing. We flew over desert with no roads, and most of the places where the land met the sea looked from the plane as if there was no beach at all. It was an amazing view, to see how dry the land was and the contrast with the beautiful clear water. I could see the land through the water along the shoreline; in places the water was a vivid blue-green and it didn't even look real... it looked like a painting.

It was warm inside the plane, and then it was hot, and grew quite noisy from the propellers, and then it became almost unbearably hot. The stewardesses wore crisp uniform dresses, with little hats perched on their perfect hair-dos. They let anyone on the plane have alcohol; there was no ice on board, so I drank warm Rum-and-Cokes in that hot plane. When we landed in La Paz for refueling we had to get off the plane, and the air on the landing strip was like an oven. The terminal was a small one-story building, and it was incredibly hot in the terminal, but at least they had ice, so I got cold Rum-and-Cokes. After we left La Paz in the same plane, there was a lot of turbulence. We flew through huge black clouds with lightening all around us, and when we descended into Guadalajara's airport it felt like we flew straight down! My stomach felt like I had been on a carnival ride.

It was evening when we arrived, and my friends from the previous year were there to greet me and the other Americans. The recent rain had left the air fresh and the streets full of quickly-evaporating puddles. I was greeted by the smell of damp earth, grilled corn and tortillas, and the sounds of guitar music and laughter.

There were cobblestone streets and artists and music and old ladies selling grilled corn on street corners; corn cooked on small wood-burning stoves and served with lime juice and chili powder. There were candy stores on the first floor of shops with dentists on the second floor. The many buses were owned by their drivers and had pictures of Jesus and Mary and altars with beads all around them right inside the bus.

I was there to teach art at Centro Cultural Jasmin; it was one of very few free learning centers in Guadalajara, and was founded by Ramona Salazar. Mrs. Salazar is reputed to have been the first social worker in all of Mexico, and her mission was to provide education for communities where there were few available schools.

Most of the free government-run public schools were filled to capacity, while the private schools were costly and usually operated by the Catholic Church. As a result, there were generations of people who had not been formally educated. These people did not know how to read, but managed still to get jobs and raise families, working as laborers, as bus drivers, artists, or street vendors. But they wanted better lives for their children, so the community welcomed the free classes that were taught at the Centro Cultural Jasmin. The classes taught there included English, cooking, woodworking, sewing, and art. I taught the children's art classes. I had brought powdered tempura paint with me in my suitcase and the children painted on newspaper with the brushes that I had also brought from America. Having the children in the art class allowed the mothers to take a class without watching their children, and for many of them this was a new experience.

Some of the students in my painting class

I stayed at a place that was similar to a youth hostel. It was the unfinished home of a doctor and was located on Calle Gigantes (Giant Street). Every afternoon at two o'clock it would rain and the street flooded several inches to the top of the sidewalk. When it stopped raining the puddles reflected the sun and the sidewalks were clean and fresh and people woke from their siestas.

Calle Gigantes and the Gate to the Youth Hostel

The American doctor who donated his house had a tragic story. The doctor's wife had died during the construction of the house, so he had moved back to America with a broken heart. There was a stairway that went nowhere because the second story had never been built.

The hostel had eight rooms, and four girls could share a room. Boys who stayed there slept in a converted stable. When we took a shower, we heated the water by building a fire under the water pipes, and then we would take a really fast shower, as there was only a small amount of boiling hot water followed by cold water! The makeshift shower was on the back patio and not very private. Our laundry was done by a lady who came every day, and she washed clothes in a pond that was in the yard of the house. She was happy to have the job of washing clothes, because as long as people stayed at the hostel she always had steady work in a clean, safe place.

I learned that when someone washes clothes by beating them on a rock that the clothes fall apart after about three washings. It made sense to pack light and bring only a few of my American clothes, and to then buy clothes in Guadalajara. Those colorful embroidered cotton clothes withstood washing, kept people cool in the heat, and were much cheaper than buying clothes in America.

One day I lost my wallet or perhaps it was stolen, so I rode the bus to the end of the line hoping that I would find my wallet. But I didn't. At the end of the line were two barrels with a board over them and some old ladies with no teeth cooking corn on a grill. I told them I had no wallet, and they helped me look in all the parked buses. When we couldn't find it, an old, old man drove me back to Calle Gigantes. I was the only person in the bus and he kept me safe and dropped me off where I was staying. I had no money, no wallet, no identification, but later I did get reimbursed for the traveler's cheques.

There were many corner stands that looked like small wooden boxcars with one open side, selling bottled soft drinks that were often warm due to lack of ice in many neighborhoods. If a person drank part of their soda and left the bottle, the owners of that shop would combine leftover sodas into one bottle and recap it.

I loved to go to the Mercado Libertad, which was the largest free market in Mexico and located in downtown Guadalajara. At the Mercado there was so much art: walnut shells cut with little doors and hinges and scenes inside of them, and yarn glued onto small square boards to make pictures. There were many sizes and shapes of metal cut into designs and jewelry and lovely weavings and embroidery and paintings. Art and creativity was a part of everyone's life with a colorful passion that was exciting and energizing.

Taking buses was very easy, and I took a bus to Lake Chapala with my group of friends. Lake Chapala is Mexico's largest freshwater lake, and is about thirty miles from Guadalajara. Driving the two-lane road through the lush countryside, I saw many one-room adobe houses scattered along the sides of the road, some with a few goats or skinny cattle in the yards. The grasses were long and lush, the countryside green and fresh-looking. There were no cars or trucks in driveways like in America, where even the poorest person seemed to have a yard full of cars and trucks. Most of the Mexican people didn't own cars, but rode buses or took taxis or walked or biked.

At Chapala we rented a motorboat with a driver to take us out on the lake. From the lake we could see the shoreline with the beautiful white adobe homes, and a tall statue on the hillside. We ran out of gas and had to spend the day and evening on a little deserted island that had many iguanas and lizards on it and no bathroom. Another boat finally came out and rescued us.

I visited newly-made friends at their home in Colonio Oblatos. There was only one school in this suburb of Guadalajara, yet there were over one thousand kindergarten-aged children, and many older school-aged children. Their neighborhood school had space for only two hundred students of all grades combined. One cold-water faucet was shared by more than two hundred people. The families who lived there made their own adobe bricks and then built their homes from those same bricks. Occasionally when it rained the roofs would collapse, crushing the people who lived in those homes.

I took a bus every day to the school, Centro Cultural Jasmin. I guided children who were passionate and thirsty to create, and they painted on newspaper with powdered tempura mixed with water. I hung up their art to dry and to show and display. The students were little girls watching their baby brothers and sisters, and little boys, some boys who were rough at eleven or twelve. There was one boy who was mixed Mexican and Chinese and the other kids called him "Chin-na, Chin-na" and made fun of him and wouldn't play with him.

I met David Horton in Mexico. He was British, very tall, and had long curly hair. He had been arrested in Palo Alto for pot, and was allowed to do volunteer service hours instead of going to California Youth Authority, which was a prison camp for teenagers. We became friends; he and I were both vegetarians and had similar anti-war beliefs. His father was a professor at Stanford University and his mother had been a Member of Parliament and we talked for hours about everything and anything.

In the evenings on Calle Gigantes, neighbors set up small tables on the sidewalks in front of their houses and ate their dinners. It was so different, so interesting to watch people eat on the sidewalks with their tables set up beautifully with tablecloths and festive dishes and flowers, right there next to the street! Then guitar players would play and sing, and the sun would set in an evening display of many colors. The neighborhood was full of music and dancing, the smells of food, and the sounds of happy children and of people enjoying life.

On a pedestrian walkway in downtown Guadalajara

with one of my Guadalajaran friends

I loved Guadalajara. There was art everywhere, and murals by the muralist and activist, Jose Clemente Orozco, who had painted vibrant political murals yet had only one hand. The University of Guadalajara was like visiting an art museum because of all the murals and statues and the beautiful building itself. The University was the second-oldest university in Guadalajara, and when I visited it one afternoon I learned about its history and I was humbled by how amazingly beautiful the campus was.

Statues and parrots were in abundance in Parque Aqua Azul, and there were small boats to rent in Parque Acalde. Siesta really happened every afternoon at two o'clock, as it was too hot to work or play. Even the fountains in the parks were turned off for two hours, starting at two o'clock. The buses quit running and everyone rested until after it rained, and then the bustle and activities of life would start again.

There was a telephone at a corner market down the street from the hostel, but we had no reason to use it. We didn't know anyone in Mexico who had a phone, and calling long-distance to the United States was incredibly expensive.

I got up every morning and went on the bus to El Centro Cultural, and then I would stop by the Mercado on the way back. I never tired of the Mercado, of the weavings, of the cotton embroidered fabrics and woven leather shoes, or of the cut-paper art and delicate silver jewelry. I could get fruits and vegetables there...I ate and drank everything and never got sick, but I drank a lot of cerveza also. Music could be heard through my open bedroom window until long after midnight, and America seemed very far away.

One Sunday morning I decided to go to church, and I ended up in a very small Catholic church. I saw only Catholic churches when I was in Guadalajara, but I knew there were a few Protestant centers. When I went into the church I caused a lot of staring because I was the only Anglo, plus I was an unaccompanied teenaged girl. I had made sure to put on a head-covering and to wear a skirt that was long enough to cover my knees; otherwise I would have offended the people who worshipped there. I sat on a hard, well-worn, and very polished bench, and laid my burlap purse on the bench next to me.

I was between two very old ladies, the kind of ladies that I saw a lot of in Mexico, with leathery skin and so many wrinkles that it was hard to see their eyes, and their scarves covered their head and most of their face. Their faces were unreadable anyway. Sitting there, listening to the priest and looking at the light filtering through the stained-glass windows, and seeing the gold and the opulence of the alter, I wondered if those ladies drew strength from the wealth of their church, if it validated their faith more than if their church would have been as poverty-stricken as they were. I thought they must get comfort and hope from the beautiful artwork and the well-worn and sturdy benches, benches that had probably held them as children, and their parents, grandparents, and many past generations.

And then I saw the cockroach. The insects in Mexico were big! There was one beetle that got stuck in our kitchen drain, and was so big it clogged the whole drain up. There were beetles that sounded like mini-helicopters when they flew, and they would bruise a person if they hit them at full flight. This cockroach in the church was no exception; in fact, it was the biggest cockroach I had ever seen! I wondered if it thought it was still night because the church was pretty dim inside. The roach skittered along the floor, and was getting closer and closer to my feet, and then it disappeared under the bench where I was sitting. I had always wanted to study insects, but that bug was more like a mouse than an insect! Then I saw it again, and it was on the bench next to me. Next to me! I felt myself recoil…the ladies on each side of me were praying and had their hands clasped in prayer and their eyes were closed. This THING, this gargantuan creature, was getting nearer and nearer and then it started crawling up my burlap purse. The strap to the purse was still on my shoulder. I couldn't help it; I started pushing against the old lady next to me, and flung the strap off my shoulder. Now I had interrupted both ladies' praying, yet they didn't even seem to notice the cockroach. I basically shoved the one lady down the bench several feet, grabbed my burlap bag, stood up and hightailed it out of that church into the hot mid-morning sun, blinking at the brightness of the daylight. I turned and made sure that the bug wasn't chasing me and checked that it wasn't on me. I hoped to never see a cockroach that big ever, ever, ever in my life again…ever. I certainly had not had any spiritual need met that morning!

In Mexico the women and girls never even thought of shaving their legs or armpits, and on Sunday they dressed up fancy and beautifully. Their husbands and boyfriends were proud of them, and if they had wrinkles or layers of fat or hair on their legs, no one even noticed, because they were families and after church they all walked together and touched and their bodies were natural.

People sat in the parks in the afternoons, playing their guitars, singing, clapping and singing some more. Women did not wear slacks or smoke in public, or even go out unaccompanied to a park. I had to be careful to act the same way, because otherwise a teenager or a woman might be mistaken for a prostitute. But I loved the dancing and the spontaneity. The poverty was intense and the young mothers were so very young; the old women with no teeth and ten children were really only in their thirties. But I was embraced as I wandered the markets and traveled on the buses and ate and drank and took it all in with my eyes, my ears, and my heart.

When I returned to America we first landed in Tijuana, Mexico, and then took a taxicab to San Diego and then flew to the Los Angeles Airport.

Everywhere I looked I saw that people did not touch each other. In Mexico a brother and sister might walk down the street with their arms around each other, talking and laughing, or two best friends would walk with their arms around each other's waists, or men would talk and hug and walk with their arms across each other's shoulders. Here in America no one touched each other unless it was a young couple at the airport frantically tongue kissing and groping each other with the neediness that came from the longing that they would have for each other when they were apart. But no one else hugged or walked touching each other, unless it was a mother holding a child's hand too tight with the fear that a stranger would grab her child and take that child away in the blink of an eye.

In Mexico the kids would run and walk in front of or behind the parents, and the families would walk out together in big groups and the children could wander off and all of a sudden would return and no one held their hand to keep them from learning how to walk and run and skip and jump.

I was so homesick for Mexico that I wanted to turn right around and go back, returning to the young men with longing in their eyes who would walk with me in the moonlight and not even try to kiss me, but whisper poetry of yearning in my ear… walking in the moonlight in flower-scented gardens with the rhythm of insects and frogs and the harmony of life. I didn't want to return to the reality of Auntie Jan being gone, or to another year of attending school, to race riots and assassinations and craziness. I loved being the art teacher at Centro Culturo Jasmin and I loved having Mexico love me.

But I did return to the reality of Auntie Jan being gone, to the sadness that had overtaken Gramma Gigi, Grandpa Bob, and my parents. I started my junior year in high school a week later, getting back into the rhythm of life as defined by school, weekends, and holiday breaks. But the weekends were now different, because Auntie Jan would never share weekends with us again.

We only saw Auntie Jan's fiancé a few times after she died. With her gone there was no reason to see him anymore.

David Horton and I began to hang out with each other; he was my friend and I liked to be with him. He had been on the same flight back from Mexico. I still had my boyfriend, Rick, and often the three of us went places together.

T elevision

We had a television in our kitchen. My mom and my sisters and I ate dinner together at the kitchen table most nights. Because Daddy often had to work late, most week nights he wasn't home in time to eat with us. On holidays or on special occasions we ate at the dining room table, but that was only about five or six times a year. The rest of the time we ate dinner with the TV on, and the TV was on before and after dinner.

My mom listened to the radio from six-thirty in the morning until the TV was turned on at around five o'clock every weekday evening. And the TV stayed on until ten or eleven o'clock at night. With a television on our kitchen counter, the shows and the news became a huge part of our lives. When I was little we had no TV; when we did get our first TV it had been in the living room and we had only watched it some evenings after dinner. Then we had received only three or four channels. Now we had a few more channels with a broader selection of shows and TV was on most nights.

We had a black-and-white television and we didn't know what shows were in color, except that at the beginning of a color show on the NBC network there was an animated peacock that had tail feathers in color for people who had color television to adjust the color on their sets. The announcer would say, "The following program is brought to you in living color on NBC." Color TVs were quite expensive. When I was a teenager I didn't know anyone who had a color TV. Besides, most of the time when we went to friends' houses, people turned off their TV because it was rude to pay more attention to the TV than to your friends or to your guests.

There was a TV show called *Sea Hunt*. While my mom made dinner, we girls took our turns setting the table and we watched *Sea Hunt*. It was a half-hour show, on from five-thirty until six o'clock, about Mike Nelson, a diver whose mission was to rescue people from trouble in the ocean or along the coastline. Most of the time he wore just a face mask, swim trunks, and flippers. In a half hour he could cut through fishing nets, help people whose diving tanks ran out of air, prevent murders, save turtles, save beautiful women, and rescue young children. It was the first TV series that centered on underwater adventures, and at the end of each episode, the star, Lloyd Bridges, spoke as himself and made a plea to protect the oceans. This was a first in television, the combining of entertainment with an environmental request.

For most kids who wore glasses, the nickname "Mike Nelson" was used in a derogatory way, making fun of their eye glasses. Mike Nelson wore his underwater goggles, and those of us who wore glasses found that we were often called "Mike Nelson." Sigh.

We watched *Sea Hunt* every weekday evening, even when it was reruns and we had seen all the episodes. There was always a happy ending and the bad guys always lost; that was one of the reasons we liked it.

After *Sea Hunt* came the evening news. The *Huntley-Brinkley Report* was anchored by Chet Huntley in New York City, and by David Brinkley in Washington, D.C. The news show began as a fifteen-minute program, but when I was in junior high it expanded to thirty minutes. We would sit down to dinner and watch the *Huntley-Brinkley Report*. At the end of every newscast, Chet and David would tell each other, "Good night." Even though they were not in the same city, they were on the same news show, and we were able to see them both on a split screen! "Good night, David," and "Good night, Chet," were the expected evening phrases, and we would say those "good nights" with the newscasters in the same manner as we had done as kids with the Mickey Mouse Club. These newscasters became a part of our evening routine.

Usually when Daddy got home he would have his dinner at the kitchen table and he and my mom would talk. We girls would already be in our rooms doing our homework or taking turns talking on the phone. I would go out with my friends many evenings, hanging out and having fun, but I would have had my dose of evening TV before I went out.

With the United States going to war in Vietnam in 1963, the nation began watching a war at their dinner tables, my family included. We had never heard of Vietnam, and now every night at dinner the story slowly, graphically, and horrifically unfolded as we ate.

During the Vietnam War, television brought real-time war into American homes. Vietnam was the first "television war," and the Saigon bureau was for years the third largest bureau the networks maintained. Dinner-time TV brought the dramatic reality of war night-after-night into our homes, eventually inspiring revulsion and exhaustion. We watched the nightly black-and-white reports about a country on the other side of the world, the small country of Vietnam. Newscasters even pronounced it differently from one another, and because they were not certain of the pronunciation, either were we:

Veetnam, Vietnam, Vetnam, Vietnum…who even knew how to say the name of the faraway country?

For the first few years of the war the news coverage was upbeat. The reporters spoke about victories and progress. However, in August 1965, CBS aired a report by reporter Morley Safer, which showed our United Stares Marines lighting the thatched roofs of the villagers in Cam Ne. Our young American soldiers were using their Zippo cigarette lighters to set a civilian village on fire! The report included critical commentary on the treatment of the villagers. We were at home watching this, and could not understand what was happening. The villagers were in their own homes, they were peasants! Why was our country doing this, why were our young American soldiers burning the homes of these faraway people?

We also saw Dr. Martin Luther King, Jr., on television. Dr. King and other leaders organized the 1963 "March on Washington," a massive protest against racial discrimination in Washington, D.C. And on August 28th, 1963, King delivered his

"I Have a Dream" speech and we saw the speech on TV. The speech expressed the hopes of the civil rights movement:

"I have a dream that one day this nation will rise up and live out the true meaning of its creed: We hold these truths to be self-evident, that all men are created equal.

I have a dream that my four little children will one day live in a nation where they will not be judged by the color of their skin but by the content of their character."

And because of television news, we could see this, we could hear the civil rights speeches, and we were inspired to make America a better place to live.

The speech and the march helped create the political momentum that resulted in the Civil Rights Act of 1964. This act prohibited segregation in public accommodations, as well as prohibiting discrimination in education and employment. It was difficult for me to believe that I lived in a country that had segregated restrooms and lunchrooms, and that in the South the Negroes were required by law to eat and drink and go to school separated from white people.

This was scary to us. Judy's best friend, Sylvia, was a Negro, and now seeing all this news on television about civil rights and Martin Luther King was sometimes making our interracial friendships a bit more tenuous. We were aware of race and racism in different ways than before. We had gone to school together with many races and didn't really think that much about what color a person was or what religion they were, but now the reality of racism was being presented on television practically every day, along with the War, and we were forced to analyze our positions and beliefs and how we really felt.

On March 7th, 1965, six-hundred people seeking the right to vote were beaten and teargassed on the Edmund Pettus Bridge in Selma, Alabama. I saw on television how scary that was and how brave people of all ages were in standing up for their civil rights. It seemed that the entire nation was on fire about rights. There was television footage of intense hatred that made me be ashamed of being a white person. However, there were also stories of intense sacrifices and love that made me proud of how honorable and loving most people of all colors were. We were going to help instigate change. This was not how the future was going to be! I was going to join in and help change America and join the civil rights movement and the peace movement with the goal to make this a better America, and television was a part of showing me how this could be done!

By 1965 television news departments had expanded. The nightly news had doubled in length, and television was dealing with stories such as civil rights conflicts, the Vietnam War and the assassination of a president.

"The Tet Offensive" was a military campaign during the Vietnam War that began on January 31st, 1968. The purpose of the offensive was to spark a general uprising among the population that would then topple the Saigon government, thus ending the war in a single blow. The operations were referred to as the Tet Offensive because they began during the early morning hours of Tết Nguyên Đán, the first day of the year on a traditional lunar calendar and the most important Vietnamese holiday. And during the Vietnam Tet Offensive, my family and thousands of other NBC News viewers saw Colonel Nguyen Ngoc Loan blow out the brains of his captive in a Saigon street.

How could we be at home eating our dinner watching this horror and not want to stop it? We watched a kneeling man with his hands tied behind his back be shot in the head right before our eyes. The next school day the Students for a Democratic Society (SDS) mobilized for anti-war marches and students all over the country protested what had been seen on television. How could we be proud Americans when we watched such shameful events like this happen? A special broadcast by the reporter and journalist, Walter Cronkite, told us about the Tet Offensive. Cronkite closed "*Report from Vietnam: Who, What, When, Where, Why?*" by expressing his view that the war could not be won, and that the United States would have to find a way out. A month later President Lyndon Johnson declined to run for reelection and announced that he was seeking a way out of the war.

Television coverage of the war continued, and reporters featured American soldiers' bravery and their skill in handling war technology. Later in the war, after Tet and the beginning of American troop withdrawals in 1969, television coverage began to change. The focus was still on American boys, but journalists started emphasizing the human costs of the war.

In 1968, reality violence on TV was relentless, including assassinations and riots such as the May student-protests which rocked France. In August, there was violent rioting in Chicago as the Democrats nominated Hubert Humphrey. In October, the Mexican government massacred hundreds of peaceful demonstrators; reporters risked their lives bringing us this news.

TV was a double-edged sword; we learned from it, we laughed with it, but we also cried and were shocked to see real violence happen before our eyes. We were not watching sensationalism or made-for-TV staged actions. What stayed in my head were the scenes recorded by news reporters who often risked their own lives to deliver stories that were so powerful as to form new opinions and change beliefs. The TV media was transitioning as a powerful tool to affect change.

And when the evening news show finished at seven o'clock, and Chet and David said, "Good night"' to each other, we would switch over to a completely different train of thought. Almost every night there was something on television that we would watch while cleaning up the kitchen after dinner. Having the television turned on while we were cleaning up made it easier to do chores compared to doing them without a TV. After all, before TV we would bicker and fight while cleaning up, but with the TV we really didn't have to talk to each other any more. We just shared the same room while the TV entertained us.

There were funny shows and entertaining shows that we watched just to escape the bombardment of horrible news about the war. It was quite a contrast: go to school, come home, set the table; eat while watching the news and seeing people getting killed, clean up the table and then watch comedy. How does anyone really process all of that?

The Flintstones was one of the first primetime animated TV shows, and it was ABC's first series televised in color. The original sponsor of the show was the R.J. Reynolds Tobacco Company, so that watching the cartoon gave viewers their dose of televised cigarette advertisement. *The Flintstones* was about a working-class stone-age man's life with his family and his next door neighbor and best friend. It was a funny show and we loved watching *The Flintstones*. It didn't take long until everyone was saying, "Yabba-Dabba-Do!" just like Fred Flintstone. We girls had sung the "Happy Anniversary" song from *The Flintstones* for my parents' thirteenth wedding anniversary, jumping from behind the couch and surprising them with our television-based rendition.

We watched *Flipper, Gilligan's Island,* and the cowboy series, *Bonanza. Bonanza* was the biggest hit series of the 1960s, a show about the fictitious Cartwright family. The youngest son was "Little Joe," and we all thought that Little Joe was REALLY handsome; on Sunday evenings we watched *Bonanza*.

Music was changing America really quickly, and sing-alongs were very popular. So when the *Smothers Brothers Comedy Hour* aired on TV, we all made time to watch it, either at home or with friends. Tommy and Dick Smothers performed folk songs, which usually led to arguments between them, with Tommy saying, "Mom always liked you best!"

Their *Comedy Hour* became one of the most controversial American television programs of the Vietnam War. The brothers were critical of the political mainstream and the War; they were sympathetic to the emerging counterculture. Their politics led to the program's cancellation.

The show had one actress who would do a skit called, "Share a Little Tea with Goldie." All of us teenagers were cracking up because most of what she said had a double-meaning about with smoking marijuana. Parents and teens who watched the skits together would be laughing about completely different things.

Pete Seeger appeared during the latter year of the show in his first appearance on network television since being blacklisted in the 1950s. In the 1950s the entertainment industry blacklist included musicians and other entertainers who were denied employment because of political beliefs or associations, real or suspected. People were barred from work on the basis of their alleged membership in, or sympathy toward, the American Communist Party. Some were blacklisted because their names came up at the wrong place and time. In 1955, Pete Seeger was subpoenaed to testify before the House Un-American Activities Committee (HUAC). Pete refused to plead the Fifth Amendment and instead refused to name personal and political associations on the grounds that this would violate his First Amendment rights: "I am not going to answer any questions as to my association, my philosophical or religious beliefs or my political beliefs, or how I voted in any election, or any of these private affairs. I think these are very improper questions for any American to be asked, especially under such compulsion as this." His refusal to testify led to an indictment for contempt of Congress and he was sentenced to ten years in jail. In May 1962 an appeals court overturned his conviction.

With all his political background, Pete Seeger's appearance on the Smothers' Brothers show was very controversial. Pete's song, *Waist Deep in the Big Muddy*, was an anti-war song, and had aired originally in September, 1967. However, CBS management censored the song prior to broadcast. Relenting in February of 1968, the censors allowed Pete to return to the show to sing the song. Those of us who had not known who Pete Seeger was, quickly developed an appreciation and respect for this performing activist. He sang tirelessly for human rights and dignity for many years and yet was punished by McCarthy-era thinking; suffering from the politically-motivated practice of making accusations of disloyalty, subversion, or treason without proper regard for evidence.

Finally, the end of the 1960s was the right time to let Pete Seeger sing again on national television.

The musical performance by The Who was another landmark moment in the series. As they often did, The Who destroyed their instruments at the conclusion of their performance. A stage hand, at the request of the band, loaded Keith Moon's kick-drum with explosives, but when they detonated, the explosion was so intense that Moon was injured by cymbal shrapnel and Pete Townshend's hearing was permanently damaged.

Hanging Out With Friends

I met David Horton in Mexico when I was sixteen, and he and I became good friends. When the French exchange student, Catrina, arrived from France and became very interested in David, I felt David's and my friendship was threatened. Suddenly David became more attractive and I did not want to share him with the short, blonde, cute and sexy French student who spoke with such an enticing and seductive accent! David had his own accent. He was British, and British was "in," what with the Beatles, the Rolling Stones, Herman's Hermits and the popularity of all the many other British bands!

David lived in a big, old, two-story house in the part of Palo Alto called "Professorville." Professorville was where many of Stanford's professors lived. David had an older brother and sister and one younger sister, and his younger sister was named Jennifer, just like my younger sister! David's father was a dean at Stanford and the head of their Aeronautical Engineering Department.

David attended Paly and was ahead of me by one grade. His best friends were Ralph and Garland. Ralph was a few years older, was adopted and his life was full of wild experiences. One of Ralph's prized possessions was a preserved tortoise that he had stolen from the Smithsonian when he was in elementary school on a field trip. Ralph's adoptive mom had been a beauty queen, including Miss Ohio State and had been a runner-up for Miss U.S.A. But as Ralph got older and after they moved to Palo Alto, his mom spent years at a time institutionalized for mental illness and Ralph learned to be independent and self-sufficient. He was a perpetual and very accomplished con-artist, with a wild imagination and a wicked sense of humor. Ralph was queer and was my introduction to "screamin' queens" and the San Francisco homosexual life style.

Garland was a few years younger and had already been busted for pot so many times that if he was busted one more time he would go to the California Youth Authority (CYA.) CYA was where child and teen offenders were sent for crimes. This was the era in which the "three seeds" rule was being enforced with rigor – if an adult had three marijuana seeds in their possession, they were charged with possession of a felony illegal drug and could spend many years in prison – not jail, but a prison like Santa Rita or San Quentin.

Along with David, Ralph, and Garland, our crowd included Rick Morton, who was a few years older and a student at Menlo-Atherton High School. Rick was my boyfriend. Rick was a "sole-surviving son," so the military could not draft him. This was because his father had been killed in the Korean War, and his mother had no other children. Therefore, her son was exempt from military service because the United States would not ask her to sacrifice both her husband and her only child. Rick's mom suffered from epilepsy, so she could not get a driver's license; she worked at a graveyard-shift job and her co-worker had driven her to work for years.

After John and I stopped seeing each other, Rick became my boyfriend. Rick and I worked together organizing the Friends Outside camps. We loved to talk for hours and we worked well together with children. Rick's life was much different from mine, as he felt a responsibility to spend a lot of time with his mom, and to do the things for her that she could not do because of her epilepsy. He did not remember his father, because Rick had been just a baby when his dad died.

Rick and I sat at the banks of the San Francisquito Creek for hours. This is the creek that divides the cities of Palo Alto and Menlo Park, and the creek was just a few blocks from Rick's house. We would sit there smoking pot, or maybe taking acid, and talk and watch the creek and the creatures that lived in the creek. Many times other teenagers hung out there as well, as it was quiet and peaceful and very far removed from daily hustle and bustle. I would ride my bike the five or six miles to the creek, and leave it parked in the pathway that ran along the top of the creek bank. There was one other boy from Menlo-Atherton in our crowd. His name was Richie. Richie had hair that went to the middle of his back. His long hair was enough to have the cops stop him frequently, because most men still had short hair that didn't even touch their shirt collar!

There was a wide easement near Richie's house in Menlo Park near Marsh Road. Rows of trees and shrubs backed up to a long fence and there was a fort that had probably been there for decades, built into those trees and bushes. We would go there at night with lanterns and candles, smoking pot and talking about the Vietnam War, civil rights, drugs, school, music, our parents, and what we wanted to do with our lives.

Richie, David, Ralph, and I went everywhere together. David had a Vespa and later a motorcycle. If we all squished up together really tightly and threw a poncho over us to hide two of the passengers, we could sometimes ride all four of us together on the Vespa!

One time we were at the Round Table Pizza Parlor on University Avenue in Palo Alto. It was after ten o'clock on a

Friday night, and Ralph said that he was going to telephone the Queen of England! We all went over to the pay phone in the back of the pizza parlor. The phone hung from the wall and we huddled closely together, listening as Ralph proceeded to make a collect call to the Queen! Thirty minutes later, he had spoken to the Queen's assistant, and was on hold for the next in line, when we laughingly gave up. There was nothing that Ralph would not attempt, and he succeeded most of the time, no matter how crazy it seemed.

Because Ralph frequently had a car, we would often all go to the drive-in movie together. The Palo Alto Drive-In Movie Theatre was right in town, on Colorado Avenue near the highway, and on warm summer evenings it was packed with families and couples and teenagers. John and I had spent many evenings there; it was a great place to go on a date!

The drive-in charged an admission fee by the person, not by a car count, so teenagers always tried to outwit the cashier by hiding at least one person in the trunk or in the back seat under a blanket or a coat. Ralph's car was the preferred vehicle for sneaking into the drive-in, as his car had a passageway where a person could easily climb from inside the trunk to the backseat without leaving the vehicle.

There were times when we were able to sneak in one or two people, and other times when we got caught. The theatre would then charge for all the people in the vehicle...there was no punishment when they caught someone in the trunk or the backseat. Some evenings watching the drive-in line was better than the movie! Cars would line up at the ticket booth, which was a one-person shack with a window and door located in the driveway entrance to the drive-in. The person in the booth would ask how many people were in the car, and many times the driver would be asked to open the trunk. There might be one, two, three or even four people who emerged, whereupon they would pay for their tickets, get inside the car, and the next car would proceed.

People knew this was part of the process, and waited in line patiently with a lot of laughter. If there was only a driver in the car usually the people in the car behind him would be guessing how many people were in the trunk, because people rarely went to the drive-in alone!

I often was the one selected to hide in the trunk, because I didn't weigh much and if the car was already full we made it through almost every time; if a person weighed a lot then the low back-end of the car would alert the cashier. And once inside the drive-in if you saw people opening their trunk and someone emerging, there usually was cheering and applause!

The drive-in had a playground for children and a snack bar which sold food and drinks. The ads for the snack bar were very entertaining; they were animated ads with dancing bags of popcorn and hot dogs and pizza, and played during intermission urging all the patrons to "...go to the snack bar and have a real good time."

Families would pile their kids into the car and take blankets and their own popcorn and drinks with them to the drive-in. It was a fun and festive way to watch a double feature. The Palo Alto Drive-In opened in 1947, and when it closed in 1969 it was a real bummer; the drive-in was nearby and had been part of the lives of an entire generation.

Another place that we went to just hang out was a tree house on Old Alpine Road. Old Alpine Road was a twisty, steep road that went up through the foothills and merged onto Page Mill Road. We would drive up Old Alpine, and from there we would turn onto a steep, unpaved road. After about one-quarter mile down that road, we would come to the tree house.

No one knew who owned the tree house. It was big enough and nice enough to live in, and eight or ten people could fit comfortably inside. Many times there would be other young people already there, so we would make new friends. Climbing the ladder was scary, but once inside the tree house, up amongst the beautiful redwood trees, it was spectacular. Every care and problem seemed much farther away when we were in the tree house. There was a tire swing hanging from the same tree, and sitting in the tire a person would swing back and forth over a deep canyon, hidden away in the coastal forest.

The builder of the tree house enriched so many people's lives. We went there often, and it was always clean and tidy. I think all the visitors valued that special place and strived to take care are of it. Maybe the owner/builder knew how often it was visited, maybe not. It was a safe and remote place, a place for talking and laughing and introspection.

The City of Palo Alto has its own park, nestled in the foothills off of Page Mill Road. The land for Foothills Park was sold to Palo Alto by Dr. Russell Lee, founder of the Palo Alto Medical Clinic, on the condition that it remain open space. The park was formally dedicated in 1965, and included a man-made lake, but swimming was not allowed.

About a year after the park opened, we snuck in and went skinny-dipping one midnight; David and I, along with a few of our friends. In the light of the full moon we swam in the new lake, leaving our clothes on the bank of the lake. It was quiet and serene and we floated on our backs, drifting in the sparkling reflections of moonlight on the water.

Part of hanging out with friends included spending time with my sister, Judy. We had become good friends, and like to spend time in Berkeley and San Francisco. The journal entry below tells of one weekend adventure.

Journal Entry

"All I have to say about the Matter is: You meet the nicest people on a cable car! It all started out Saturday morning. My sister, Judy, and I caught the 7:08 train, and spent the morning in Berkeley, looking at an art exhibit. Then the afternoon was ours — mine, Judy's and Esther's (our good friend.) So back to San Francisco we went; I was just tingling for an Interesting Experience, and nothing could stop me!

After we ate a quick lunch, I was all for going down to the wharf. So off we went for our first Big Adventure Saturday Afternoon. I saw the cable car coming so we ran, and just caught it at the beginning of the line. A lot of the operators don't let girls hang on the sides, but luck was with me, and the conductor had no comment but, "Hang-on-the-out-sideeee..!" My sister and Esther got seats, but I was happier hanging on the outside.

There was, on this cable car, standing directly opposite me, a man eating pistachio nuts. I didn't mean to stare, but I guess I was, because pretty soon he asked me if I wanted some. I said, "Okay," and that's how I met Rusty Evans of the The New Christy Minstrels!!

I accepted his pistachios, and pretty soon we had an interesting conversation going. I discovered that he had just gotten into San Francisco that morning, that he was a member of the The New Christy Minstrels singing group, that he lived in New York, and that he and his group were doing a show both Saturday and Sunday night, then leaving the St. Francis Hotel for somewhere else.

Rusty, I found out, has been with the group for around a month. He will be on the next album jacket, and will have three speaking lines on the "Red Skelton" TV Show in two or three weeks. He also is a good friend of Bob Dylan and Joan Baez.

Well, we got to the end of the line, and I asked Rusty if he'd like to be shown around the wharfs. He said he'd really love it, and we thus spent an hour or two at the shops, the ship Balclutha, and just sight-seeing.

However, he had a rehearsal at 4:00, so we all ran and caught the trolley. On the way back, my sister, who is going to Foothill College, asked him for his autograph. So I did too, and he wrote to me: "To Jane, Best Wishes Always, Rusty Evans"

We got off at the end of the line and as we finished a loaf of French bread, Rusty remembered that his agent had told him to quit eating! I asked him if he thought New York and San Francisco were similar. Rusty said emphatically "Yes!" mainly because of the vast conglomeration of people in both cities. One thing New York can't boast, however, is hills and trolley cars! When we got to the St. Francis, Rusty said he'd send us autographed copies of the book he wrote, which is being published in a couple of months. So I gave him my address, and even if he doesn't write, it's not everyone who meets a singer, author, actor on a cable car, is it?"

I didn't get the book, but it had been a very exciting afternoon. I thought that Rusty had probably lost my address. The song *Eve of Destruction* made the pop charts in 1965. It was an anti-nuclear anthem by the former New Christy Minstrel member, Barry McGuire.

The Establishment, Brownies, Be-Ins and Love

I had grown up taught to respect adults, respect authority, and government. But in my household we also had been encouraged to be politically involved, to question what the government was doing, and to pay attention to the issues of the day. We were particularly involved with issues that related to human rights and dignity and fairness. And the First Congregational Church in Palo Alto was a cornerstone in non-violent political change and in helping to frame the importance of speaking up for others and for standing up for what was right. As the 1960's continued, those tumultuous times became my teachers.

Our local police department had been staffed by honest, reasonable officers that expected to be obeyed. They felt that they were an important part of protecting both society at a large level and Palo Alto at a small level from outside forces that could corrupt and destroy family values.

However, the behavior of police all over the country began to destroy the feeling of trust between communities and their police departments. At first it was little things that happened locally. I was hitchhiking and the cops, who had always been fatherly figures who protected everyone, began to change. Those same cops began telling young women that if they hitchhiked they could be charged with prostitution. They were telling young women that if they might be a little friendly to the cops, well the cops might be a little understanding to female hitchhikers. Those who were sworn to protect were now those who were sworn to harass and occasionally molest with a big smile on their faces! And cops were becoming aggressive and violent, even to unarmed pacifists.

We began to call the police officers "pigs." The more overtly peaceful people became, then the more violent the pigs became. Students were beaten up by the pigs; not by stressed-out police officers who were in the middle of a riot, not by cops who were being shot at, but by narrow-minded cops who were standing over long-haired hippies who smoked pot, flashed the peace sign, and promoted peace.

Cops didn't know anymore how to protect peacefully. They felt that everyone was out to get them, so they better get every one else first! At least that was how it seemed. There were still good cops, but there was a lot of tension between those of us who preaching, "Make love, not war," and the cops.

One Christmas I went over to a friend's house and we made pot brownies and put them in a nice cake pan and took them to the Menlo Park Police Department as a Christmas treat. The cops took them and thanked us and we hoped that they ate the brownies, got stoned, and mellowed out and enjoyed their Christmas....but of course we couldn't easily go back and ask!

"Be-Ins" and "Love-ins" and "Happenings" were spontaneous gatherings of people that were occurring everywhere. If one hippy-looking person sat somewhere and took out a guitar, well, pretty soon there was a group of people gathering in the same place, people who were happy and felt like they knew each other. Often a Be-In would happen just through word-of-mouth: "There's a Be-In this afternoon near Stanford..." and just like magic, people would congregate. Most of these gatherings were anti-war, pro-love, and non-violent. There would be music, drugs, and a sense of euphoria and hope.

On January 14th, 1967, the "Human Be-In" happened in San Francisco's Golden Gate Park, and I was there. Peace symbols and peace signs were every where, including peace symbols fastened to tall poles that waved high above the crowd. The crowd grew to more than thirty-thousand people, people who were peaceful and hopeful and full of love. There was a stage and the poet Allen Ginsberg and some others spoke and read, but most of the people were sitting on the lawn singing, talking, and smoking pot.

The Diggers were a political activist group in San Francisco who distributed food and resources to all people. And at the Human Be-In they passed out a lot of food and a lot of LSD. Musicians such as the Jefferson Airplane, the Grateful Dead, Moby Grape, and Janis Joplin with Big Brother and the Holding Company performed.

San Francisco was where it was happening, and we hitchhiked there and joined in the music, the dancing, the drugs, and the smiling love fest that held so much hope for a non-violent, sharing, and caring future. Children ran free, dogs and their owners romped, and the sparkling hope of peace and non-violence filled my heart.

Rick, David, and I hung out together and were great friends. Rick was still my boyfriend. However, one afternoon when the three of us went to Pescadero Beach together, the relationship between us changed.

David went for a walk up the beach, and Rick and I were talking when Rick turned to me and said that I needed to choose between him and David. Rick said that he could tell that David was in love with me and that it was destroying our friendships. I was stunned. Rick was my boyfriend…I thought we all were friends. Rick took me in his arms and said that whatever choice I made that Rick would always be my friend.

I felt like I couldn't breathe. In that one unexpected moment I was presented with a choice that I had not planned to make and that was the furthest thing from my mind on that chilly afternoon at Pescadero Beach.

I liked both of them so much…they were both so close to me. I felt like my heart was breaking. Rick told me that he couldn't stand any more to feel his heart breaking.

Then he poured out to me that he knew he would always have to live with his mother to care for her and that he felt he was holding me back. He let go of me and told me to go find David, that my future was with David and not with him. Rick said this with much kindness and wistfulness. I began to cry. Rick said not to cry, that it had been a while since he had realized that I should be with David and that he had been just been waiting for the right moment to tell me.

And then I realized that Rick was right.

Road Trip to Georgia

David Horton's family moved to Atlanta, Georgia, when David was a senior at Paly. His father had accepted the position of head of the Georgia Tech Aeronautical Engineering Department and also a position as a dean at the college. David refused to move with them to Atlanta; he wanted to stay in Palo Alto. The minister at the Unitarian Church said that David could stay with him and his wife, so that was settled.

David spent his last year in high school with a lot of freedom to do what he wanted to do and not much supervision. That was fine with us! However, when he got busted for pot things got pretty scary. David was not an American citizen, nor were his parents. They didn't even live in the same state, and David was a minor. He called me in the middle of the night from the Palo Alto police station. My parents slept upstairs and luckily did not hear the phone.

The next day I took all my savings out of the bank and helped hire a lawyer for David. Eventually David was released to a program and the minister agreed to be responsible for David. His parents and my parents never even knew about the bust. But now David had to be really careful to never get in trouble again. He would be deported to England if he got caught with drugs.

When David's parents and younger sister moved to Atlanta they still owned some property in California; a piece of land with a trailer and a boat at Clearlake in Northern California. David's dad, Wilf, decided to come get the boat and take it to Georgia as there were a lot of Georgian lakes that were good for water skiing. They missed having their boat and wanted to start water skiing again.

Wilf asked David if he wanted to drive with him back to Atlanta. It would be a fun road trip and they would tow the boat and share the driving. David said he would go if they agreed that he would come back to California and not stay in Atlanta, and also if I could go too.

I had just turned seventeen when the three of us headed out to Georgia in a new pickup truck, towing the boat on its trailer. We drove through Nevada, Utah, and the Salt Lake desert, and somewhere near Denver the trailer tire shredded and David and I sat on the side of the road with the boat while Wilf drove to the nearest town to get a replacement tire.

We saw beautiful American scenery on the way to Georgia and ate at coffee shops that were at freeway exits. When I traveled with my family we always ate from the old aluminum ice chest, but with David and his dad we ate at Stuckey's and other roadside diners, the kind of places that were open around the clock, twenty-four-hours, and had pink-uniformed waitresses that called all the men "Hon" and all the women "Ma'am."

All three of us smoked. We smoked our way across thousands of miles until I got bronchitis and couldn't smoke any more. But I drank Robitussin® cough syrup to stop my cough. At the time Robitussin contained codeine and was available over the counter, so I spent several days in a codeine-induced daze, drinking bottle upon bottle of codeine-rich cough syrup.

When we got to Atlanta I found it to be different than I had ever imagined. It was a tapestry of trees and beautiful homes – homes built from bricks on huge lots with no fences between properties. It rained almost every afternoon so there were lush plants and greenery everywhere.

And what David and I also discovered was that there were paved side roads in the city; those roads then changed into dirt roads, and the homes along the roads degraded until they were almost shacks. It was like going back in time…it was where the blacks lived. There were entire neighborhoods that were hidden away all through the city. Because David and I were not from the South and were exploring Atlanta I think we happened upon places that many Atlantans either didn't know existed or chose to ignore. When we drove down the rutted dirt roads and we only saw people who were black, there was a lot of staring from both inside the pickup truck and outside the pickup truck! I think the people we drove past were afraid we might be young rednecks out for an afternoon of fun, but we were just California kids stopping to talk, meet people, and find out about their lives.

As we drove through these small, hidden black communities the road would change back from rutted mud and dirt, to hard dirt, and finally to paved road. And the paved road would merge with a main street. Driving past all the side streets we had no way of knowing how many of them led to segregated black neighborhoods that looked like black-and-white snapshots from the past.

David and I stayed in Atlanta for about six weeks. It was summer and I liked his parents and his sister and I liked the south. It was so green and beautiful. But it was HOT! The first night we stayed in Atlanta the fan in the window was left running all night, and the room cooled off just a bit by morning. During the night I had awakened to see a lightning bug flashing on and off as it flew around the room! Without my glasses on it seemed like a huge flashing light, and it reminded me of Kansas when I was a little girl. In the morning on the floor in front of the fan there was a little pile of bugs…the unfortunate ones who had not made it through the blades of the fan. It was gross.

When I took a shower for the first time and afterwards dried myself I thought that there was something wrong with the towel; perhaps it was not absorbent, because I couldn't get dry. David's mom, Margaret, just laughed and said it was the humidity….that no one could ever dry off in the summer in Atlanta because it was too hot and too humid!

The second evening we were there Margaret prepared a proper British tea. She made a tray of elegant little sandwiches and used her beautiful china cups and saucers. The tray also held lemon, sugar and cream. Tea was an evening snack to assuage hunger; after tea we could delay dinner until nine o'clock or nine-thirty when the temperature was cooler. That was how David's family had always done meals, even in Palo Alto. They had partaken of tea in the evening and eaten dinner later at night when Wilf came home from Stanford.

I had never had British tea before even though I had been to David's house when they lived in Palo Alto. Margaret poured the tea, and I added sugar to my tea. Then I added lemon. Then I added cream. After all, the three condiments were on the tray and I thought that I was supposed to add all three. Of course, adding lemon to the cream caused the cream to curdle, so I had a swirling mass of coagulated cream in my cup, looking more like cottage cheese than like tea. But I didn't want to be rude, so I drank up the disgusting mess without looking at anyone, thinking all the while that it was gross and that I could never develop a taste for British tea!

After I had excused myself from the living room and left, they all looked at each other, shaking their heads, until Margaret said that she couldn't believe how the Yankees could stand to drink their tea like that!

David and I would go to the back of their large garden and smoke pot after dinner, and just sit there and talk. We had to sit on chairs when we were outside because if you sat on the grass the little chiggers, the "no-see-'ums" would bite you and the next day you would be covered with an itchy rash.

One of the things we did while in Atlanta was strip the paint from the boat that we had towed from California and after it was sanded and repaired we painted it. I was using the electric sander when my long hair got caught in the sander and the sander climbed right up my hair, right to my head! It was ripping out my hair and starting to sand my scalp; I was screaming and David leaped over and unplugged the sander! It had happened so fast I hadn't known what to do. The sander was full of stinky burnt hair and my head had a bald and bloodied patch on it about the size of a quarter. I was lucky that my glasses hadn't gotten tangled up in the process.

Once the boat was painted, we towed it to Lake Altoona and went water skiing. I had never water skied before, and had only been on a ski boat once, the time Gramma Gigi had taken me to Lake Berryessa and I met some boys and went out with them in their boat. Water skiing was a new experience. David's dad launched the boat, which was scary; I wasn't confident about the safety of backing up the truck until the tail pipe was submerged, unhooking the boat from the trailer and then accelerating as fast as possible to get back up the launch ramp.

David's dad drove the boat while the rest of the family took turns skiing. David's mom looked gorgeous in her swimsuit. She was tall and slim without one ounce of fat anywhere on her body; she was tan and had shockingly white hair, hair that had started turning white when she was just in her twenties. Margaret was an excellent skier as was David and his sister, Jennifer. They all skied on one ski and skimmed across the surface of the lake, jumping back and forth over the wake from the boat.

I actually learned to water ski, to get up out of the water and to keep standing on the skis as I too skimmed across the surface. I wasn't brave enough to try it with only one ski, but it was fun! The warm water of the lake made it the ideal place to learn to ski. The Georgia soil is bright red, and perfect to use as natural dye; every place the red clay gets on clothing it leaves a reddish brown stain that doesn't wash out!

We visited Stone Mountain, Kennesaw Park, and other Civil War sites. We also drove to Tennessee to visit the Great Smokey National Park.

The visit to Kennesaw National Battlefield Park was very thought-provoking. The Atlanta Campaign of the Civil War started there in 1864. The park presented reenactments of the war, and the tour included walking up hillsides and seeing the trenches that had been dug more than one-hundred years ago by young soldiers. There were cannon emplacements and the ground was still littered with shells from the thousands of bullets that had been fired there. On one small hill, more than five thousand soldiers were killed in a battle that lasted less than two weeks. Standing there in the stifling heat I felt such sorrow for the young soldiers dressed in their hot woolen uniforms, many away from home for the first time, the many teenagers who had ended their lives so long ago. War. War. War. Coloring my life in subtle and not so subtle ways and having shaped those young men's destinies. Visiting the South gave me a much different perspective on the desires of the South to secede from the

Union and of the complicated economic times that contributed to the Civil War.

When we went to Stone Mountain, the sculpture was still being carved on the side of the mountain. The largest bas relief sculpture in the world, the Confederate Memorial Carving depicts the three Confederate leaders of the Civil War: President Jefferson Davis and Generals Robert E. Lee and Stonewall Jackson. We went up a tramway from the ground, raising six-hundred feet to the top of Stone Mountain, passing right over the work-in-progress. The tour guide told us that a man could stand inside the carving of the horse's mouth and still have plenty of room, but it was difficult to comprehend the size of the sculpture. The carved surface measures three acres, about the size of three football fields. The work was started in the 1910s, was stopped in 1930 and not resumed until 1963, when the state of Georgia purchased the mountain and established a state park. The carving was completed in 1969. It was strange to me that these men were heroes, as I had been educated with the perspective that the South had been wrong. Yet throughout the South, we saw many Confederate flags and signs and billboards that "The South Shall Rise Again!" The Southerners were proud of their part of America, and spoke about it as if it was their own territory or country.

While in Atlanta we went to the Lowes Tara Theatre, a plush and opulent movie theatre that since 1939 had shown only the movie, *Gone with the Wind*. The Lowes Tara played *Gone with the Wind* three times a day to a full house, playing continuously from 1939 until 1976. And I found out that the 1939 premiere of the movie was so huge that the governor declared it a Georgia State holiday! The night before the premiere, a "Gone with the Wind" costume ball was held and during the event, a boy's choir sang for the guests. One of the singers was young Martin Luther King Jr. Nearly a million people crowded to witness the premiere but only twenty-five-hundred were able to attend inside the theater. Ironically, Hattie McDaniel, the black actress who portrayed the role of Mammy, was prohibited from attending because of Georgia's segregation laws.

Visiting the south in 1967 was an eye-opener in that segregation was overt. There were signs telling people who could sit where and who was and wasn't allowed. David and I had long discussions about what we should do. We thought that we should stand in the "Colored Only" lines just to see what would happen, but after a few weeks of staying in Atlanta the hot, humid weather and the slow life-style made us feel sleepy and even lethargic. We felt a complacency and lack of urgency about all the causes that we usually were intensely passionate about. Each day went by in a rhythm of southern leisure, with breakfast on the front porch in the shade, neighbors sweeping the street in front of their homes with their straw brooms, and of long afternoon naps.

However, one afternoon, Margaret shouted at us to open all the windows, and to then stand by the fireplace. A tornado alert was sounding, with sirens blaring everywhere. The wind was strong and wild, but the tornado missed the house by a few blocks. I found it difficult to reconcile that this British-born gentlewoman now lived where she routinely knew how to react in a tornado!

Downtown Atlanta was an exciting metropolitan area, and I felt quite out of my comfort zone. At noon Atlanta was bustling with professionals in their stylish and fashionable clothes, much like downtown San Francisco on a weekday. But about seventy-five percent of the businesspeople were black, and I realized that in San Francisco or Oakland I was not accustomed to seeing blacks as the majority of professionals. Atlanta was vibrant and stylish, full of energy and excitement.

There was a huge department store downtown, Richey's, which spanned both sides of the street with an enclosed pedestrian walkway on the second story to join the two sides together. Margaret worked in their fabric department during half of the year; she did excellent needlepoint and embroidery and loved to teach others her art. She also substitute taught in the public schools. With the two jobs Margaret would save up enough money to go traveling four or five months of the year; she then wrote magazine articles about her travels. Shortly after they moved to Atlanta, David's parents had separated and each of them had their own homes for the rest of their long marriage. Margaret gained the freedom to travel on her own, but she would have given up that freedom in the blink of an eye to be able to go back and share the same house with Wilf.

David and I saw Jimi Hendrix while we were in Atlanta. We hitchhiked to Fourteenth Street and Jimi was playing there. It was amazing! Seeing him in Atlanta was an unexpected surprise, and a part of music history that we didn't fully appreciate at the time.

The South had a way of getting under my skin, resonating as part of American history. I often thought of my mother's ancestors who settled in Tennessee in the late 1700's, and visiting the Great Smoky Mountains opened up my eyes to the ephemeral beauty of the south, part of my family history that coursed through my blood.

David's parents didn't want him to go back to California; they wanted him to stay in Atlanta. But David wanted to go back to California and live in Palo Alto with me. David and I drove back to Palo Alto in time for me to start my senior year at Cubberley and for him to attend San Francisco State University.

The WAVE and Passionate Thinking

When Ron Jones started teaching at Cubberley High School in 1968, it was considered the most innovative of Palo Alto's three high schools. That was why the twenty-six-year-old graduate student in the Stanford Teacher Education Program wanted to teach there. Mr. Jones's methods were experimental and his goal was to bring social studies to life. Because it was the '60s, Mr. Jones became caught up in a whirlwind of student activism.

Eventually, Ron Jones earned an international reputation because of his technique in which students were taught about Nazism and obedience to power. During a discussion on Nazi Germany, Mr. Jones formed the idea for his experiment when a student insisted, "It couldn't happen here." Mr. Jones began thinking of ways to prove that student's assertions as either true or false. At Cubberley we believed that we were smart, free-thinking, and that we had minds of our own. We thought that we were different from past generations and that what Hitler had done in Germany could never happen here; we could not be manipulated like Germans had been during WWII.

Suddenly posters began appearing all around campus: "The WAVE is Coming." Soon students and teachers were wondering what The WAVE was and who was behind the signs. There were rumors about The Third Wave, which spread quickly around campus. We didn't know what this was, but students, teachers, and even the principal were speculating and wanted to find out more about The WAVE and what it meant.

Meanwhile, in the classroom, Mr. Jones transformed his group of students into an efficient youth organization, which he called The Third Wave; within his class some students became informers, and others were forbidden to go specific places on campus. Mr. Jones insisted on rigid posture and that questions be answered formally and quickly. The experiment was initially scheduled for one day, but it stretched out to five days.

"It was strange how quickly the students took to a uniform code of behavior. I began to wonder just how far they could be pushed," Ron Jones wrote in *No Substitute for Madness*, a book about his teaching experiment. Mr. Jones was surprised that students recited facts more accurately in his authoritarian environment than in his usual classroom, and that he also had no discipline problems.

Five days into The Third Wave, at a Friday school-wide assembly, Mr. Jones announced that together…"We can bring a new sense of order, community, pride, and action. Everything rests on you and your willingness to take a stand." And students shouted, "Strength through discipline!" After a long silence, Mr. Jones began to speak. "There is no such thing as a national youth movement called The Third Wave. You have been used. Manipulated. Shoved by your own desires into the place you now find yourselves." Mr. Jones then showed a movie of Hitler at the Nuremberg Rally, and students and teachers saw that they had easily adopted many of the behaviors they were witnessing on the screen. They realized the possibility that it could happen here, that what a person thinks he is or isn't capable of may be much different than reality.

This was an incredibly valuable lesson for everyone involved. Those of us who were not students in that specific class were still affected. I knew Mr. Jones and had him for other classes. The signs and posters, and the assembly that resulted from The WAVE were strong lessons. Never, never believe that you are immune from being led by expert persuasion, and do not judge those people in the past without judging first yourself.

Mr. Jones showed that it was both easy and possible to compromise one's belief because of the desire to conform and fit in, to get a good grade or to have peer or teacher approval. Mr. Jones allowed students to think and examine values and actions and decision-making processes. He actually encouraged real thinking and dialogue.

Mr. Jones also sponsored the SDS organization, the Students for a Democratic Society. In the tumultuous times of social change, turmoil, racial strife, civil rights, and feminism, the SDS provided an avenue to organize, talk, discuss and mobilize. At Cubberley we were still segregated by gender in some of our school activities. But when we went to SDS meetings and discussed and planned strategies for making the world a better place… well, we could also discuss how to make our school a better place, a more equal place for all students.

Our dress code ruled the length of boy's hair and if they could wear beards. In spite of dress codes, teen-aged boys wore bell-bottom pants, sandals, ruffled shirts, and Nehru jackets — the styles of the Beatles and Jimi Hendrix and the Rolling Stones. The boys were battling out-dated dress codes like tucking in button-down shirts and only being allowed to wear T-shirts that were solid colors with no writing on them. And the girls? We wore mini skirts and sandals, but wanted to wear pants, Levis, and hip-hugger pants. We wanted to go braless and wear T-shirts. We wanted change!

We were busy volunteering in our community, our state, and internationally, yet girls and women were still way behind in equal pay, in job equality, in the control of their own bodies, and even in the clothing we were allowed to wear!

Birth control was finally somewhat accessible, but only through great effort and deceit and unknown health risks. Women were expected to be chaste, yet women by the thousands died at the hands of backroom abortionists. If a girl wore no bra and a mini-skirt, then society perceived her to be marketing her body. So The WAVE also illustrated the dangers of following popular opinion blindly. We needed to learn to think for ourselves and make choices that would have a positive outcome for the future generations.

The SDS developed and expanded rapidly in the mid-1960s before dissolving at its last convention in 1969. During the late 1960s, the University of California, Berkeley, exploded into the free speech movement. Mario Savio was the Berkeley leader, and there was TV news coverage about the movement, the ban by the university, sit-downs, demonstrations, meetings, and strikes. The SDS effectively shut the university down through peaceful protests, and we at Cubberley joined students across the country in watching and learning about non-violent protests. The SDS urged all citizens to express their views about the Vietnam War.

In February of 1965, President Lyndon Johnson bombed North Vietnam. SDS members all over the country started to lead and participate in demonstrations against the war. On-campus recruiting for the military was a huge issue on college and high school campuses. U.C. Berkeley became a center of radical strikes and demonstrations over the University's repressive anti-free-speech actions, and an effective student strike occurred. Campuses all over the country protested the Secretary of Defense, Robert McNamara.

'Third Wave' presents inside look into Fascism

- By Bill Klink-

"A mirror is a deadly weapon," reflected Cubberley history teacher Mr. Ron Jones regarding a revolutionary concept of teaching history that is the basis for his "The Third Wave" -- a form of Fascism employed two weeks ago by his second, third, and sixth period sophomore Contemporary World classes.

The theory of the movement was "that man has basically an authoritarian nature. He likes to be led and be select." Mr. Jones reinforced in his students the idea that through dis-cipline and involvement they would become select. Furthermore, he convinced them that their "Third Wave Movement" would become a national movement which would eliminate democracy, a form of govern-ment that, according to Mr. Jones, "has many unnatural aspects since the emphasis is on the individual instead of a disciplined and involved com-munity." Hence, the motto of the "Third Wave Movement," "Strength through discipline, strength through involvement" originated.

Guards were posted at the door of C-3 during each of the three periods involved in the movement. Students were taught to salute each other with a curved hand similar to the salute used during the Nazi regime. They were often or-dered to sit at attention with their hands clasped behind them in back of their desks when "Fuhrer" Jones spoke. To avoid rebellion, rules were made which made it illegal for any party members to congre-gate in groups larger than three outside of class.

Despite such strict rules, there were offenses. Unruly members were banished to the library and their grades were reduced. One group reported-ly had 500 parents backing a boycott to remove Jones as a teacher because of "a move-ment they didn't quite under-stand." His fifth period sen-ior government class launched the most successful coup d'etat on Wednesday, April 5, the last day of the movement, as they kidnapped Jones and threatened to deliver lectures on democra-cy to his sophomore classes. However, he persuaded them to let him go, telling them he had planned to end the move-ment that day with a rally at lunch.

As a large group of "Third Wave" supporters assembled for the rally, Jones announced that they would hear their na-tional leader speak. He turned on the television to static and the movement came to a crash-ing end. Most were dis-illusioned. As one second per-iod Third Waver, Joel Amkraut, put it, "Everyone feels stupid about it. He sure made fools of us. I guess I expected a national leader." Another, Todd Austin, Mr. Jones's per-sonal bodyguard, expressed the opinion that "I really kind of liked it. I went to the rally because I was curious." Steve Coniglio was pleased with the outcome. "It was probably the most interesting unit I've had. It was successful in its goal to achieve the emotions of the Germans under the Nazi reign."

This is undoubtedly not the last attempt at a three party system as it came to a halt due to a disillusioned leader and not a disenchanted membership.

259

The games people play ...

Culminating a soft-sell lecture on "cultural shock" in the United States with a blunt "plea for revolution," Cubberley history teacher Mr. Ron Jones played games with his first, second and fourth period Contemporary World classes by exposing them to a "simulated" environment two weeks ago, resembling last year's Fascist "Third Wave" movement.

Admitting to being a "regional head of the Student's Democratic Society," Mr. Jones announced SDS "plans" for a four million man demonstration in Washington D. C. on Christmas Day. "The Pentagon demonstration was a sort of 'dry' run for the December 25th demonstartion. We now know that the National Guard

units that will be called up against us are infiltrated by 12,500 of our members. I myself am in the Guard."

Convincing the students of the actuality of the situation, Mr. Jones went on, "In 1964, some people got together and formed the SDS. We got short hair cuts, joined the National Guard, and got jobs as teachers. At Cubberley, there are three other 'undercover' teachers besides myself."

Upon bringing the sophomores back to reality by revealing that the previous day's address was a sham, Mr. Jones stated that the simulation's purpose was to "provide a situation similar to China's in the 1900's. The simulation also let the students experience the con-

sequences of value change, revolution, and revolutionary fervor."

Although Mr. Jones asked the students if they would participate in the march, he did not disclose how many said yes, as "it would be an unfair analysis."

After the "game," Mr. Jones confirmed his statement about being a member of the National Guard. As the SDS, "I belong to every club I can belong to."

The "revolution," first of two simulations to be presented by Mr. Jones to his sophomore classes this year, was "planned and programmed, but crude." The next game, a kit developed by Scientific Research Associates, Inc., will be "played"

(Cont. on Page 7)

Mr. Ron Jones, pictured in the social studies office, can rarely be found here because of his active part in SDS, classroom experiments, and school activities. Photo: SCOTT

Keeping up with Jones

(Cont. from Page 1)

in February. "It is formulated, sophisticated, learning material." The students will know this time that the situation is a mockup.

The game, Inter-Nations Simulation, "calls for a wide range of student activity, from waging war to waging peace." Once the game is finished, the students should have "more understanding of international relations and the consequences of international reactions."

Responding to a question on the two unannounced simulations Mr. Jones held that "neither had gotten out of hand. If one had, I would just have refuted it, said it was a lie, or just said, so what?"

As to overzealous student participation in the simulations, he commented, "There are going to be cases in which students become involved. But there was no intended infringement on other classes." Mr. Jones added, "Students shouldn't be regulated into one hour thinking blocks."

The two types of simulation, informed and noninformed, both have their places, according to Mr. Jones. "The teacher must decide if simulation would be good for his classes. Simulation provides students with some present criteria for judging all statements. It also brings decision making about, followed by satisfaction and pride.

Sitting in front of the television we were appalled by the war and by the support given it by the Secretary of Defense. McNamara was recruited to run the Pentagon by President Kennedy in 1961. Yet even McNamara's son, a Stanford University student, protested against the war while his father was running it. Additionally, the fact that McNamara's middle name was "Strange," provided additional fuel for mocking him. Everyone knew what McNamara looked like and what he sounded like. He was on the news, on the cover of magazines, and he talked about using enough American firepower to cause the Communists to make peace. And we did not want our friends and fellow students to join the dramatically-rising number of war causalities. The SDS was helping students to mobilize and to find their united voice. Robert McNamara later denounced the Vietnam War as "terribly wrong."

One of the reasons that this war was so unpopular was because of the draft. Many young people were torn between "doing their duty" and opposing what was an undeclared war. My friends and I could not understand why American youth were being required to intervene in the policies of Vietnam.

In the 1960's America-at-war was not the norm. War was not standard operation; war was not part of our national policy. America had not yet transformed into a country which considered war a part of national planning and of our budget. We were not yet immune to war.

Anti-war actions escalated all over high schools and colleges. A series of demonstrations against the draft happened in Berkeley, San Francisco, Oakland, and in Palo Alto. After conventional tactics of peaceful pickets seemed to have failed, the "Stop the Draft Week" ended in violent skirmishes with the police. Night-time raids on draft offices began to spread.

In the spring of 1968, national SDS activists led an effort on campuses called "ten days of resistance," and local chapters cooperated with the student mobilization committee in rallies, marches, sit-ins and teach-ins. This culminated in a one-day strike on April 26th, when about a million students boycotted classes, the largest student strike in the history of the United States. And at Cubberley, we participated in the strike as well. "SDS" became a household name in the United States.

We held our off-campus SDS meetings at Kathy Moore's house. Her parents had a beautiful old Spanish-style two-story house on the corner of Lincoln and University Avenues. The house had a full basement, and we would have our meetings in the basement. We discussed with passion our anti-war feelings and what peace activities were happening locally. We combined forces with a group from East Palo Alto, and started meeting with some of the Black Panthers, including Bobby Seale and Huey Newton. Founded in Oakland in 1966 by Bobby Seale and Huey Newton, the Black Panthers called for the protection of African-American neighborhoods from police brutality. The organization promoted a core belief in the interest of African-American justice and "Black Power," and self-defense for blacks.

The peace movement and the black-student movement and the Black Panthers were trying to determine how to work together and decide if, in fact, the groups wanted to work together. Some of the intensely emotional discussions were disturbing and draining, especially when it became evident that there were a lot of very angry people on all sides of these issues.

I was meeting more interracial couples, young people the same age as me. And listening about the prejudice that they encountered here in the Bay Area was shocking. It seemed like black families didn't want their children living with or marrying white people, and the same was true with white families. But most of us who had cross-racial friends and lovers managed to have dialogue and respectful conversations.

Kathy's house was the perfect place for our meetings. Her father had been blacklisted during the McCarthy era, and as a result lost his business and deeply suffered both economically and emotionally for years. He and his wife had a deep interest in politics and in the peace movement. Their home was a hub of liberal and creative thinking.

Kathy's sister-in-law, Carol, was an incredible artist, and Kathy's home was full of amazing paintings done by Carol. There was one painting that was riveting: It was a family sitting at the dinner table in what at first looked like a happy family setting, but then as you spent time looking at the painting, you saw starving people peeking from under the table. It was done so subtlety that at first the viewer did not notice it, and then the juxtaposition of the well-fed and the starving was engrossing.

Carol was also a great illustrator and her art was in many children's books. She could look at a person and quickly sketch them with remarkable skill and accuracy. Going to Kathy's house meant art and political discussions late into the night; many nights I stayed all night, spending the night on a hide-a-bed in the basement.

Kathy drove a French car, a Citroën, which her parents had brought over from France because they liked the car so much. It was much different that American cars. When the car came to a stop, the front of the car would slowly lower. Kathy and I would cruise around town in the car, smoking and talking and listening to the radio.

Kathy and Leandra were really good friends with each other, and the three of us were starting to spend more time together. Leandra was one of those natural blondes whose hair is so blonde that it is almost white, and she had very pale skin. She always wore a grungy Levi jacket and smoked non-filter Camel cigarettes…the style of cigarettes that always leave a piece of tobacco on your tongue. Leandra habitually stuck out just the tip of her tongue and used her fingertip to flick off the little pieces of tobacco. She was a terrific artist, in addition to Carol and I, painting with wild abandon and creating intense paintings that were free-form and intriguing.

The three of us used to cut school together. One time we cut school on a warm spring afternoon near time for the end of the school year. We decided to go for a hike in the foothills. Already the hills were dry, with golden grasses that smelled like warm bread in the afternoon sun. We saw several tarantulas, and watched them cross the path as if they were in no hurry to reach their burrows, and then, in a blink of an eye, they would disappear down into their underground nests. We walked for about an hour, and then decided to rest on a log under a huge old oak tree. It was cool in the shade, and Leandra rolled a joint and we sat there smoking pot in the shade of the oak tree.

Kathy leaned over to me and took me in her arms and kissed me. I was so taken by surprise that I did nothing but kiss her back. It was the strangest thing, because when a boy kissed me there were all these other things going on as well, so that I didn't really focus on the kiss, but all I could think of when Kathy was kissing me was how incredibly soft her lips were.

But then I jumped up and started to walk away, and my two good friends came after me. I wasn't sure what had just happened and I didn't know how to react. They started both talking at the same time of how Kathy had wanted to kiss me for a long time, and about how the two of them were lovers and had been lovers for quite a while.

I stood still in my tracks. They both had boyfriends. In fact, Kathy had a boyfriend that was a biker in his twenties. And yet my two girl friends were lovers? I had not had a clue! They started kidding me about how dense I was and they said they couldn't believe that I hadn't known about the two of them. I was dumbfounded, but we all ended up laughing about it.

Kathy said she hoped I wasn't mad at her. We hugged each other and decided that our friendship was more important than any misunderstanding, and they would still be lovers but I wasn't sure that I was interested in having that kind of relationship with them. But I did think about how soft Kathy's lips had been and how different it felt to kiss a woman than to kiss a man.

The next time that we had an evening meeting at Kathy's house and it ran long into the night, I was dreading her offer to spend the night at her house. It had always been so interesting and we would stay awake and talk for hours and hours, but now I wasn't sure if she would want to kiss me again.

I think Kathy sensed that, because we were talking and she suddenly threw a pillow at me and started laughing, and pretty soon we were having a big pillow fight, and she told me that she just wanted to be my best friend if that was all that I wanted. So I spent the night and we remained best friends and everything was fine between us…and sometimes we found ourselves laughing for no reason, as if we had played a secret joke on ourselves.

About a year later, Kathy's sister-in-law, Carol, died. Carol had been such an inspiring artist, but had coupled her artistry with methamphetamine addiction. Carol ended her life by walking out onto the Mojave Desert and never coming back. It was as if her art and her passion for life was more than she could at times bear.

Hitchhiking, Driving, and Lookout Hill

All I had to do was to go out to the street, stick out my thumb, and someone would pull over and give me a ride. Even before the "Summer of Love," hitchhiking was the norm. I would leave school, stick out my thumb on Middlefield Road, and quickly get a ride to Menlo-Atherton High School in Menlo Park where my boyfriend, Rick, was a student. Or I would catch a ride to San Francisco to go hang out in the Haight.

Driving the Coast Highway, it was wall-to-wall hitchers; hitchhikers would meet other people going the same direction and hang out together. A lot of times a hitchhiker would hold up a hand-made sign with a destination and easily get a ride.

There were only a few times that I had weird hitchhiking experiences. One night a creepy middle-aged man picked me up and started asking me questions like if I was afraid, or if anyone had ever tried to rape me. He told me that he heard that girls hitchhiking at night were just asking for it. I responded that all people were good and that no one would ever do that because there was good in everyone. It was kind of scary, so I decided then not to hitchhike at night by myself any more.

But before that happened I had an odd experience when I got picked up by a male model. Life in general had been somewhat of a roller coaster for a while, and one night I decided that I wanted to just take my sleeping bag and go to the coastal mountain range and escape there and hide out and not deal with all the pressures that were weighing on me. I took my trusty S&H Green Stamp sleeping bag and sat on a street corner in East Palo Alto. I had been staying at a commune there, and the corner was right down the street from the commune. Two minutes later a man stopped and asked me if I wanted a ride. "Sure," I said, and I got in the front seat of his car. He had a big black dog in the back seat. Then I noticed that the man had no pants on. "Stop the car, I have to get out!" I told him. He said not to worry, he was a male model and had just gotten off work and had never picked up a hitch hiker, but saw me there looking so forlorn that he decided I might need a safe ride. We drove to a park where he walked his dog with just a sweater and shoes on, and then he started talking to me about life and what was going on and he convinced me to go back to the house where I had been staying. He drove me back and dropped me off at the house and wished me a great life.

How I got my first car was a result of hitchhiking in a round-about-and-unexpected way: I was hitching in Palo Alto and who came around the corner but my dad! Oh crap. I didn't even bother to hide that I had been hitching a ride, so when my dad pulled over and said, "Get in!" well, that's what I did. I was on the defensive and full of explanations waiting for the parental lecture, but the lecture did not happen. Daddy simply looked at me and asked me not to hitchhike for one week, to promise him that I would not hitchhike for one week.

Well, that was really weird, because almost everyone's parents just spent all the time yelling at them and telling them what they did wrong, so for my daddy to ask a relatively simple sacrifice like not hitchhiking for a week…well, I could do that. So I said, "Yes," and he drove me to where I was going.

And I had a week to think about my promise. It was a long week, because I couldn't get any place I wanted to go!

Well, the week was over and guess what?! My daddy had gone to the town of Gilroy, south from San Jose, and he bought me a car! I had my first car! Instead of yelling at me, he had solved what he felt to be a problem by buying me a car. It was a Rambler…a really uncool, not-groovy car, like a car that old people would drive, but that didn't matter, because it was a car just for me!

And do you want to know what was really funny? The front seats were two side-by-side seats, not bucket seats. Each seat folded down towards the back seat, and the way that they folded down made the car one big seat! It was like having a big bed when the seats were folded down. And I am quite sure that my daddy never even realized that. What an unexpected feature!

My friends and I would drive to "Lookout Hill." That was a hill in the foothills off of Page Mill Road, and it was called Lookout Hill because once a person was on the top of the hill there was a 360-degree vista and anyone could be seen coming from a long distance away. There was only one road to the top of the hill, a rough dirt road that created a lot of dust when traveled. Lookout Hill was a favorite place for teenagers to park, to smoke pot, to drink, and just party and have fun!

One time I was part of a group of five or six cars parked on the top of the hill, and we could see two cop cars slowly coming up the dirt road. One teenager had brought a case of beer and we had just started drinking cold canned beers. We drank faster and faster, trying to drink all the beer before the cops arrived. We could see their headlights in the reflected dust; it was obvious that they were taking their time. Cops really didn't want to have a confrontation on the hill.

By the time the two cop cars arrived and the four cops slowly got out of the cars, most of the beer was gone. The cops helped us dump out the rest of the beer and asked if anyone needed a ride home or if anyone was too drunk to drive. We all said, "No," and the cops left, taking their time slowly navigating down the dirt road. They had made their point and no harm was done. By the time we all left much later no one was too drunk to drive.

Having a car meant mechanical responsibility. I had to make sure the oil was checked and that there was enough gas in the car. After I had two fires in my car because of passengers who were smoking, I created two beautiful "No Smoking" signs and posted the signs in the front and back seats of my little car.

The first fire was in Menlo Park, when I was driving near Rick's house with David in the front seat with me. I noticed a smell that was similar to incense…and so did David.

"Wow, something smells really groovy…like incense."

"I know, I was just groovin' on the smell too."

"I wonder where it is coming from……"

We were driving in the residential area of town when David shouted that the back seat of the car was on fire!

The moment we realized there was fire in the car, I slammed on my brakes in the middle of the street. We opened the car doors, and David and I pulled flaming floor mats from the back of the car and threw them into the street. It wasn't the back seat on fire, but the floor mats! It was dark, the flames were bright, and we couldn't believe it when a cop drove right past us without even stopping! Later we found the cigarette butt that had started the fire.

The second time I had a fire in the car happened when David and I were crossing the Dumbarton Bridge. The Dumbarton spans the San Francisco Bay connecting the cities of East Palo Alto and Fremont. And once again we were in the car commenting about the good smell.

"Something smells like incense…wonder what that good smell is..?"

Then David yelled that the back seat was on fire, and this time it WAS the back seat that was burning up! There we were on the bridge, water all around us, and we were cut off from water by a chain-link fence! Once we got to the causeway of the bridge, I stopped the car to go get water to put the fire out. I was panicking – I had no container for water, so I dumped out the small car ashtray and ran over to the water's edge and filled the ash tray with about a half cup of water, which was all that the ash tray held. David took off his size-thirteen motorcycle boots, filled each boot with Bay water, and put out the fire with two boots full of water!

The next day we went to Tadlock's junk yard in East Palo Alto and bought a new back seat for the car.

I then made the "No Smoking" signs and quit smoking in my car and didn't allow any one else to smoke in my car either.

It was too much trouble! I was seventeen and had been smoking for three years, but two fires in the car was two too many!

One time I went to the beach with some friends and my car smelled like it was overheating on the way home. I stopped at the top of Skyline Road and Highway 84 at Alice's Restaurant and checked under the hood. When I checked my oil it looked like strawberry yoghurt…there was so much water in my oil that the oil was pink and frothy. My friends and I had dropped some acid at the beach, and we all stood there in the parking lot of Alice's saying things like, "Oh wow!" and "Far out!," and "Oh wow, man, do you see that oil?" So I decided instead of driving from the top of Skyline that I would coast, trying to save the engine. I put my car in neutral and coasted about nine miles down hill, until I reached Stanford University and started my engine back up. I made it home safely. We changed the oil and my car was good for quite a bit longer.

The Rambler had a hole in the radiator, just a small hole, so I put a can of Stop Leak in it every now and then. Stop Leak was an additive poured into the car's radiator and it guaranteed to stop small leaks. Yet the hole was getting bigger and bigger and I was adding Stop Leak more frequently. Daddy would take the car to his friend's gas station for a tune up and a lube, but it had been a while since I had had that done.

One morning when I went to start the car the radiator blew up!

There was so much Stop Leak in the system of the car that every thing was plugged up and pressure had built up, exploding the radiator. No one was hurt, but that was the end of the car. There were pieces of radiator all over the driveway – it had exploded under the car and blew out the front of the grill. I had that car for about a year and a half.

Jerry Garcia (later of the Grateful Dead) taught music lessons at Dana Morgan Music Shop.

Music

Folk-music changed my life. My parents had listened to Frank Sinatra, Perry Como, Rosemary Clooney, and Dean Martin. But I was listening to Pete Seeger sing the song, *Little Boxes*. This song was about the houses in Daly City, just south of San Francisco; houses which clung to the hillsides and were like boxes, mass-produced boxes, representing how society was homogenized and becoming all the same. *Little Boxes* parodied the development of suburbia and its conformist values. When Pete Seeger sang that song, we heard it and understood it and it hit a nerve with people across the country.

Where Have All the Flowers Gone? was an anti-war song that touched my heart. It spoke of youth and hope, wars and graveyards, starting with flowers being picked by a young girl and ending with the flowers on the grave of a young soldier, and because we were dealing with the draft and a war, the truth of this song could not be avoided.

Folk music was the message: Pete Seeger wrote a song about wading through rivers in Vietnam, wading across the Big Muddy. The Smothers Brothers gave Pete the opportunity to appear on TV to sing the *Big Muddy*, and for many Americans, Pete's music was the impetus for change. This was not a defensive war, we had invaded another country, and folk music was a peaceful and uniting way to refine and verbalize our thoughts about this military invasion.

On television we saw young people dying and the horror of burning villages and Napalm and casualties. America was ready for musical activists led by people like Pete, Joan Baez, and the Smothers Brothers who dared defy the Establishment. We needed music and rhythm to rally people together, in the way that music has been used for generations to inspire and unite. Music was a rallying mechanism to help bring our soldiers home.

I listened to *Bring Them Home* on TV and radio, and sang it at my church and at impromptu sing-alongs. The war was good for the economy, but it was not fought by old, fat, white, and secure men. It was mostly the young men, the men who had no voice, the young people without money or representation who were our soldiers. There were also young men who believed that what they were doing was right and that they had a patriotic duty; all these young men were at the mercy of the old white lawmakers who were deciding their fates.

Joan Baez sang folk songs with a voice that was so pure that it would take my breath away. I had started going to the Quaker Meeting, the Friends Meeting, on Colorado Avenue in Palo Alto. Joan Baez attended the same meeting, and later she started the Peace and Justice Center in Palo Alto, and went on to be recognized internationally as a singer and peace advocate. Joan had attended Paly, and was a common participant in many activities around town, often an evening visitor to Kepler's Bookstore in Menlo Park. Joan's music helped to fire up the anti-war movement and to keep it going once started. Joan Baez and Bob Dylan...their music helped end the war. It was impossible to think about music when I was a teenager without thinking about anti-war songs and songs about injustice.

I had gone to the Buddhist temple on Louis Road; as a child I went to the Obon Festival and won a fish and magic ball of surprise, but now I went there to find a peaceful religion. Because I was a white teenage girl, they looked at me as a freak. Later, I went to the Catholic Church in downtown Palo Alto; it was ornate and dim, but I didn't understand the sermon.

The Quaker belief was consistent with my beliefs, but sometimes an entire meeting went by with no one talking, and I felt invisible. I was searching for spiritual grounding that would guide me and my beliefs that people were good and that war was not the way for people to solve their problems. Music tugged at my heart with immigration issues, hope for peace and free love, with a new message of responsibility for the environment and for taking care of the earth – and dreaming of a good future.

There was the pivotal song, *We Shall Overcome*. Pete Seeger met Martin Luther King Jr. only two times, but the message of overcoming resonated with Dr. King and went on to become a signature song of the civil rights movement. Pete Seeger sang *We Shall Overcome* with an incredible sweetness and an innocent hope. I was looking for my place in the world and trying to figure out who I was and where I belonged, and hearing *We Shall Overcome* opened up a well of hope in my heart that never disappeared or dried up. There was a hope that no matter what, everyone would overcome badness and despair and injustice because of the deep beliefs that were inspired and then stored safely in people's hearts.

I loved that song. It was how I felt and how we all were feeling.

> *"We shall overcome, we shall overcome,*
> *We shall overcome some day*
> *Oh, deep in my heart, I do believe we shall overcome some day*
> *We shall all be free; we shall all be free...*
> *We shall live in peace; we shall live in peace..."*

Teenagers were hitchhiking, taking LSD, going on peace marches and wanting strongly and earnestly to fix all the wrongs in the world. Martin Luther King Jr. was marching for civil rights, César Chávez was marching for civil rights, and as a teenager in Palo Alto I marched in peace marches, marched with the grape workers, marched with the civil disobedience workers who wanted change.

"We Shall Overcome…"

I could be anywhere and if I started singing, soon I was singing in a crowd, a crowd of people singing together. There was always someone carrying a guitar, and it was common to see regular people, not professional musicians, carrying a guitar. A person might just sit down on a bench, take out their guitar, and start singing and soon there would be an impromptu song fest. People of all ages and races enjoyed the music that brought them together to sing any place, any where.

Several years later the country singer, Loretta Lynn, surprised everyone with a song about birth control! We never listened to country music; we thought that country music was for hicks and people that were ignorant. So it was hard to fathom that this back-woods woman wrote and sang about a topic that was both radical and not a subject for general discussion. Loretta Lynn was a woman who understood how birth control changed lives dramatically, and she was gutsy enough to sing about the Pill.

"You wined me and dined me when I was your girl
Promised if I'd be your wife you'd show me the world
But all I've seen of this old world is a bed and a doctor bill
I'm tearing down your brooder house 'cause now I've got the Pill

All these years I've stayed at home while you had all your fun
And every year that's gone by another baby's come
There's gonna be some changes made right here on Nursery Hill
You've set this chicken your last time 'cause now I've got the Pill

This old maternity dress I've got is going in the garbage
The clothes I'm wearing from now on won't take up so much yardage
Miniskirts hotpants and a few little fancy frills
Yeah I'm making up for all those years since I've got the Pill

I'm tired of all your crowing how you and your hens play
While holding a couple in my arms another's on the way
This chicken's done tore up her nest and I'm ready to make a deal
And you can't afford to turn it down 'cause you know I've got the Pill

This incubator is overused because you've kept it filled
The feeling good comes easy now since I've got the Pill
It's getting dark it's roosting time tonight's too good to be real
Aw but Daddy don't you worry none 'cause Mama's got the Pill
Oh Daddy don't you worry none 'cause Mama's got the Pill"

Many radio stations refused to play *The Pill,* when it came out. It was too controversial. Religious groups taught that taking birth control was the same as murder. I thought that having baby after baby after baby was akin to murder. I had seen women in Mexico who were in their early thirties with ten or twelve children, women who had no teeth left and their bodies were haggard and worn out from having a baby every year. And their babies were busy taking care of each other while their parents struggled. Having babies in poverty with not enough to eat and little hope for a change of life... well, those politicians and ministers weren't taking care of the babies, so how dare they dictate that women couldn't control their own bodies! And Loretta Lynn wasn't singing about a foreign country, she was singing about birth control in America!

Unfortunately, the reality was that we still listened to lines from other songs like this: *"If her daddy's rich, take her out for a meal; if her daddy's poor, just do what you feel..."* But guess what? All women could embrace Lorettta Lynn's message.

One morning there was a guitar case on our front porch, with a beautiful guitar inside it and a note apologizing for not returning it sooner! However, it was not our guitar, so we put an advertisement in the "classified" section of the *Palo Alto Times* newspaper, saying that someone had left a guitar by mistake on our porch. No one responded, so we ended up with one more guitar at our house!

On Saturday mornings everyone listened to the DJs on KYA Radio count down the week's "Top 30." KYA would start with song number thirty and play it, and count down until they would play the number one song of the week. Teenagers liked to listen to this show, guessing ahead of time what the number one song of the week might be.

I usually was at home Saturday morning doing chores. We girls had to put clean sheets on our beds and rotated other chores like cleaning the bathrooms and vacuuming the living room. I was still stuck cleaning out the stupid parakeet's cage. Whatever parakeet we got, no matter what, that was still my job. And I still hated it. But at least I could do my chores with my transistor radio plugged into my ear!

There was usually live music at Be-Ins. We would hear a rumor that a Be-In was at a park or a field, and that's all it took for hundreds of people to congregate spontaneously. We would have flowers in our hair and the aroma of incense and marijuana would perfume the air... people shared food and drugs and music. Balloons and Frisbees were tossed, games would start...dogs and babies ran freely and it would just be something that happened. And guitar-playing, sitar-music, harmonicas and drums and singing were the scene.

Hippies across Northern California came together to celebrate all of life at the Be-In in Golden Gate Park in January of 1967. Almost all of the major San Francisco bands were there, including The Grateful Dead. Jerry Garcia, their guitarist, had been teaching guitar at Dana Morgan Music on Ramona Street in Palo Alto.

The other place that the Grateful Dead played was Frost Amphitheater at Stanford University. The Frost Amphitheater was one of the Grateful Dead's usual stops for years. In May of 1967 they played there, along with Santana and Jefferson Airplane. Other bands that played there included The Chambers Brothers, and Creedence Clearwater Revival. In 1967 Santana and The Chambers Brothers were the headliners, as Creedence was still a local unknown band. There were Be-Ins and Love-Ins hosted by the Hells Angels at El Camino Park across from Stanford Shopping Center and those free concerts also included The Grateful Dead and Jefferson Airplane.

The Chambers Brothers were a soul music group known for their eleven-minute long song, *Time Has Come Today*. The strange sounds heard on this song were meant to replicate the sounds of the Vietnam War. My friends and I bought their album, and would sit on the floor with a chair on each side of us and put stereo speakers on the chairs. We sat between the speakers and cranked the music up all the way and listened to the ticking sounds and screaming voices of that powerful song.

There was a coffee house, The Underground, on El Camino in Menlo Park near Kepler's Book Store, and Jerry Garcia used to come there and play on Sunday nights. That's where he met Johnny Dawson, and as a result the New Riders of The Purple Sage was formed around 1968. Their best known song is *Panama Red*, referencing marijuana grown in Panama.

In April of 1967, Cubberley hosted a concert with Neil Young's band, Buffalo Springfield, and also with the Sopwith Camel. Sopwith Camel was the second San Francisco band to get a recording contract with a national record label and the first to have a Top 40 hit. Sopwith Camel's only hit single, *Hello, Hello*, became the first hit title to emerge from the San Francisco rock scene. More obscure than that, Stevie Nicks sang at Cubberley's 1967 Christmas dance as the vocalist in the Fritz Raybine Memorial Band. Santana played at Cubberley's graduation in 1969.

"Garage Bands" became popular, and I was the tambourine player in one of those many bands. The other band members were guys from Paly, and we would get together in a garage on Sunday nights to practice. We were actually pretty good, and even got some paying gigs in San Jose. I wore mini-dresses and managed to hit the tambourine at the right time.

300,000 people attended the "The Altamont Speedway Free Festival," held on December 6th, 1969. David and I went there with some friends.

The concert was supposed to have been held at Golden Gate Park in San Francisco. Then the venue was changed to the Sears Point Raceway, but the location was switched one more time on the night of Thursday, December 4th. The information about the change spread like a wildfire; the only thing people could talk about on December 5th was the free music festival that would happen the next day.

Headlined and organized by the Rolling Stones, it also featured musicians that were local or who had played locally: Carlos Santana, Jefferson Airplane, The Flying Burrito Brothers, and Crosby, Stills, Nash and Young. The Grateful Dead were supposed to have played, but cancelled at the last minute.

On Saturday, December 6th, my friends and I drove to the speedway. It was a drive of less than one-hundred miles, but the last twenty-five miles of the drive were gridlocked. The festival organizers had expected 100,000 people, but as we crept slowly along in the traffic, we ended up on a hilltop, where as far as we could see in all directions every road was bumper-to-bumper, packed solid with young people on their way to the festival. People hitchhiked and walked, getting in and out of vans and vehicles. The aroma of pot was everywhere, and impromptu picnics and dancing happened along the roadsides. We knew there were more than 100,000 people there. Saying "one-hundred thousand people" and actually experiencing a crowd the magnitude of Altamont are two completely different things. It is difficult to even conceive of that many people outdoors on the rolling hills as far as one could see.

When we finally arrived at Altamont the parking was haphazard, with thousands of vehicles in the dusty fields. Throngs of people were carrying food and sleeping bags, walking towards the sloping hillside where the newly-erected stage had been erected. The sea of people was colorful and everyone that I saw was happy and excited about this amazing free concert!

About half of the time we couldn't even hear the music, but the music became less important than the event. People blew huge soap bubbles, juggled, ate, shared food and drugs, and were amazed that so many people were in attendance. It was hard to fathom and to understand the burst of rage and violence that marred the concert and affected future free concerts and gatherings. My friends and I and those who were sitting and dancing around us were unaware of the violence that came to be synonymous with Altamont, and until we heard reports on the radio the next day about the death of eighteen-year-old Meredith Hunter, we had no idea that it had happened.

Within minutes of starting the Rolling Stone's third song, *Sympathy for the Devil*, a fight erupted at the foot of the stage. Mick Jaggar paused the song, and pleaded with the audience for people to remain calm. The motorcycle gang, the Hell's Angels, had been recruited for crowd-control, and when Meredith Hunter attempted to get onstage, one of the Hell's Angels grabbed him and chased him back into the crowd.

Hunter drew a revolver from his jacket, and was then stabbed by Hell's Angel, Alan Passaro. Just like most of the audience, the Rolling Stones were unaware of the killing, and completed the remaining eight songs of their set.

In addition to the homicide at Altamont, there were three accidental deaths: two caused by a car accident and one by drowning in an irrigation canal. Four births were reported during the event as well.

The media subsequently analyzed what happened and many people concluded that Altamont became, whether fairly or not, a symbol for the death of the Woodstock Nation.

In 1971 singer and songwriter, Don McLean, released the song, *American Pie*, and many interpret part of the song to be about the stabbing death at Altamont. Alan Passaro was arrested and tried for the murder in 1971. Passaro was acquitted after a jury concluded that he had acted in self-defense.

"And as I watched him on the stage
My hands were clenched in fists of rage
No angel born in hell
Could break that Satan's spell

And as the flames climbed high into the night
To light the sacrificial rite
I saw Satan laughing with delight

The day the music died
He was singing..."

Kezar Stadium at Golden Gate Park in San Francisco was the end-point for several anti-war marches that I went on in the '60s. Both the San Francisco 49ers and the Oakland Raiders got their start at Kezar Stadium, but by the early 1970s each football team had their own stadium. With the loss of professional football in the 1970s, the stadium became an outdoor concert venue with many well-known acts performing there, including Led Zeppelin, The Doobie Brothers, Jefferson Starship, Tower of Power, Joan Baez, The Grateful Dead, Carlos Santana, and Neil Young.

Living and going to school in Palo Alto, we thought that the whole country was enmeshed in anti-war, pro-drug, free-love music. It was certainly OUR music!

'Concert master'

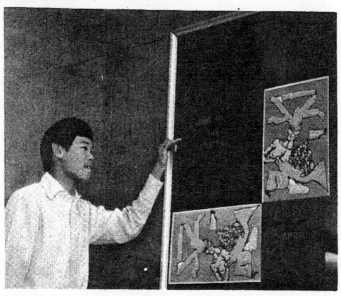

Student coordinator for Cubberley's tri-school concert, Rod Jew, points out the flourescent colored posters, designed by Bill Perry for publicity.   Photo: SAMPSON

Buffaloes, Camels booked for tri-school concert

With the Junior-Senior Prom behind you, it's time to make plans to attend the Spring Concert featuring "The Buffalo Springfield" and "The Sopwith Camel," who will perform on Thursday, April 27.

The doors of the pavilion will open at 6:30 and because ticket sales have begun, one may purchase a ticket for this terrific show for $2.75 with SB card and $3.50 without. Tickets will also be sold at the door but the price of $3.50 will remain constant, regardless of a SB card.

. Due to the expense of the program, it will be sponsored by Gunn, Paly, and Cubberley High Schools. The proceeds will be equally divided and donated to each school's American Field Service (AFS) and School Affiliation Service (SAS) programs.

Don't be left out in the cold! Buy your tickets now.

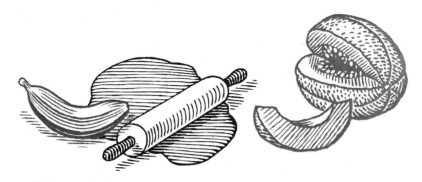

Can You Get Stoned on Cantaloupe Rinds?

Cubberley had an open campus. During lunch time we would go to the houses and apartments of students who lived near campus to get stoned, and we would try anything!

Rumors abounded about smoking cantaloupe rinds and banana peels; someone said you could get stoned on dried banana peels. In fact, we sang and listened to *Mellow Yellow* sung by the Scottish folk singer, Donovan. *Mellow Yellow* was about smoking dried banana skins, which were rumored to be hallucinogenic. We peeled bananas, dried the peels in the oven, shredded them, rolled them into cigarette papers, and smoked them to see if it was true. All we got from our Mellow Yellow cigarettes were headaches and a stinky mess.

Students en masse were smoking pot at lunch time or experimenting with trying to get high on something else. There were many different varieties of pot, and an explosion of hashish as well. Hanging out with friends meant getting stoned on pot, on hash, on anything we could get our hands on. "Head shops" were popping up in every town and city around the Bay; places where anyone could buy a water pipe or cigarette papers or cigarette rolling machines, and pipes for smoking pot. It was the new way of life – leave school at lunch, get stoned, and then return back to school.

With all the cigarette and pot smoking happening on school campus, Cubberley finally implemented a no-smoking-on campus rule, although it was never rigorously enforced. Students still smoked in the restroom, on the field, in the parking lots, and in their parked vehicles.

The Federal Cigarette Labeling and Advertising Act of 1965 required that the warning "Caution: Cigarette Smoking May Be Hazardous to Your Health" be placed in small print on one of the side panels of each cigarette package. The act prohibited additional labeling requirements at the federal, state, or local levels. In June 1967 the Federal Trade Commission (FTC) issued its first report to Congress recommending that the warning label be changed to "Warning: Cigarette Smoking Is Dangerous to Health and May Cause Death from Cancer and Other Diseases."

```
CAUTION: Cigarette Smoking May Be
     Hazardous to Your Health
```

In 1969 Congress passed the Public Health Cigarette Smoking Act, which prohibited cigarette advertising on television and radio and required that each cigarette package contain the label: "Warning: The Surgeon General Has Determined That Cigarette Smoking Is Dangerous to Your Health." We had grown up listening to and watching cigarette advertising. That Congressional act was huge in changing the behavior around smoking.

The following articles from our school newspaper highlight some creative problem-solving that took place in the three Palo Alto high schools to address smoking on campus.

By BOB MELOSH

WARNING: Smoking on the Cubberley campus may be hazardous to your health.

The tensions and pressures of grade-grubbing drive many students to the smoking of tobacco and other assorted weeds. But state law doesn't allow campus flames without a permit. This law both puts out the cigarettes and dampens certain boy-girl relationships. Under the law the smokers at Cubberley continue to do a slow burn.

Gunn and Paly high schools both reacted to the problem of campus smoking with bureacratic imagination. The Gunn administration compromised its principle by declaring one Gunn hill as "off campus".

Paly vigorously tried to stop smoking by increasing their campus area. The administration consecutively declared that the residential area, the Stanford campus, and the Town and Country Shopping Center are part of the Paly campus. No smoking allowed. It looked like Paly's principal had succeeded, until the Paly school paper published a photo of three jolly green students smoking on the Southern Pacific tracks. Paly's administration has not yet succeeded in annexing the Southern Pacific Railroad as a further extention of their campus.

Catamount lavatory research has proved that even at Cubberley smoking has not been stopped. However, smoking on campus does remain hazardous to your health. The smokers could give up smoking and find new ways to relieve their tensions. Possibly, they could take up chewing tobacco with student power providing a spittoon in every room. Or they could start group knitting at Cubberley, where the byproduct might be new band uniforms. But if anyone finds it impossible to give up smoking they can always go to Gunn or Paly.

Underground cookbooks for cooking with pot were starting to be sold, and the psychedelic style of art and clothing was exploding. I had sewn clothes for a long time, and now I was sewing clothes for David also. I bought bedspreads from India at the store, Cost Plus, and made dresses for me and shirts for David from the bedspreads. They were cotton with beautiful colors and patterns, and the clothing made from then was light-weight and airy and looked exotic.

Men's fashions burst out with color, texture, and with ribbons and lace. I made David a deep-green velvet shirt trimmed in wide embroidered ribbon. I sewed him a blue corduroy shirt with puffy sleeves and wide cuffs and a big collar and decorated it with rows of ribbon. My skirts were as short as possible, and I had purple and turquoise boots and a Nehru paisley jacket in psychedelic colors.

Judy Gets Married

It had been a few years since Judy had graduated from high school. She was attending junior college and studying to become a nurse. Judy was twenty-years old and had fallen in love with John Johnston. They were going to get married! It was exciting that she was getting married. John was handsome, tall, had a beautiful smile and he and Judy were very happy together. John had a motorcycle that he drove to San Francisco State, where he majored in microbiology. But since Judy and he were spending a lot of time together, John needed a car. He didn't want to take Judy places on his motorcycle, especially if it was cold or rainy.

Our next-door neighbor, Sandy Jensen, drove a Rambler Metropolitan all during high school, but now her car was for sale. John bought the car from the Jensens. Sandy had given me rides to school in that car and now it felt odd to see John driving it instead of Sandy.

John and David commuted together in the Metropolitan to San Francisco State. David was in college already; I was still in high school. David and John had similar mellow personalities.

John had a soothing way about him and there was an amicable relationship between David and John during their daily commute to the university.

The family was happy that Judy had found such a nice person to love. Judy and my mom spent a lot of time planning the wedding. There was a guest list to create, invitations to order, sewing of dresses, and food and menu planning. My mom made all five of the bridesmaids' outfits and a new dress for herself.

The ceremony was held at the Congregational Church, and Lou Riley officiated.

Judy and John drove away from the church in the Metropolitan. The car was decorated with shaving cream and soap, and tin cans were tied with string to the tail pipe. As they drove away and the sound of the cans hitting the road grew fainter and then disappeared, I knew that I would miss Judy. She was married and she and I would never live in the same house together again.

Judy and John left, and my mom, Daddy, Jennifer, and I finally went home together without Judy. Grandpa Bob and Gramma Gigi drove home. I was tired. The wedding and its preparation had filled our lives for weeks, and now it felt like the day after Christmas….there had been so much anticipation, then finally the event, and now I could let my breath out.

I had not stumbled while walking up the aisle. I had remembered to do everything that I was supposed to do. I was happy for Judy but I missed that she was gone. She and John would come back from their honeymoon to live at an apartment on Wilkie Way in Palo Alto.

My sister was now Judy Johnston. I liked the sound of her new name.

"I have a dream that one day this nation will rise up and live out the true meaning of its creed: 'We hold these truths to be self-evident, that all men are created equal.'"

More Assassinations

A Baptist minister, Dr. Martin Luther King, Jr. became a civil rights activist early in his career. His efforts led to the 1963 March on Washington, where he delivered his "I Have a Dream" speech. In 1964, at the age of thirty-five, Martin Luther King, Jr. became the youngest person to receive the Nobel Peace Prize. It was awarded Dr. King in honor of his work to end segregation and racial discrimination through civil disobedience and other non-violent means.

In 1965 we watched on TV civil-rights marches and protests and saw how the country was seemingly divided on the issue of segregation. There was a fifty-mile voting-rights protest march planned to go from Selma, Alabama, to the state capital of Montgomery. The goal of the march was to draw national attention to the struggle for Negro voting rights in the state. It was hard to believe that I lived in a time when Negroes had to fight for the right to vote! We watched in horror as the police beat and tear-gassed the marchers just outside of Selma. This day came to be known as "Bloody Sunday."

Two weeks after Bloody Sunday, more than three-thousand people, including three-hundred marchers who made the entire trip, set out toward Montgomery. They arrived in

Montgomery five days later, where Martin Luther King, Jr. addressed more than twenty-thousand people in front of the capitol building. Also in 1965, Dr. King joined the growing number of antiwar activists who were publicly criticizing America's foreign policy in Vietnam.

Dr. King was an adherent of the philosophies of nonviolent civil disobedience as described in Henry David Thoreau's essay of the same name, and used successfully in India by Mahatma Gandhi. Dr. King's role as the leader of the civil rights movement was questioned by younger blacks who argued that Dr. King's protest strategies and idealism were useless in the face of sustained violence by whites. Black Power advocates looked more to the beliefs of the slain Black Muslim leader, Malcolm X, than to the beliefs of Dr. King. Malcolm X had been assassinated in February of 1965; he had insisted on self-reliance and the right of Negroes to defend themselves against violent attacks. And here in the Bay Area, we were listening to the Black Panthers and their support of Black Power.

At school and at homes we met with Bay Area leaders such as Huey Newton to try and form coalitions between white and black activists. As a member of the SDS, I met frequently with people who were described on TV as dangerous thinkers, but who in person were working hard to avoid violence.

Throughout 1966 and 1967 Dr. King increasingly turned the focus of his civil-rights activism throughout the country to economic issues. In fact, Dr. King was spending time and energy on ending poverty and opposing the Vietnam War, both from a religious perspective. His emphasis on economic rights took Dr. King to Memphis, Tennessee, to support striking black garbage workers in the spring of 1968.

On April 4th, while Martin Luther King, Jr. was in Memphis, he was assassinated by a sniper.

I was with a group of students returning from a retreat in the Santa Cruz Mountains. The retreat had been about unity and peace, and we were all energized about our futures.

We were in the car trying to get radio reception; a static-filled message about an assassination kept fading in and out. In the car we stopped talking so we could hear the radio. The car was driven by one of the retreat's host teacher, and in the car with me were several members of the Executor Car Club. It was a moment frozen in time, as if things were in slow motion, as if I had misunderstood what the radio announcer had said. I looked at the other passengers and as our eyes met in stunned disbelief I felt the horror that indeed what I heard on the radio was the same that all of us heard, that my ears had not played a trick on me. Yet my mind denied what I had heard; we couldn't be in the midst of another political assignation of an American leader!

When we heard the confirmation, it was almost too much to bear. Was our country going insane? News of Dr. King's assassination resulted in shock and anger throughout the nation and the world, prompting riots in more than one hundred United States cities. Martin Luther King, Jr. was thirty-nine years old and left a widow and four children.

On April 4th, the day of Martin Luther King's assassination, Robert Kennedy was campaigning for the 1968 Democratic presidential nomination. Kennedy had spoken at the University of Notre Dame and Ball State University earlier that day. Before boarding a plane to fly to Indianapolis for one last campaign speech, Kennedy learned that Martin Luther King had been shot. However, Kennedy did not learn that Dr. King was dead until they landed in Indianapolis. Kennedy decided to go ahead with his speech, and he spoke for just five minutes.

Kennedy acknowledged that many in the audience would be filled with anger, especially since the assassin was believed to be white. Robert Kennedy told the audience that he had felt anger when his brother, John F. Kennedy, had been assassinated. Kennedy continued, saying that the country had to make an effort to "go beyond these rather difficult times," and concluded by saying that the country needed and wanted unity between blacks and whites.

President Lyndon B. Johnson declared April 7th a national day of mourning for the lost civil rights leader. And we sat before our TV for days, watching the story of the assassination unfold. It was beyond my understanding. How could this man, this unheard of man named James Earl Ray, be so full of hate to kill Dr. King?

The more I heard about James Earl Ray, the more disgusted I became.

The assassination of Robert Kennedy, a United States Senator and brother of assassinated President John F. Kennedy, took place shortly after midnight on June 5th, 1968 in Los Angeles, California. Dr. King had been assassinated exactly two months previously. We thought and hoped that the horrible assassinations of President Kennedy and Martin Luther King, Jr. were the end of gun-driven hysteria, this belief that if a person disagreed with a political position that killing the other side's proponents was the obvious solution.

Robert F. Kennedy was killed during a celebration of his successful campaign in the Californian primary elections while seeking the nomination for President of the United States. Kennedy was shot three times, with a fourth bullet passing through his jacket. He died nearly twenty six hours later. Five other persons at the party were also shot, but all recovered.

We could have had another Kennedy in office, another Kennedy as President, someone who had been behind the scenes during his brother's presidency, someone whose life had always been directed towards this high commitment to serve his country. The perpetrator of the murder was a twenty-four year old Palestinian immigrant named Sirhan Sirhan. Because of the number of reporters at the scene, the shooting was recorded on audio, while the aftermath was captured on film.

Robert Kennedy's body lay in repose at St. Patrick's Cathedral in New York for two days before a funeral mass was held on June 8th. His body was interred near his brother, John, at Arlington National Cemetery. Robert Kennedy's death prompted the protection of presidential candidates by the United States Secret Service.

For the next several weeks the news was full of conspiracy theories. And we learned all about Sirhan Sirhan in the same way that we had been bombarded with media information about Lee Harvey Oswald and James Earl Ray.

Robert Kennedy had, like his brother and Malcolm X and Dr. King, sacrificed his life to politics.

I was getting ready to graduate and thinking about my future. Both San Francisco Art Institute and the Oakland Art Institute had offered me partial art scholarships, but it was hard to focus on the future with the stress and confusion and disbelief of another assassination!

A week after the murder of Robert Kennedy I graduated from high school.

My friends and I decided to wear nothing under our graduation robes. I wore sandals, my gown and the silly looking hat. David sat next to me even though he had graduated from Paly the year earlier. We managed to spill a bottle of patchouli oil by mistake, and the strong scent caused the evacuation of several rows and the disruption of the ceremony.

Grandpa Bob Retires

When Grandpa Bob retired from Southern Pacific Railroad after a long career as an accountant, he got another job instead of staying at home. He went on to work at Stanford Research Institution (SRI) in Menlo Park as an accountant for the next five years. But now Grandpa Bob and Gramma Gigi were ready for him to retire permanently.

Ever since Auntie Jan died, my grandparents had been very sad living in their same house in San Carlos. Auntie Jan had lived in that house for some of the time they had been there, and there were so many memories of her in the house during happier times that they were too grief-stricken to continue living there. In the two years since Auntie Jan's death, their neighborhood had changed, and most of their friends had moved away. They no longer had neighbors that would drop in on them for an afternoon cocktail and visit, or that they would drop in on.

So when SRI offered Grandpa Bob retirement, my grandparents decided it was the time to take retirement and to think about moving away from San Carlos. They decided that they would move to a brand-new retirement community, a place called Oakmont that was on the outskirts of Santa Rosa, about one hundred miles north of Palo Alto.

What a huge change this would be! All three of us girls had spent countless weekends at my grandparent's house, and Gramma Gigi was always there for us at the drop of a hat. Having my grandparents move one-hundred miles away was a difficult and uncomfortable idea. My mom talked every day on the phone with her mom, so that would not change, but the house on Emerald Avenue in San Carlos was the only place I had ever known my grandparents to live, as they had moved to San Carlos from Oakland when I was quite little.

I would miss Gramma Gigi's bedroom with the big plate-glass window. I would miss the century-old oak tree in their back yard, the oak tree with the swing in it. Their back porch was the porch where I had danced the Indian rain dance until I had made it rain, and their lilac bathroom, the old linoleum kitchen floor, and the steep, steep driveway were as much a part of me as my own house. But they had too many memories at their house and they needed a fresh start in life.

My grandparents packed up their things and moved to Oakmont. Their new house wasn't finished when it was scheduled to be, so Oakmont paid for my grandparents to stay in a hotel about seven miles away until their house was ready. And when they moved in they had a huge housewarming party! The party was catered at an inn, and I danced with Daddy for the first time in my life. I was grown-up enough to now dance with my father; he was a natural dancer and it was a very special moment in my life.

Grandpa Bob and Gramma Gigi's new house was on the edge of a golf course, and their patio faced the east. Every evening there was a beautiful rosy sunset reflected off the cliffs that were in the distance. They had California quail wander through their yard, and watched deer roam on the golf course during the mornings and evenings.

Grandpa Bob learned how to play golf, and Gramma Gigi started swimming every day. They made many, many new friends and were busy all the time. And once a month I would drive there and spend a Friday or Saturday night and come back the next day.

Moving to Oakmont had saved their lives. They started to be happy again.

They then began traveling and went on several ocean cruises, each time to Hawaii. My grandparents fell in love with Hawaii, and with cruising on the Lurline cruise ships. What a luxurious change! To celebrate their first cruise, we had a family dinner at a restaurant in San Francisco. It felt so extravagant for my parents and sisters and grandparents to be dining out in the City. It was the second time we had all eaten together at such a fancy place. The first time had been when I was little and we had taken Grandma Ruth to eat in Chinatown.

Because Oakmont was a retirement community, my grandparents made many new friends that were in their same age range, people who had experienced both WWI and WWII and had their lives shaped by those global events. They met people from all over the world who shared their life stories and knowledge. They even reunited with some long-lost friends who moved to Oakmont.

It was both exciting and comforting for them to live in that brand-new community. There was a clubhouse and a restaurant within walking distance, and the restaurant overlooked the golf course. They were so busy with their new lifestyle that each day was full of visits with friends, eating lunches with others, and swimming, golfing, and taking classes.

Their house had a spare bedroom and a hide-a-bed couch, and they always welcomed guests and visitors.

Gramma Gigi started a guest book when they moved into their new home, and as the years flew by, the book filled with hundreds of entries from all their visitors.

Peace Groups and Bombings

Not only did we have the two family-owned Kepler's Book Stores within biking distance, but in 1965 the Midpeninsula Free University was formed as a reaction to the growing influence of the military-industrial complex on American universities. "Mid-Pen U" or "Free You" required no certification to teach there; once a member, anyone could teach what ever they wanted to teach, and students would take whatever classes they wanted. It was a great way to meet like-minded people and to experience classes that were definitely not main stream!

Roy Kepler helped instigate the Institute for the Study of Non-Violence and the Mid-Peninsula Free University. The Mid-Peninsula Free University began life as the Free University of Palo Alto. Some of the classes that the Free You offered included:

Tantra: The Yoga of Sex
Touch Marathon
Toward Revolution; An Inquiry into the Tarot
Counter Counter Insurgency
Techniques of Massage
Acid Yoga
The Art of Giving Away Bread

In a very short time enrollment at the Free You reached three thousand students. By May of 1966, students could register for classes at Kepler's. Roy Kepler was in charge of the curriculum committee, and led a recurring class entitled "An Inquiry into the Theory and Practice of Non-Violent Resistance." David and I signed up for some classes through the Free You. It was a great opportunity to meet people who were interested in new ideas and personal growth and in shaking off old, stale ways.

My friend Carin and her family were friends with the Kepler family and the Duveneck family, so I heard a lot about what these iconic Bay Area families were doing. Hidden Villa Ranch was founded by Frank and Josephine Duveneck, who purchased the land in 1924 and offered it as a gathering place for discussion, reflection, and incubation of social reform. The Duvenecks established the first youth hostel on the Pacific coast, the first multi-racial summer camp, and also Hidden Villa's Environmental Education Program. These were creative thinkers in the peace movement, the core of what helped make the Palo Alto area liberal and innovative.

Kepler's Book Store was the place that everyone wanted to go to hang out on a Friday or Saturday night. Roy Kepler was not only instrumental in the local peace movement, but he helped develop the nation's first public radio station, KPFA, which aired in 1949.

On the evening of October 15th, 1968, a thrown hatchet smashed through the window of Kepler's Menlo Park store. At the time, the store featured a window display of Chinese books and a poster of Mao Tse Tung. About ten days later, a bomb blew a four-foot hole in Kepler's Los Alto store.

Events got worse with a series of bombings at the Free You, the Tangent Coffeehouse on University Avenue and the home of City Council member Kirke Comstock. Comstock was a vocal opponent of the Vietnam War and a strong supporter of gun-control. The bomb that blew the door off Comstock's house was a pipe bomb spiked with nails. "We were out of town that weekend," Comstock recalled. "We were very fortunate … if anyone had answered the door, they would have been killed." Bombings happening in our community was scary…it signaled a new conservative backlash in the area; a group of people who believed in killing and maiming instead of dialogue.

I marched in the Kezar Stadium Peace March, which was part of the 1967 Spring Mobilization. At that one march, there were over sixty-seven thousand people protesting the Vietnam War, marching through San Francisco. The protestors took over entire streets, and when I stopped and looked behind me, there were peace marchers as far as I could see. Many people joined in the march as it progressed. After the march there were speakers and music at Kezar, with peace symbols everywhere, including some large symbols festooned with paper streamers.

In 1970 my birthday ended up being a landmark day in history, not because it was my birthday, but because of Kent State University.

On May 4th, Kent State University in Ohio was holding student demonstrations against President Nixon's decision to invade Cambodia. Why was our country so intent on invading Cambodia? Students were exercising their right to protest when twenty-eight National Guardsmen fired on the students.

Four students died, one student was permanently paralyzed, and eight others were wounded. This was a school, a college, and colleges should have been safe places where students could debate and discuss and enjoy the freedom to disagree! That our National Guard could occupy a college and open fire on unarmed students was horrifying! Students were the hope for the future, students were the children and grandchildren of people who loved them, and had dreams and hopes shared in those students.

Neil Young's song about Kent State, *Ohio*, became a rallying cry for students and peace-lovers all over the country.

> *"Tin soldiers and Nixon coming*
> *We're finally on our own.*
> *This summer I hear the drumming,*
> *Four dead in Ohio.*
>
> *Gotta get down to it*
> *Soldiers are gunning us down*
> *Should have been done long ago.*
> *What if you knew her*
> *And found her dead on the ground*
> *How can you run when you know?*
>
> *Tin soldiers and Nixon coming,*
> *We're finally on our own.*
> *This summer I hear the drumming,*
> *Four dead in Ohio."*

David

When David's parents moved to Georgia and David stayed in Palo Alto, some things were complicated because of his age. He was seventeen and not an American citizen and had been busted for pot several times. Each of these by themselves caused difficulties, but the combination was starting to make his future in America questionable. We realized that we needed to learn more about laws and rights so that David could continue to stay in the Bay Area.

David rented a small room at the back of Kleins Workingmen's Store on Castro Street in Mountain View. The store sold cowboy boots and hats, men's working clothes, and a lot of equestrian gear. Built in 1874, Klein's was said to be the oldest commercial structure in Mountain View, having survived the 1906 earthquake.

David was still going to San Francisco state, but the rent for the room behind the store was cheap enough that it made sense to rent in Mountain View. Mr. and Mrs. Klein allowed him to work in the store in exchange for the rent.

There were three small rooms in the back of the store with a communal kitchen and bathroom, the same bathroom that the customers used. David's room had bars on the window and overlooked the parking lot that was behind the store, between Castro Street and a small alley named Wild Cherry Lane. His was the only room of the three that had a window; so the monthly rent was fifty dollars instead of forty-five dollars.

There was an old, old lady named Mae who rented the second room. She had lived there for what sounded like forever. She cooked her meals in the tiny kitchen and ate in her room, and the TV was on all day and all night. I think she only left a few times a month when she went to the post office to collect her social security and when she did a bit of grocery shopping at the grocery story that was on the corner of Villa and Bryant Streets. David did his grocery shopping at the same store, and it was the site of our first argument.

David and I were going to cook something, and we were buying the ingredients when I said that we could just use three teaspoons to measure out a tablespoon if we couldn't find a tablespoon. Well! David said no, there was four teaspoons in a tablespoon, and I said three, and pretty soon we were like the "Question Man," asking random shoppers how many teaspoons were in a tablespoon, and most of the shoppers didn't know either! Then David used a pay phone to call his mom long-distance and asked her, and she said four!

It turns out that in England there are two teaspoons to a dessert spoon, and two dessert spoons to a tablespoon! So we were both quite right, thank you. For years we joked about our first argument, the argument in a grocery store about teaspoons and tablespoons!

The person who rented the third room was a young man that we just called "Weirdo," because he was snoopy and odd and would say strange things. And one day David saw that Weirdo had drilled a hole in the wall between the two rooms so that he could spy on us. What a creep!

There were times when I worked the sales counter and the cash register of the store. The Kleins liked to travel, and they would have David and I take care of the store when they were gone. I knew nothing about the merchandise and neither did David, but most of the customers came to the store because they knew exactly what they wanted, so it worked out okay.

At night there was a small street sweeper that cleaned the parking lot directly on the other side of David's room. David thought that would be a perfect job if he could get it; go to school during the day and work the late shift in town. But when he applied for the job he was told that he had to be a citizen to work for the city. A non-citizen couldn't have the responsibility of a street-sweeper. There was a bit of irony in that decision!

Canadian-born S. I. Hayakawa became president of San Francisco State College in 1968. He was controversial for allowing and encouraging the San Francisco police to go on campus to break up peaceful student demonstrations. During 1968 and 1969 there was a student strike at San Francisco State University led by the Third World Liberation Front, supported by SDS, the Black Panthers, and others. The strike demanded the creation of a Black Studies Department, an end to University's complicity with the Vietnam War and an end to racism. The five-month student-led strike was the longest campus strike in United States history, and laid the groundwork for establishment of ethnic studies and similar programs at other universities throughout the country.

Clashes between the strikers and San Francisco Police Department's tactical squads made national news. David was one of the students who participated in a student demonstration when the tactical squad came on campus, armed with their shields and batons.

David was beaten pretty badly, and came home with a swollen, black-and-blue bruised face. His tongue looked like hamburger meat. He had been sitting non-violently on the ground in passive resistance when the tactical squad came on campus and attacked the students.

The University of Berkeley was experiencing similar clashes between demonstrators and police, and for the first time police started using both mace and tear gas to break up demonstrations. It was a time of polarization; parents didn't understand students and the government seemed to be attacking the youth of America.

I was spending most of my nights at David's room, but one night when I slept at home my daddy woke me up early in the morning. "That idiot is out in front of the house with a weather balloon, the thing must be twenty feet tall. He's been there for hours. Go see what he wants!"

David had seen a weather balloon falling from the sky and tracked it down and found it. He wanted to share it with me and tell me all about it. It was whimsical and magical all at the same time.

David could fix anything. He had the ability to look at machinery and easily figure out the working mechanisms. He was good at trouble-shooting car engines too, having the needed patience to diagnose a problem and then repair it properly. It was fascinating to me, because I had never been around anyone who had that mechanical talent, and through David's eyes I began understanding a whole aspect of the world that I had never been exposed to. It was fun and interesting when David explained how things worked and how to troubleshoot them.

Even though he was in America with a green card, David was a permanent non-citizen and still eligible for the military draft. Like all our friends, he dreaded checking the mail each day, afraid there would be a draft notice from the Oakland Induction Center telling him to report for a physical and to bring a toothbrush and toiletry kit in case he was inducted immediately. The prospect of being drafted hung like a shadow over our future and the future of our friends. We had friends who had been inducted through the Oakland Center; they went there for their physical exam and we never saw them again.

The Vietnam War overshadowed our lives. We talked and talked about draft resistance and went to many protests against the draft and the war. We were worried that David might get deported; he had drug charges against him. Many war-protestors were being jailed and charged with crimes, crimes that could justify deportation. Because of our fear that he might be sent back to England, David and I were thinking about getting married. If he was married to an American citizen, it would be much easier for David to stay in the United States without threat of deportation.

In order to get a California marriage license, David needed his parents to notarize a permission document which would be presented to the county clerk. The law was that men under the age of twenty-one could not get married without their parent's permission. I was eighteen and therefore did not need my parent's permission, as California allowed women over eighteen to freely marry. Even my father had needed his mother's permission to get married; he had been nineteen when he married my mother and could not get married in California without Grandma Ruth's written consent.

Because of the draft, David and I were thinking of homesteading in Canada, of leaving the United States and therefore totally avoiding the draft. We had friends who had already left America because they did not feel this was a war they wanted to fight, so we knew that it was possible. And because David was British, going to Canada would be easy for him. And if I was his wife it would be easy for me also.

We bought a wood-burning stove at a flea market, along with a 1906 foot-treadle sewing machine. We thought that if we were going to homestead that we should start weaning away from our dependency on electricity and gas.

We both liked the Bay Area. But if staying there meant David would be drafted, we thought we should leave.

Our plan to leave to Canada didn't happen in time. David received his draft notice and had to go to Oakland for a physical exam. I was nervous all that long, day, hoping to see David come out of the Induction Center and worried sick that they would take him in, shave his head, give him a uniform, and send him to Vietnam where he would perhaps kill or be killed or wounded. I waited in the parking lot, watching young men enter the Induction Center, holding their paperwork and toiletry bags.

They didn't induct David. He wore a size thirteen boot. This was not a standard military size for boots. Soldiers were standardized, uniforms were standardized, and boots were standardized. They wanted only young men who fit standard-issue uniforms and boots. David's big feet kept him out of the military. I gratefully drove him home at the end of that long day, so relieved and happy that he did not get inducted.

First Real Job

I began working at a contract-drafting sweatshop named Guralnick & Lee straight out of high school. We drafted eight hours a day with a half-hour lunch, sitting on high, backless stools, our work resting on light tables which we hunched over while we drew. I drafted contract jobs such as cabling diagrams for the phone company and electrical diagrams for other customers. Guralnick & Lee was located on the Palo-Alto side of East Palo Alto, on a road known as Whiskey Gulch, so named because of the abundance of liquor stores.

The drafting was done on Mylar, a plastic sheet which had 1/8-inch squares lightly printed on it, and we drew with ink-filled rapidograph pens. The rapidograph pens were expensive and we had to provide our own. The pen points would wear out quickly because we were drawing on plastic, and a worn-out pen would scratch the Mylar. Scratches in the Mylar affected our ability to create quality work, and because our job would be microfilmed when completed, our work had to be perfect.

When any of us thought that we were done with a job, we would take it to the team lead-person who held the position of "checker." The checker's job was to put the drawing on a light table and check it through a jeweler's eyepiece for accuracy. Most of these drawings were 36" x 24" and two people often carried them to keep the Mylar from bending. The checker would circle in pencil all the areas of the drawing that needed correction. If a line was not consistently light and dark, then it had to be redone. If a line was not uniformly thick or crisp or the ink was too light or too dark, then it had to be redone. Not only did the content of the drawing have to be perfect, but so did the 1/8-inch tall block letters. These large drawings were reduced to very small microfilm to be sent all over the country and accuracy was an absolute requirement of the job. One mistake and an entire building might not function properly because of a bad drawing!

I used an electric eraser for the first time, learning to apply pressure just right; otherwise the fast-spinning eraser would melt a hole in the Mylar.

After the corrections had been made and re-checked, the drawing was microfilmed. Then the Mylar was washed for reuse. There was a big tub in the back of the shop for washing the Mylar sheets. Ideally the same draftsmen (there was not a title of "draftsperson") washed and reused the same piece of Mylar many times.

The job gave me nightmares. I would dream that I was sitting on a drafting stool, and in front of me was 1/8-inch gridded Mylar, spread to the horizon in all directions – up to the sky as far as I could see, and down below as far as I could see, and to the left and the right to infinity. And I was suspended in space in front of this Mylar, with my little rapidograph pen and an infinite drafting job that I could never finish!

It reflected the real job pretty accurately. If employees were six minutes late, they were docked fifteen minutes; sixteen minutes late, one-half hour docked pay, and thirty-one minutes, we were docked one hour pay. And thirty-two minutes? Out the door and fired. We punched in on the time clock for the morning, got a ten minute break at nine o'clock, and had to punch out for our half-hour lunch at eleven o'clock. By the time sixty people punched out, a person could have wasted five minutes of their lunch! Then we had to punch in at the end of the half-hour, but had to start punching in at eleven twenty-five so that we would not punch in late for lunch, because we would be docked similar to what happened in the morning. That left only twenty minutes of actual lunch time.

Most of the people who worked at Guralnick & Lee would cash their paychecks at the Bank of America in Whiskey Gulch, which was right across the street. It was the only bank I had ever seen that had an armed guard outside the bank, a turn-stile to enter the bank, and another armed guard inside the bank. These were tense times in East Palo Alto, there was a lot of racial tension, and Whiskey Gulch was known for crime, robberies, prostitution, and blatant heroin usage. On Fridays when people got paid, we would sometimes spend our entire lunch standing in line at the bank to cash our payroll checks.

There was one young woman who worked there who would try to cash her check before her husband came to meet her at the bank; she wanted to keep some of the money for herself, but usually he was waiting for her outside of work and would walk across the street to the bank with her and then take all the money from her check. She was left with nothing and had to beg him for a few dollars to buy milk for their baby.

It was a man's world. None of the checkers were women, and less than five-percent of the draftsmen were women. Everyone smoked on the job, and balanced their ash trays on the light tables. It was a job that paid hourly, and we were expected to produce non-stop.

In my parent's backyard at our wedding reception
Daddy, Mom, John, my sisters Jennifer and Judy,
my friend Barbara

David's sister Jennifer (7ᵗʰ from the left), Jane, David,
Wilf and Margaret

Grandpa Bob, Gramma Gigi, Daddy, Mom, Jennifer,
Barbara, Jon, Reverend Lou Riley

I Get Married

My parents didn't like the idea of David and me "living in sin."
It was causing them a lot of anxiety, along with my grandfather.
I didn't see what the big deal was…if people loved each other,
why did they need a piece of paper? I loved my family and
didn't want them to be agitated about David and me; there had
been enough traumas in their lives and I didn't want to add to it.
Besides, David and I had been taking about getting married
anyway, so that his situation in America would be more stable.

So we decided that we would get married.

I worked at Guralnick & Lee on Friday and David and I
got married Saturday morning at San Mateo County Memorial
Park. My drafting supervisor would not give me Friday off; I
had been sick and used up all my vacation and sick time, and I
didn't have even a day off to prepare for my wedding or for my
honeymoon.

I made David's wedding suit. It was a wine-colored
cotton suit with bell-bottom hip-hugger pants, a vest and a

jacket. His shirt was cream-colored cotton with a V-neck, yoke, and puffy Renaissance-style sleeves.

The eve of the wedding I was still sewing. My friend Marcia had let me use her sewing machine. David had already gone to the park to be in a meditative mood, spending the night at the park, camping in the forest on his wedding eve. Ralph was to pick up David's wedding suit and shirt and take them to the park and camp in the woods with David. I couldn't find the piece of fabric that was the back of David's shirt. Because the shirt had front and back yokes, the sleeves and the front and the collar were all complete. The vest I had sewn would cover David's back anyway. However, just as Ralph arrived to pick up the clothes, I found the shirt-back; it had slipped between the sewing machine and the wall. Ralph waited while I finished the shirt, and then I wrapped the finished outfit in paper.

David and I had taken a copper-enameling class at junior college, and I during the class I had made him a beautiful copper belt to wear with his wedding suit. The belt was rectangles that were enameled red and gold, and each rectangle was wired to another enameled piece. I wrapped up the wedding belt in paper with the rest of the suit and gave that to Ralph. Ralph put the package under his jacket and joked that he and David might be there in the morning, or that perhaps they might not be. Ralph drove away on David's motorcycle. I felt the same pre-wedding jitters, not certain that either one of them would be there at nine o'clock the following morning for the wedding.

My mom had made my dress. It was white fabric with pastel flowers all over, and I had new pastel pink shoes. David had new motorcycle boots, so we were all set.

San Mateo County Memorial Park is in the redwood forest near the small coastal town of Pescadero. The wedding guests and family drove to the park in several cars, winding through the forest road in the morning fog. Lou Riley and his wife, Skip, were there, and Lou performed the ceremony. Our friends played the guitar and the cello, and we read poetry. It was a wedding all about Love, Joy, Peace, and Happiness.

Then we drove back to Palo Alto to a reception in my parent's back yard. It was mostly family and a few friends. David's parents and his younger sister had come from Atlanta for the wedding, and Grandpa Bob and Gramma Gigi were there too, as were Judy and John. Grandpa Bob did not like the British; after all, Grandpa Bob had been born in France and there was a long-standing feud between France and England, so Grandpa Bob shook his head in disgust and muttered a lot about my poor decision to marry a damn Limey. I wished that Auntie Jan could have been with us. That would have made it perfect.

Daddy opened champagne and everyone ate and drank and visited, and then David and I left for our honeymoon. We drove away from my parents' house in our 1949 Chevy pick-up truck with the floor starter. The truck had only one good panel on the bed of the truck because David had gotten in a wreck a few weeks earlier, smashing the passenger-side of the truck. But both of the truck's doors had "Just Married" written on them.

Honeymoon shot of David next to our truck

We headed south on Highway 101, through San Jose, through Morgan Hill and Gilroy, and drove several hours until we arrived in the prison-town of Soledad, where we turned west towards the ocean, driving on a two-lane road towards the Los Padres National Forest. As we gained elevation, the road got narrower and there were no other vehicles. We passed a hitchhiker out there in the middle-of-nowhere, and decided to back up to offer him a ride.

The hitchhiker had visibly deformed hands which were partially covered in heavy gloves. It was a hot afternoon and we knew the man must have been tired and thirsty, but he refused to sit on the cab of the truck with us and made himself comfortable in the one-sided truck bed. Several miles later the road narrowed to one-lane and turned to a dirt road. The hitchhiker tapped on the back window of the cab; we stopped and he asked us to let him off in about a half mile. He said we should watch for a fence and to drop him off at the gate.

When we dropped him off at the gate, he did not look at us or say anything. The fence had signs on it which read, "Caution, Leper Colony. Do Not Enter." We figured that his hands had been covered with the gloves on that hot afternoon because of his disease.

We reached the crest of the mountain range as the afternoon was turning to evening. We were deep into the Big Sur Forest, and along both sides of the road were beautiful blooming century plants. Those cacti bloom every forty or fifty years with flower stalks at least fifteen or twenty feet tall! We stopped frequently to look at the plants and the forest. There were some parts of the road where we could see all the way to the Pacific Ocean in the far distance.

The afternoon was quiet and peaceful, and civilization was forgotten. There was one place we stopped where we could hear far-away voices and laughing. We looked far down into a canyon, and in the river at the canyon bottom were six or seven people skinny-dipping, laughing, and playing in the hot afternoon sun, far below us. We hollered and waved at them, and they waved back, but we had no idea how they had gotten there or how to get there ourselves.

David and I spent our first night as a married couple in our sleeping bags in the one-sided bed of our pick-up truck. We ate a picnic and drank champagne, watching shooting stars in a pasture that we shared with cows.

But by four o'clock in the morning the mosquitoes were getting the best of us, so we packed it in and got back in our truck and started driving. And then we began to see some odd things. The first one was a sign that was fastened to a tree: *"Caution, Military Crossing."* The one-lane dirt road had almost disappeared, and we forded several streams driving on the faint road. Then we came to a large cleared area that was so full of military pup tents that the ground was completely covered. The tents were empty. We saw another sign, one that said *"Caution, Tank Crossing."*

I was hungry and somewhat hung-over, and my hands and face were covered with mosquito bites. Plus I had to go to the bathroom and hated going in bushes because I didn't want to get more mosquito bites or poison oak!

David and I were getting rather anxious; we didn't want to run out of gas and we had no idea where we were, and the sinking feeling in our stomachs made it difficult to be upbeat. Finally we saw a building in the distance, but as we got nearer we realized that it was a guard shack, and that there was a chain-link fence with razor wire on the top of it. The fence appeared to continue as far as we could see in either direction. We drove along the perimeter of the fence....and along the perimeter...and along the perimeter! Eventually we saw towers with more guard shacks on them; then about fifteen feet above us were soldiers in camouflaged fatigues pointing rifles at us.

We were questioned, initially at rifle-point, for about ninety minutes. There we were in our pick-up truck with "Just Married' painted on it, and we somehow had managed to drive into the highly-secured Hunter Liggett Military Firing Range. The military personnel that pointed their guns at us and questioned us wanted to know how we had broken their security perimeter and gotten on the range. We sure didn't have an answer. After asking us over and over again what we were doing on their installation, they finally let us go through a heavily-guarded gate. We were given a stern warning to never show up there again and told that we were lucky that they believed us and that we were allowed to leave. It turned out Fort Hunter Liggett is the largest United States Army Reserve Command post with over 165,000 acres, and that we had managed to enter it and had been trespassing!

I doubt too many people spent a honeymoon there. That was a pretty interesting first day of marriage.

We continued on the one-lane road, which eventually became wider, then was paved, and we meandered through beautiful forests. We spent several more hours driving that curvy road, lowering in elevation until we finally came to the Pacific Coast Highway, where we headed north towards Monterey and enjoyed a coffee-shop lunch of pancakes, coffee, fruit and eggs. We then drove through Monterey and to Watsonville. I introduced David to the artichoke stand in Watsonville, the stand that my family had visited when I was little. It had the largest cement artichoke in the world, and sold every kind of artichoke, cooked any style that you could imagine.

We drove back on the highway, with fields of strawberries and artichokes as far as we could see on either side of us. We ate French-fried artichokes and baby artichokes and marinated artichoke hearts, and then stopped and bought strawberries and ate those as we drove.

When we started off on our honeymoon, I didn't know if David had a destination in mind or not. Perhaps he had; but it didn't really matter. Our trip together seemed symbolic… it was the journey that was important, much more important that the destination. If we got lost on the way, then that became part of our journey.

We arrived home to our tiny apartment in Palo Alto late Sunday night. I had to be at work at seven o'clock on Monday morning, and I would go to work as Jane Horton, not Jane Richter any longer.

Jane with Indigo, the cat

Married Life

David and I were living in a car. After six months of marriage we couldn't pay our rent at the apartment where we had been living. I was the only one working, and had to be at work in East Palo Alto at seven o'clock in the morning. Some times I would just throw a coat over my pajamas and go to work.

I would hitchhike to and from work most of the time, because David used the car that we were living in to go to and from San Francisco State college. Judy's husband, John, was now on a different schedule than David and they were no longer commuting together.

My gross pay was three-hundred three dollars a month. The rent on the apartment that we had lived in had been one-hundred twenty-five dollars a month. That left us about one-hundred fifty dollars a month to live on. After six months we realized that we couldn't afford to buy food, gas, school books, and registration, have a phone, auto insurance, and health insurance all for one-hundred fifty dollars a month.

We could buy onions for three cents a pound, Campbell's tomato soup for eleven cents a can, and beans and rice were cheap. We had decided to live on only fruits, vegetables and grains…no dairy, eggs, or meat or fish. But we still couldn't afford to live on what I was earning plus pay rent.

So we lived in a 1940's Ford with our cat and fish tank and all that we owned. We lived in the car while David built a camper on the back of our 1947 Chevy-with-a-column-shift-and-a-floor-starter that we had purchased from the tropical fish store owners who had their shop in the Sears' Shopping Center on San Antonio Road. We had bought the truck several months before we were married. While our camper was being built we spent a lot of time at Marcia's house. Marcia was married to Thom. Marcia lived in the house where her sister, Carin, and their family had grown up, near to Cubberley.

One really hot afternoon we got into a backyard water fight at Marcia's house, squirting each other with the hose and throwing water balloons. David made a mad dash for the house, and for some inexplicable reason Thom, who was inside, slammed the door shut just as David reached it. David's arm went through the glass window that was the top half of the door, and then he pulled his arm out again.

I freeze up around blood. Ever since I had cut open the top of my head in elementary school I stop functioning when confronted with gushing blood injuries. David knew this, so he yelled at me not to look, to just go start up the car because we had to go to the clinic.

We were both soaking wet; I was barefoot and wearing a skimpy India-print dress. David was wearing his cut-offs with no shirt and he was also barefoot. But he wrapped his arm in a towel and we sped off to the Palo Alto Clinic, where they had an emergency room open on Homer Avenue.

By the time we got there, the towel was soaked with blood, and they took David in right away. And I sat in the air-conditioned waiting room, listening to the sounds of pieces of glass as they were dropped into a steel dish. The doctors removed hundreds of glass shards from David's arm during the next several hours, and it took more than fifty stitches to close up his many cuts and slashes.

I was freezing cold and worried sick, sitting there listening to glass hit the pan. When David finally came out the doctors said he would need physical therapy once the healing started, and that he had to sleep sitting up and to keep his arm in a sling until the stitches came out.

That night we slept sitting up in the car, with David's arm in a sling, sharing the space with our cat and our fish. The fish were none the worse even after their car ride that day.

The following day I started coughing. Having been in the air-conditioned waiting room the previous day probably contributed to how ill I felt. After several days I had a high fever and was coughing so badly that I couldn't go to work, and David had to drive me to the emergency clinic. He had his arm in a sling and I couldn't stop coughing…what a pair we were. When we arrived, I couldn't get out of the car. My hands were contorting inward and had frozen in that position, apparently due to lack of oxygen. Someone came with a wheelchair and took me in. It turned out I had a bad case of double-pneumonia and they started me on antibiotics.

Marcia let David and me stay in her house for a few days; she was expecting her second child so we knew it was an imposition. I was still trying to smoke even with the double pneumonia, but I physically could not inhale the smoke, as my lungs didn't have the strength. So I lay on Marcia's couch and watched the historic "one small step for man…" when the astronauts landed on the moon. It was live on TV, on July 20th, 1969. Neil Armstrong was the first known human to step on the moon. With more than half a billion people watching on television, he proclaimed, "That's one small step for a man, one giant leap for mankind."

My mom had always been interested in science and the space program. She was so excited to watch this on TV. When the Apollo 11 crew splashed down off Hawaii on July 24th, I was still sick and staying at my parents' house, watching the command module splash down in the Pacific Ocean and the Apollo 11 crew being picked up by the USS Hornet. The Apollo 11 crew was quarantined for eighteen days to ensure that they had not picked up any infections or diseases from the moon. One of President Kennedy's challenges had been met: Men walked on the moon and returned safely home.

Within a few weeks there were conspiracy theories and speculation that this event had never happened. Some of the people at work said that there was no proof that the earth was even round, and that Hollywood could have easily produced this whole event in order to show that America was ahead of Russia in the race to get a human to the moon. Tabloid newspapers at the grocery store check-out line started repeating the speculative stories. Since the assassination of Kennedy there had been many conspiracy theories and now it seemed that the United States Space Program was also the subject of the conspiracy theorists.

When I returned back to work I was an ex-smoker. I had started smoking at fourteen and now, at barely nineteen, I could no longer smoke. I wanted to, but the healing of my lungs from the pneumonia took a long time.

I found out about a volunteer project at Napa State Hospital, so David and I started going to the town of Napa during weekends to volunteer at the hospital. Some times we were able to recruit our friends to go, driving in a caravan of several vehicles for the eighty-five-mile drive. Napa State Hospital was in the wine-country town of Napa, and had opened in 1875. It was a tree-lined facility that looked like a college campus from the outside. The hospital population peaked in the 1960s with over five-thousand residents.

There were many patients that touched my heart. We volunteered to do simple tasks, like taking patients outside. There was one girl/woman who lived her life in a crib and her physical needs were met, but there were too few staff to take patients, including her, outdoors. David and I took her outside for the first time in two years, after the staff helped put her in a buggy and secure all of the tubes that were fastened to her. This tiny person was blind, deaf and mute and her limbs were contorted, but when we went outdoors and she felt the sun and the wind her little face broke into a smile and she turned her head side-to-side and we knew it was a good experience for her. That entire summer we would take her out when we volunteered. It was heartbreaking that she had spent her life there since infancy and would spend her entire life there and that the resources were not available to take her outdoors except through volunteerism.

One other experience made me forever cringe when I would hear people talk about their hyperactive children. There was an entire ward at the hospital devoted to hyperactive children. These children literally did not sleep, and most died by the time they were eleven or twelve years old…they just burned out. The nurses warned David and me to remove all our jewelry, hair clips or rubber bands, and to strip down to our basic pants and shirts. They also said that although they tried to keep the children dressed, many of them would remove their clothing and preferred to be naked. I wasn't sure of what to expect when I entered their play room.

The play room was chaos, and when I walked into it ten or twelve children surrounded me as if in a pack and several started to climb me as if I was a tree. I realized too late that they wanted my eye glasses. One child ripped my glasses from my face and they all seemed to be in a frenzy of climbing me, looking for anything that glittered or that they could remove. David managed to rescue my glasses, but not before I was scratched pretty badly. All the children in the hyperactive ward were a flurry of activity, running non-stop, spinning, swaying, and pushing and climbing. There were some balls and soft toys, and I could partially engage a child by rolling a ball to them, but after just a few times they would lose interest. Many children had open wounds that they constantly picked at; the staff had warned us that the children removed band aids and picked at themselves without stopping.

As children lost immediate interest in me and I had a chance to really look at them, what astounded me was that there were three boys who looked as if they were brothers about one year apart in age. The three boys actually were dwarfs and were affected with microcephaly, more commonly known as "pinheads." That is an actual condition that I had no idea existed. Their heads were about half the size of a normal head and almost pointed at the top. People with this condition are often born with a head half the size as normal and the head fails to grow while the face continues to develop at a normal rate. These three boys suffered from seizures which contributed to their wounds and bruises. And looking at those three brothers I wondered what their parents had been like. Nothing in my life had prepared me for this...to think that there were lives spent entirely in this hospital, that this was their world. I wondered how many of these children had families that visited them.

Most of these hyperactive children did not talk, but instead made shrill noises or moaning noises. Some would grab me and drag me. But when David and I volunteered it gave the staff time to focus on specific children, the children that could not even go into the playroom! The children in the playroom were better off than some of the other children; there were children there that could not socialize at all.

We went through wards of adults who spent their lives in cribs, bearded men in diapers who were shaped like the cribs where they had lived since infancy. Tiny bodies with feeding tubes hooked to them. There were wards full of cribs for adult women as well, but they didn't reflect their biological age the same way as the men, most of whom had full beards.

The patients were clean and the wards were quiet in general, with the soft hum of equipment that kept patients alive. Patients lay in cribs, some alert, but most sleeping. Watching the staff in operation it seemed that they spent most of their time feeding and cleaning patients, slowly traveling the rows of cribs, pushing a cart of equipment and stopping at each crib with a smile and a conversation. The nurses and staff were mostly Filipino ladies. I talked with one for a while as she did her routine tasks, and she told me that many of the workers were women who had married American soldiers during WWII and when they came to the United States with their husbands that care-giving was one job that they could get. As I watched this woman I saw her gentle concern for each patient; she would talk to each of them briefly, not knowing if they heard her or not, and I thought of her doing this year after year and perhaps being the only contact the patients ever had.

When David and I volunteered we would spend the night in the parking lot at the hospital because we couldn't afford to stay any place else. When we volunteered at Christmas time we were invited to a festive volunteer-appreciation dinner, along with other volunteers. There were long tables set up in the auditorium which was decorated with lights and ornaments.

And we had the opportunity to talk with staff and doctors and heard that our volunteering was appreciated and that it had a positive impact on the patients and on the staff.

We left early that evening. The Napa River was predicted to reach flood level and people were being urged to evacuate. We drove home in the rain, our windshield wipers making a comforting slap-slap-slap sound, and the lights from oncoming cars reflecting like jewels in the falling rain. The downpour was non-stop and heavy at times, but we were snug and warm together.

Next Job

My friend Marcia worked at Fairchild as a circuit designer, and when they had an opening in her department for an entry-level position, she referred me. The drafting job that I had at Guralnick & Lee was a no-where job and I finished each day with so much tenseness between my shoulder blades that it would take all weekend to recover.

David was still going to school, so I worked to support both of us. Applying for a job was much different during that time than it is today. Many places still considered married women to be a liability in the work force. The mindset was that women of child-bearing age would cost the company money to hire and train, and that women would get pregnant and then leave, not giving companies a return on their investment.

The application and hiring process at Fairchild certainly reflected that mindset. The paper application asked questions that would be illegal today, but that women, including me, had no choice but to answer. My application asked if I was married, how many children I had, what the ages of the children were, and if I was pregnant. It went on to ask the date of my last period, and if my periods were regular and if I planned to get pregnant in the near future. There were questions about who would babysit children if I was hired, and also there were questions about if I had reliable transportation to get to work. These were standard and typical questions corporations large and small asked female applicants; many of the same questions were also asked at the in-person job interview.

This chauvinistic and male-oriented attitude was so ingrained in women as part of the employment process that it was difficult to acknowledge that this was blatant discrimination. And Fairchild had its own on-site dirty-old-man doctor who performed physical examinations on the women who applied for jobs. This was business-as-usual for the day. Women were just happy to have jobs and to get a portion of the pay that men got! But the broader issue of double-standards and gender discrimination was difficult to discern. Women felt empowered to be working any jobs that were the same jobs as men... it gave a superficial illusion of equality.

I was hired at Fairchild, working swing shift, and I started out doing keypunching. Keypunching was a process similar to typing (which I HATED) where special paper cards were put into the keypunch machine and the operator looked at codes written on paper and punched the same codes onto the keypunch cards. The codes were created by the circuit designer and indicated the layout of each layer of the integrated circuit.

After keypunching, the cards were taken to the high-security computer room and fed through a card reader by a computer technician. The computer scanned the cards, and the data was converted to the layout of each layer of the circuits that were designed by the mask designer in the group. "Mask" referred to each layer of the circuit. When I started at Fairchild there were only five layers in a semiconductor circuit and the circuits were small, about one-hundred mils square or less.

Any mistake on the keypunched cards translated into loss of time and money. When the data was transferred, a large automated table drew each layer. Part of my job was to position the three-foot square paper on a plotter table, and make sure the suction that held the paper worked properly. I would check the pens that were anchored in the drawing arm and then monitor the drawing of each layer. It was fascinating. The machine drew faster than my eyes could process, hitting the paper with the exact pressure to draw without either being too deep or too shallow. The pens switched between the colors, again faster than I could actually see it happen.

After a few months I started designing metal-oxide-semiconductor (MOS) circuits. One circuit would take between four and six weeks to layout and design. It was fun! The engineer created the schematic drawing, and the mask designer was responsible for the layout with the resistors, capacitors, metal, diffusion, and contacts, taking into consideration speed paths and size constraints. Smaller was better, as the more circuits that could fit on each wafer translated to more money. I would put a red pencil in one hand to draw the diffusion layer and blue pencil in the other to draw the metal layer, and I would draw them simultaneously…it was like doing a big puzzle. And once again I was drawing on Mylar, but this was completely different from using the rapidograph ink-filled pen on scratchy and used Mylar!

When a design was finished and had been reviewed by the engineer, then the same machine, the CalComp Machine, would be used again. However, instead of drawing with pens, this process used exacto knives, and instead of paper, a Rubylith was placed on the table. The Rubylith, which we called a "ruby," was two layers of film sandwiched together. The bottom layer was clear and the top layer was translucent and red, and the ruby was only a bit thicker than a regular piece of paper. The CalComp would cut only through the top layer, and the precision was amazing. Then the ruby had to be stripped.

It was the designer's job to strip the ruby. That meant first transferring the ruby to a light table. Usually the rubies were three-feet square, and two people worked together to move the ruby to the light table to prevent damaging the ruby. Then each cut that had gone through the red layer had to be removed, or stripped, leaving the clear layer intact. The designer put masking tape, sticky side out, around their left hand and used an exacto knife in the right had to delicately pick the cut layer off of the base layer and stick it on the masking tape. Static electricity made the job more difficult, and it was important that each piece of ruby did not get attracted by static and get pulled back on to the larger ruby sheet. The contact layer was the hardest to strip: the contacts were less than 1/8-inch square and had to be removed perfectly. If even one of the hundreds of contacts was missed, then the circuit would not work.

After each layer was cut and stripped, the engineer inspected them, and when all five layers were done they were stacked together and inspected one last time. Once perfect, they were sent to be photographed by a special camera; the photos were then reduced and duplicated and became the templates for each layer of the circuit. The structure of the MOS was through growing a layer of silicon dioxide on top of a silicon substrate, and the templates determined where the growth happened. When the circuits were done, they had to be cut apart, and the women on the assembly line would solder the circuits into their packages. There were so many steps in the process that it was amazing when we heard that the circuit worked, the pass rate was high, and the speed was on target!

Because my boss worked days, his shift overlapped swing shift by only few hours. We had a design team-lead in charge of swing shift, and we called him "Chief." Chief hardly said a word, did his job, and always had a pack of cigarettes rolled in his T-shirt sleeve. Chief was a muscular chain smoker, which meant he lit each cigarette from the still-smoking butt of the previous cigarette, and was never without a cigarette hanging from his mouth. The ashtray on Chief's table overflowed by midnight, which was the end of our shift. I was one of the few designers that didn't smoke; smoking was accepted in the workplace and the company provided ashtrays.

One evening I needed special lead for my pencil. The final draft used special pencil, and the boss kept those in his office because they were expensive. So I went looking for the pencil lead, and when I opened his desk drawer there was a report listing all of his team and their salaries. I didn't think he would have left a confidential paper in his unlocked drawer, as he knew we went there to get lead. Before I could stop myself, I saw that the three women in the team were all paid only half of what the men were getting. Two of the women had been there longer than most of the twelve men in the department.

I took the paper out to the women and shared it with them. They had been assured by our boss that they were getting equal pay for equal work, and their work was definitely as good as if not better than the men's. The next day copies of that report mysteriously appeared on many desks throughout the company. It resulted in some parity in pay for women at Fairchild, at least in my department.

Fairchild was a reflection of the times. Most of our team would go to the parking lot and smoke pot during their breaks. People were sleeping around, and there was a gossip/rumor mill that provided entertainment and speculation about who was sleeping with whom. At least several times a week someone would ask me to sleep with them...often people I didn't even know at all! But there was also a lot of energy and excitement, because we were involved in new technology and the future of the industry seemed guaranteed and solid and innovative.

Companies were unschooled about the storage and disposal of chemicals, and that resulted in a lax and blasé attitude. On the assembly line chemicals were readily available and not kept under lock and key. While I worked at Fairchild, there were three separate occasions when assembly-line workers drank chemicals to successfully commit suicide. The rumor mill would confirm this before any supervisor would.

One night there was a chemical spill in one of the parking lots, and the tires on all the vehicles parked in that lot dissolved. There were hundreds of vehicles affected. Within less than an hour, the parking lot was ringed by tow trucks pulling out vehicles and installing new tires. Managers were writing checks to the employees to "...compensate for the inconvenience." As I either hitchhiked to and from work or got a ride from someone, I was not affected. The parking lot was rimmed with anxious employees who had left their work areas to watch what was happening.

Later the parking lot was hosed down with water for hours, all of the run-off going into the storm drains. During the following week there was a reported dying out of some fish in South San Francisco Bay, but no correlation was made.

Decades later Fairchild and eight other companies were part of a Superfund Site, declared Superfund by the federal government. Tens of thousands of tons of TCE-contaminated groundwater were cleaned, and the polluters were ultimately held responsible for the cost of the clean-up. But during the time the pollution was taking place, the regular people who worked those three different shifts had no idea of the long-term impact the carelessness and lack of knowledge about solvents and other chemicals would cause.

Life in a Commune

David and I lived in a commune for a couple of years, most of the time staying in our home-built camper. We often cooked our food over an open fire and slept in our six-by-eight-foot-little-house with its wood-burning stove.

The commune was on a several-acre piece of property on Grant Road in Los Altos. The property was owned by an old couple who rented it out for eighty-dollars a month. There was a big, circular dirt driveway with a huge palm tree in the middle of the circle. The old farm house was situated more than one-hundred feet from the street. The house had three bedrooms plus a garage that was converted to a room, but there were always a lot of people staying there, either in the house or in campers or vans. We had a big garden and a pond made from a discarded gas station sign, and there were ducks in our pond.

There was no phone at the house; if someone needed to make a phone call we went to the gas station that was about a mile away and called from the phone booth there. We had a large kitchen with double windows that opened out to the garden behind the house… the kitchen was the hub of the commune. People would just drop by and hang out and stay as long as they wanted.

Our friend, Ralph, who had changed his name to Simon when he escaped from Agnew's State Mental Hospital, was the core of the commune.

Simon was adopted, and his pride and joy was a dried up tortoise that he had taken from the Smithsonian on a classroom field trip when he was in elementary school. Simon could charm anyone with ease, and always had a scheme or a wild plan which was one step away from happening. Simon was gay, but in those days we didn't say gay, we would say "queer" or "screamin' queen," or just "queen." At the commune there were all sorts of people: musicians, queens, old people, straight people, singles and couples, and an ebb and flow of energy there that made it an exciting place to be.

David, Simon, Jane

There might be a week when no one spoke; we might communicate non-verbally for a week just as an experiment. Or maybe we would eat food that was Zen Macrobiotic for a week, or stay up and play music all night just for the fun of it. We all used heroin one week, and I traveled from this planet to the farthest ends of the universe and back again. Using it once was all I needed; we had so many new drugs to try, it was no big deal.

One day when we came home there was a pregnant goat tethered to the front porch. We named her "Aggie with the crazy yellow eyes," and she stayed with us at the commune long after she gave birth to her two kids. It was a difficult birth and David ended up acting as a midwife, helping poor Aggie deliver two kids.

Aggie weighed almost ninety pounds and was quite aggressive. If she wanted to get inside the house she would butt her way through the back door, then butt her way into the kitchen. There were many times that I had to chase her out of the kitchen with a broom, as she was too big and heavy for me to drag her out by her collar. There she would be, eating everything off the counter and the kitchen table, and Aggie would head-butt me when I tried pulling her by her collar. After a while I realized how fond she was of tobacco. Aggie would chase every smoker who came over, some times even grabbing their lit cigarette and eating it! I kept cigarettes in a drawer to entice her out of the house.

As I worked swing shift at Fairchild, I didn't have to be at work until three-thirty in the afternoon. I had most of the day to hang out, smoke pot, and do what I felt like. David moved in and out of the commune…sometimes he was there, sometimes not, and he went to school during the day.

David and Aggie

She's going for the cigarette

There were days when we body-painted each other, days when we did communal art projects and days when we gardened and laughed and played. I would often go out with one of my co-workers, riding on the back of his motorcycle on warm summer afternoons, winding through the foothills, wearing a dress made from a silk scarf. I got a pretty severe motorcycle burn inside my knee, and had the scar for many years. My friend was a Vietnam vet, only twenty-four years old, with long shiny black hair and his smoky black eyes sparkled in the sun. We rode that motorcycle on warm afternoons, leaning together in harmony on the twisty foothill roads.

My boss at Fairchild was a former CIA agent and was as straight as could be. He had been in the military and sported a crew-cut and had razor-sharp creases in his khaki slacks. One day he asked me if he could buy some pot. I told him I didn't sell pot. I wasn't sure what his motives were or if he might even be an undercover cop! The next day I talked with the commune, and everyone decided that it was okay to have him come over; maybe he was looking for a life-style change!

I told my boss to pick a time when he wanted to visit the commune. The evening he decided to come over, my boss and I drove together in his car during our dinner break. When we pulled into the circular driveway, the commune was crawling with FBI agents. Recently Simon had a phone installed at the commune, and when he had gone to the phone company to pay the bill, he got impatient and asked the clerk if anyone had ever tried to bomb them. Well, that was considered a bomb threat, so the FBI rushed over to check out all the radicals that were living at the commune and took Simon to jail, and of course my boss hightailed it away as soon as he saw what was happening.

Simon got out of jail a few days later.

There was a lot of suspicion and prejudice and hatred against homosexuals/queens/queers, and there were several times when Molotov cocktails were thrown into the yard of the commune. We finally built a street-side fence because we were getting anti-queer anti-hippy hate notes. Someone in the neighborhood was upset about the people at the commune.

I was almost shot when I was sitting inside the house one weekend evening. A car pulled into the driveway and the people in the car opened fire at the house. A bullet came through the front window and into the wall, and missed my head by about two inches, leaving a round bullet hole in the wall behind me When the cops came out they only asked what did we expect... after all, they said, with our alternative life styles, the police could not do anything to protect us.

We added a plywood gate to the street-side fence, turning the commune into a locked compound where the gate was opened only for passage in or out.

We would pool our money together on the weekend and hitchhike to the huge San Jose Flea Market to spend the day, buying fresh produce, tortillas, and bread. The San Jose Flea Market was founded in 1960, when George Bumb bought one hundred and twenty acres; today the San Jose Flea Market is the largest open-air market in the United States. When we went there in the late 1960s and early 1970s, there was music, food, beer, and hundreds of vendors. There was one stall that had clothes and costumes from the 1930s. I purchased a floor-length red velvet coat with shoulder pads, and it was the greatest- looking coat I ever had! The Flea Market was where David and I purchased our wood-burning stove and our antique, treadle sewing machine.

Usually we met someone who would give us a ride back to the commune in exchange for dinner or pot or whatever might be the thing they wanted. One time a lady picked us up when we were hitchhiking back and she talked about how President Kennedy's father had made a pact with the devil and that was why the Kennedys had such bad luck. She told us that she hated police and was going to become a policewoman to infiltrate the cops. We couldn't wait to get away from her!

Another time a teacher from Peninsula High School, a free school up on Skyline Boulevard, gave us a ride home. His name was Suleiman, and he stayed at the commune after he drove us home. The first night his car was parked at the end of the driveway, and each day when he returned from his job he would park his car nearer to the house. Finally he moved in and became the lover of one of the women at the commune.

I would hitchhike to work, but hitchhiking home at midnight was a real drag, so I would try to get a ride home from a co-worker who was going my way.

Tommy

Simon's boyfriend was Tommy. Simon called Tommy "Arnold the magical pig," and Tommy called Simon "Bunny." Pretty soon we all called them by their pet names. Tommy was from Portland, Oregon, and he loved the Bay Area, especially San Francisco. Tommy and Simon would go to the City every weekend, to go to the baths and to night clubs. They were excited about the acceptance of queers in the counter-culture of the City. Going to San Francisco was like a holiday escape from prejudice for Simon and Tommy. But they themselves had no tolerance for lesbians, which seemed so hypocritical to me.

Tommy taught me to dance. I thought I could dance until I met Tommy. He would look at me and say, "Oh, honey, you gotta fix those moves, come on, let me show you, come on, dance like THIS!" We would play music and dance up a storm, laughing and smoking pot and just enjoying being alive. We had an old piano at the commune, and Tommy and many of our other friends could play piano beautifully. Some afternoons we would simply lie around and listen to piano-playing.

Tommy's driver's license was issued by the state of Oregon, and Oregon did not have a photo on their licenses, only the person's name, date of birth and address. Because we were now doing a lot of dancing, we wanted to go clubbing, but I was too young to get in. There was one club in Mountain View, St. James Infirmary, where we wanted to go. It was known for its thirty-foot tall Wonder Woman that hung from the ceiling, and an extensive assortment of beers. Because it was very near to Moffett Field, it was also a military hang-out.

One night we all went to the Infirmary and I got in using Tommy's Oregon driver's license. At home Tommy and David had dressed me as a man, rubbing soot on my face so it looked like I needed to shave, and tucking my hair up under a bandana. I wore a motorcycle helmet over the bandana. I made it past the bouncer at the door and into the Infirmary! Once inside I hurried to the women's restroom and changed into a mini-dress and boots that had been in my backpack, undid my hair and washed my face. I partied and danced and drank beer with my friends and had a blast! That system worked for several years until I turned twenty-one and didn't need phony I.D. any more.

When Simon and Tommy would get in fights it was usually because they were testing their relationship and their trust levels with each other. And Tommy would come to me all in a huff and bitch and moan, and then we would end up laughing. It was like having a best girl friend except that Tommy was in a guy's body. He loved to dress up and we teased him about being a drama queen. He could play any character you could think of, only with a sharpness that made his mimicry seem better than the real thing. He would act out Bette Davis, Liz Taylor, Debbie Reynolds, and Anita Bryant, the anti-queer former Miss America. Then Tommy would dance like Carmen Miranda; he could parody and imitate them so well! There were times when we held non-stop talent competitions to see who could do the best and funniest imitation, and who could create the best costume.

We laughed a lot and had a lot of fun. There were few boundaries, unlimited laughter, and compassion. I think all of us

expanded our comfort levels and tolerance by living together the way we did.

David on our house.

The truck is parked at the commune.

More Sorrow

Judy and her husband John were thrilled because John had been accepted as a professor and would begin teaching microbiology at the Cal-Davis campus in the University of California system. John was only twenty-three and this was quite an achievement. He had been studying non-stop for several years, and he was ready for a break before his teaching career started in the fall.

Judy and John were staying at my parent's house for a few weeks, as the housing in Davis wasn't quite ready and they had moved out of their apartment on Wilkie Way in Palo Alto. With all of the exams and studying John had been through before graduating, he was exhausted and glad to take a break before starting his professorship. Everyone was so proud of John and what he had accomplished; he was the first college-graduate in his family.

Judy was taking an afternoon nap on the weekend when Daddy, John, and Jennifer decided to ride their bikes down to the Eichler Swim Club for a well-deserved swim. They were enjoying themselves, but as John got out of the pool he told Daddy that he just couldn't catch his breath.

And then John leaned over into my daddy's arms and stopped breathing and John died in Daddy's arms, next to the swimming pool on a warm weekend afternoon.

Jennifer rode her bike home as fast as she could and woke Judy up. Jennifer didn't know yet that John had died but she told Judy that something was terribly wrong. By the time Judy got to the swim club, an ambulance had arrived.

David and I just couldn't take it in. We had been away for the weekend at the trailer in Clearlake when John died. My family had contacted the sheriff's office to find us and tell us, but that hadn't happened. We returned home to our friend's mother asking us if we had heard the news, the devastating news that John had died.

We went to my parents' house, and then we heard the news from my family, their explanations as to what had happened. There was so much crying, so many tears.

The next several weeks were a nightmare. The county coroner said that John had drowned. The coroner cited fluid in his lungs as proof of drowning. Judy had been taking nurse's training and argued with the coroner, telling him that John had gotten out of the pool and spoken, and that everyone who dies gets fluid in their lungs. The family demanded an autopsy.

After battling for weeks the coroner agreed to perform an autopsy. It was from the biopsies that John's cause of death was determined. He had a fatal disease that attacks every vital organ in the body, but could only be diagnosed through biopsy. That was why he had been so tired for the several months prior to his graduation. The name of the disease was Sarcoidosis.

Judy and John had been ready to move to Davis, ready to start a new and exciting chapter in their life together. Now Judy was a twenty-one year old widow. Judy and John had been married a year and a half.

My parents took care of the funeral arrangements. Once again we went to Roller and Hapgoods on Middlefield Road in Palo Alto for a funeral service. Seeing my brother-in-law so young and handsome in his coffin was heart-breaking. And seeing John there meant I understood and finally believed that he was really dead. He was laid to rest at Alta Mesa Cemetery, the same place as our beloved Auntie Jan.

After the memorial service, Grandpa Bob and Gramma Gigi whisked Judy away on an ocean cruise to Hawaii. They wanted to help her get her balance back and to allow her some time to recover.

Daddy's hair turned white overnight. He had loved John as a son, as the son he had never had. John dying in Daddy's arms was almost more than Daddy could bear.

Inside the camper
Our wood-burning stove and the couch/bed
Behind my head is the crawl space into the cab;
our storage drawers are behind my feet

Road Trip

David and I lived in our home-built camper which we parked at the commune. I had one drawer for my clothes, and David had one drawer for his clothes. Our home was six-feet by eight-feet, with an ice chest for our food and a wood-burning stove to keep us warm. Our bed was a couch in the day, and at night we folded it down, screwed in a table leg for support, and had a three-foot wide bed. David was tall, and he could never stretch out to all of his height when he went to sleep in our camper.

But it was our home, with a flower box, the wood box, a light on the back and our spare tire tied above the wood box. There was a crawl space between the camper and the cab of the truck, so we could actually go between the camper and the truck cab without even having to go outside!

I was pregnant. We were trying to decide if we would stay together. In a very short time things had changed to where I was the full-time worker and supporter of my husband and he often forgot to pick me up at midnight when I got off work. His new friends were students, and most of them were not married. He was with a party crowd and it was hard for him to step back and be married.

And I was the same way. At work everyone was sleeping around with everyone else; when you worked with people eight hours a day they became like your family. People brainstormed together, solved the circuit layouts and circuit speed paths together. We took our breaks and lunches together and went out to the parking lot to smoke pot together. We partied after work, and the men were always flirting with the few women in the department.

It was a different world in the work place. Fairchild had three shifts: there was day shift, swing shift, and graveyard shift, and most of the people working swing and graveyard were women. Their status was identified by the color of the anti-static smock they wore: blue, pink, or black. "Blue-smockers," were the assembly workers whose skills included the ability to solder a PC board and follow detailed instructions. The "pink-smockers" were the select few who checked the work of the blue-smockers. And the "black-smockers" oversaw the shifts; they were the shift leaders. If a person did not wear a smock, then they were not a shift-worker, but a designer, a layout artist, a secretary or a manager. The designers in our team were not required to wear smocks, but often we would wear a smock to keep our clothes clean while we drafted our circuit layout.

David's world and my world were increasingly different worlds. We hardly ever saw each other. With the disconnect between circuit designer and student, David and I decided to take a road trip. We needed to know if we were suited to be together for the next part of our life.

I asked my boss for a leave of absence, not certain if I would get it. But it was granted. David and I were ready for a road trip in our home-built-camper-on-the-back-of-the-1949-Chevy-Apache-pickup-truck-with-a-foot-starter!

We left with our cat, Indigo, nine-hundred dollars in traveler's checks, and a determination to see if we were meant to spend our lives together.

We drove through San Francisco, a challenging drive with the heavy camper on our truck. We had manual transmission, steering, and brakes, yet David drove without any problems up Nineteenth Avenue and across the scenic Golden Gate Bridge. We were excited to start our adventure together.

David and I spent our first night along the coast a hundred miles from home, cooking canned vegetarian links over a camp fire. There was a moonlit, starry sky and the sound of waves lulled us to sleep. It was very magical to have that sparkly scene right outside the door of our traveling home.

We traveled up the Northern California coast, stopping at ancient redwood groves and family-owned coffee shops, taking local family-operated tours of small roadside attractions. Every day of the trip I would sketch on a postcard a plant or flower that I saw on our journey. When we drove through towns I mailed the postcards to Gramma Gigi, challenging her to identify the plants. I thought that I might be able to stump her, but the first time I saw her after our trip I found that she had identified the common and Latin name of every single sketch I sent her!

During the first few weeks of our nine-week trip, I would think of my co-workers and what they were doing. But gradually work and circuit design began to fade away as if it was a dream, as if it was not even real. I still had my Fairchild access badge with my name and photo on it, but that didn't seem important any more.

We traveled leisurely, stopping at Bodega Bay, the town where Alfred Hitchcock's movie, *The Birds* had been filmed. We stopped at Point Arena and Fort Bragg, at Eureka, Trinidad, and Crescent City. We stayed at a small park near Coos Bay, Oregon, and there we met a sheep shearer.

It was so interesting to talk to the sheep shearer; he was from Spain but now traveled the Oregon coast during sheep-shearing season, making scheduled stops at sheep ranches. We shared a campfire meal with him, listening to his stories about Spain and his travels, and he showed us the tools he used. His tools had been passed to him from his father and to his father from his grandfather. We watched the sun set into the Pacific Ocean from the hilltop. The grass was green and fresh-smelling and the colors of the sunset transformed the water, the sky and the hillside into a pink and orange glow of colors.

I was experiencing morning sickness to the point that I was only able to eat in the evenings. When I got pregnant I weighed about one-hundred pounds, but now weighed less. The doctor had given me some medicine to stop morning sickness, but it didn't really help; mornings were an interesting routine of eating soda crackers and trying to keep them down. And of course we had tea with our breakfast!

Most of the places we stopped there were people who were interested in our camper, especially older people. Many times we were treated to a meal while we talked with other travelers or locals about our lives and their lives and what was going on in America. Our camper was a great introduction and conversation starter!

We were on a two-lane logging road in Washington State when the right rear wheel of the truck completely sheared off. The wheel went down the hill, and we spun around, going side ways on the road. It seemed as if everything was in slow motion... I was saying to David, "Can't you stop this thing?" and his response was in slow motion too... "I am trying my best!" The steep hillside was in front of us instead of to our right, and behind us was a very steep embankment with a river at the bottom. We started sliding backward down the embankment and came to an abrupt halt.

Our heavy-duty bumper had bent and twisted, embedding itself in the embankment. It kept us from going further backwards...backwards down the steep hillside and into the river! And all I could think about was the baby, if the baby was all right.

There was a sudden silence in the truck. No engine sound. There were creaking noises that were unfamiliar, as the truck was slowly settling into the roadside embankment. We were balanced precariously, with the rear of the truck facing the river and our cab facing the side of the road, which was about twenty five feet above us. I was scared out of my wits, but I started laughing, and then David started laughing too. We were afraid to move to hug each other. We were afraid to open the doors. We just sat there for a moment and did nothing.

Then a shout came from above, a shout from a person on the road. A man had seen our wheel go down the road, traveling in a straight line as if it knew where it was going, and our wheel flying past him is what had alerted him to our accident! He was shouting at us, and we heard him say that he would go up the road a bit to the gas station and send help. The man shouted that he would try to find the wheel and that he would drop it off at the gas station if he found it.

We sat in the truck. The dust around us settled. We began to hear birds. I was afraid to move because I was afraid that the truck would start sliding backwards. David wanted to get out of the truck, but I pleaded with him to stay put until help came, and so we waited.

After what seemed like forever, a middle-aged man with a heavily-lined face, wearing greasy overalls and a stained baseball hat approached the hood of our truck. He was half walking, half sliding downhill in the dirt path that our truck had created. As he came towards our truck, we could see that he was pulling behind him a thick steel cable which had a huge hook attached to it. As he slid nearer to the hood of our truck I was relieved to see him, but also very nervous, because we were obviously at his mercy. Without any conversation, the man kneeled down, and we could feel and hear him wrapping the cable around parts of the front of the truck. After several minutes he turned around without saying anything and hiked back up to the road.

We heard and felt the cable tightening, and we knew that the man was attempting to pull us up the embankment. David and I had gone through a truck weight-station a few days earlier and weighed our truck. We had a half-ton pick-up with a three-quarter ton bed and extra-heavy leaf springs, and we weighed more than three tons. The man at the top of the embankment had a lot of weight to pull up that hillside, and I was fearful that the cable might snap. Our rear bumper had kept us from sliding down the hillside, but it was so embedded that it was also keeping us from being pulled up!

We couldn't see what was happening, but heard later that the man increased his tow truck's power and began driving straight into the road while simultaneously using a wench. This was a two-lane logging road, and we had gone down at a curve; the driver was pulling his truck right out into the road at a very dangerous spot! But he needed to get as much power as possible to pull us up.

Meanwhile our truck was protesting, creaking, and swaying side to side. The lurch that happened next was terrifying! For one breath-stopping moment I thought that we were going to tip over sideways, but a second later the bumper was freed from the embankment and we were being pulled up the hillside. Getting from the dirt up onto the road, my heart was in my throat! And once we were on the road, we saw that he was using a commercial-sized tow truck. The driver had to release us and maneuver around so that he could tow us from the back. Because we were missing a rear wheel we could not be towed from the front. David and I got out of our truck to look down the embankment, and then we saw how lucky we had been. Our truck had torn a swath down the hillside and if we had not stopped where we did, we would had gone several hundred feet and landed in the river. David had welded on a heavy-duty bumper with a heavy-duty vise fastened to it. The bumper was folded down but had remained attached to the truck and saved our lives.

The man who rescued us was named Mr. Bob. We found out that Mr. Bob took our truck's lack of cooperation as a challenge, so he had been intent on pulling us up that embankment, come hell or high water! He knew his work and what to do and was accustomed to his tow jobs running perfectly. There was no way he would have failed in his attempt to tow us up and get us to safety.

Mr. Bob owned a combination gas station, tow service, and coffee shop in the middle of nowhere. He told us that he would put our truck behind the gas station and that we could stay there until we got it fixed.

Our poor truck! Because of the weight of our camper, the rear wheel had sheared off. All six wheel studs were broken. The man who had shouted from the top of the road that he would get help actually did drop our wheel off at the gas station. And the gas-station family invited us in for dinner. We ate with them and spent the night in our camper, with it resting on a heavy-duty jack, parked behind the gas station.

Mr. Bob did not have the repair parts we needed, which meant we had to go to a town to get parts. It was then we found out that it was illegal to hitchhike in Washington State! David wanted me to stay at the camper while he hitchhiked to the nearest town, but I told him that if he got picked up hitchhiking and got arrested what did he think I would do, just sit there in the camper for the rest of my life?! So we cautiously hitched to a town together and found an auto-parts store. We were anxious about leaving Indigo in our truck, but we left her plenty of food and water and put clean dirt in a litter box for her.

Of course the auto-parts store did not have what we needed; wheel parts and brake parts and special lug parts and studs, but they ordered the parts. We spent the next day and a half in the town, drinking coffee and walking around, spending the night in the all-night coffee shop. We met many locals and talked with men who had lived in the small town all their life and were enmeshed in the logging industry. Talking with them was interesting, as they had a perspective much different from mine.

We hitchhiked back to the gas station, and a few days later we were ready to continue on our journey. Mr. Bob would not let us pay him, but that year at Christmas I mailed a book about the Bay Area to "Attention Mr. Bob c/o the Gas Station" along that stretch of highway. I sent him cards and presents for many years.

We stayed at a park near the Olympia National Forest where we collected salmon berries! I had never heard of salmon berries until then; they were like raspberries but when ripe they were salmon-colored. David and I had never been in a forest like the Olympia forest before, with its variety of plants and trees. I did many sketches of those plants and mailed them to Gramma Gigi.

We wanted to pass into Canada at a large border crossing where there was a constant flow of people and we would not be conspicuous. Many young American men were avoiding the draft by going to Canada, and crossing the border into Canada from the United States had become difficult. David was a British citizen; therefore we expected to cross without any problems. England and Canada were ruled by the same queen, but because of stories we had recently heard about people being turned away at the border we were apprehensive.

The border guards did not like our hippy looks, and pulled the camper over for additional inspection. But when they saw David's British passport and our traveler's cheques, they let us in. People were not being allowed into Canada unless they could prove they had money with them, as Canada did not want any freeloaders. Our trip was a good opportunity to see if we liked Canada enough to move there.

David and I drove past fields of flowers and pristine white houses and farms. We stayed at a beautiful spot along the St. James River, a place that was miles and miles down a dirt road next to the wide, swift-flowing river.

We crossed the Canadian border the Fourth of July weekend. Yet as we drove farther north into Canada towards Prince George, we were caught in a snowstorm! David and I stayed at a pullout by the side of the road for three days while it stormed and snowed. We were thankful for our wood-burning stove. One day we cooked pea soup in our cast-iron kettle and David said that in England they didn't call it pea soup, that they called it "pease porridge," similar to how they called oatmeal "porridge!" We snuggled under our comforter and ate hot pea soup while our wood-burning stove kept us warm. When the storm finally stopped and we opened our camper door, we were awestruck by the new-fallen snow and the pure white clouds in the stormy sky. The high mountains around us were beautiful, nothing like I had ever seen.

Crossing the Fraser River in Prince George, Canada
The two-way bridge was barely wider than our truck, as can be seen from our truck's hood in the foreground. We had to fold our truck's side mirrors flat, and the railroad bridge touched the side of the vehicle bridge.

We drove north to Prince George and then headed west towards Prince Rupert. The highway was under construction, and there were parts where instead of a bridge over a river, there were floating pontoons. Driving over those pontoons was scary and unsettling. The highway became narrow, and then gravel, then dirt, and as we traveled farther west the road was rutted and we bounced and shook every moment that we drove. The truck's shock absorbers were no match for that road, and combined with the manual steering and brakes it was an exhausting drive for David.

I couldn't go further on that road; it was a horrible rough ride. I was still morning sick every day, and the rough ride made me feel sicker. So we turned around and headed east on the same road, and traveled until we hit Calgary. The Calgary Stampede had finished, but Calgary was still crowded with cowboys and trucks towing trailers of horses filled the roads. We had seen billboards advertising the largest rodeo in the world, yet we had never heard of it until that week! I never thought about Canada and cowboys in the same sentence until our Calgary visit, so it was an eye-opener for me.

We traveled onward through the plains of Canada until we came to a very isolated border crossing. It was merely a booth between Canada and Wyoming, on the side of a two-lane road that was seldom traveled.

The two border patrol agents kept us at the crossing for more than five hours! They made us give them the case of beer that we had bought in Canada. The Canadian drinking age was eighteen, and we had drunk in bars and bought beer legally. The border agents searched our camper, sniffing at and then throwing out our oregano, our parsley…every green herb that they could find. They pawed through our drawers, and emptied out our ice chest and our wood box and looked inside the guitar.

They examined all of our kitty's papers, as I had brought Indigo's immunization records with us. While we were searched, Indigo sat on the top of the backrest of the seat in the cab. She liked to sit there, riding behind our heads and was comfortable in that location.

When they finally let us go we knew they were disappointed. They had joked about how they were getting a big drug bust. And David and I started laughing about five miles down the road. Indigo the cat had done a good job of guarding our stash of marijuana, sitting on it during the entire search.

We spent only one night of our road trip at a motel, and that one night was in Wyoming. Right after the border patrols let us into Wyoming from Canada, the weather changed quickly into a major thunder, rain and wind storm. We were afraid that we might blow off the road, as the highway was narrow with deep ditches on each side, ditches designed so that winter snow could be plowed off the road and into the deep ditches. After our previous adventure with steep embankments we were anxious to prevent another similar disaster.

We checked into the first motel we saw, in a small town about fifty miles from the border-crossing. The desk clerk told us we had made a wise decision; a wind storm had blown the roof off of their high school the previous year, and the winds on that part of the high prairie became violent quickly. The new school roof had just been finished and the town celebrated the reopening of their school, a school which served students from as far away as forty miles.

All night long we listened to the wind, safe inside the motel room. There was non-stop thunder and the wind literally howled. Brilliant blue lightening flashes were almost constant.

The next morning the storm was gone, and when we opened the door of the motel we could see that some nearby billboards had been torn to shreds. There were deep puddles every where and a lot of debris from the storm.

When we checked out, the desk clerk told us to be careful. He explained that the storm had torn off the brand-new high school roof, and had completely blown away the screen of the town's drive-in movie theatre. Most of the power was out for miles. David and I were really thankful that we had arrived at that town when we did, and that there had been a vacancy in the motel. We left a five-dollar donation with the desk clerk to help their town rebuild the school roof.

We headed east, and suffered several more mechanical problems, but we were always rescued one way or another. One time we were on a desolate road when the truck broke down.

David suspected that we needed a part for the carburetor. We managed to start and restart the truck enough times to make it to an isolated farm... a farm with a lot of abandoned-looking vehicles. It turned out the farmer had an old Chevy, and he let David take the part we needed from his Chevy. David asked him how much we owed him for the part, and the man said to pay him what it was worth.

David and I went back to the camper. How could we decide what the part was worth? It might have been worth our very lives. In an auto-parts store it probably would have been three or four dollars. So we gave the farmer a five dollar bill, thanked him profusely, and went on our way. At the time, five dollars was the cost to fill our gas tank, and we thought that it was a fair trade.

We visited Mount Rushmore and also watched the sculpting of the Crazy Horse Memorial. And when we drove through the Badlands I was amazed by their starkness and beauty. Seeing the Badlands and trying to visualize how pioneers had crossed in covered wagons through those steep canyons and rock formations just astounded me. As day turned to evening and then to night, we watched the light and dark and shadows change, and the beauty of the Badlands filled my head with a serene, almost surrealistic, peace.

We traveled onto an American Indian Reservation and while we were at the "trading post" a handful of the locals wanted to see inside the camper. We invited them in, and soon we were part of a group sitting in the parking lot playing guitars and singing and talking and visiting and exchanging stories. They invited us back to their homes for dinner. The Reservation homes were depressing-looking. The government built homes for the Indians and gave them the homes...just flat-out gave the homes to them! But there were no jobs, no landscaping, no trees, and just these stucco houses out in the middle of nowhere in a barren land. Nothing to do. Their children had to take school buses to schools about forty miles away every day, waiting in the hot sun or cold snowy weather for buses.

The rate of alcoholism and depression was very high on the Reservation. There was no alcohol sold there. The government declared it illegal to sell alcohol on the Reservation. We drove in a car with some of the Indians to the nearest town to buy beer. Along the highway there were several crosses with plastic flowers and sun-faded photos attached; memorials to Indians who had died in automobile accidents while drinking. They told us on hot days they couldn't wait to get back to the Reservation to drink, that they would drink in their cars on the way back from town, and that was why there were the many memorials along the road.

The liquor stores in town were government liquor stores. Even beer or wine could not be purchased in a grocery store, only at the government stores, which were closed on Sundays. We went in the store and looked around. The salesperson was joking around with the Indians, reminding them to not drink on the way back to the Reservation. We piled back into the old station wagon and headed back to the Reservation, the sun shining in our eyes. They had some great pot and so did we and we started smoking pot and drinking the cold beer. There was no radio reception in their car, but we all started singing, driving westward in the sunset with the windows rolled down, the heat like an oven, laughing, talking, smoking and drinking.

That night we built a campfire and there were about ten or fifteen of us sitting around the fire, watching shooting stars, lying on our backs on the warm prairie, where the land was flat and nothing blocked the view of the sky. There were millions of stars and the air was finally cool. The Indians from the Reservation were beautiful with their long black hair and brown skin, and we all felt young and as if we were in a moment in time that was special, sharing our histories and our differences but bonding and wanting to be united in goals of peace and love. Never before or since have I seen such a sky, a deep black sky with millions of stars, feeling like our earth was connected to the giant universe. We played guitar, and then everyone got drunk and woke up the next day with painful hangovers.

We drove through South Dakota and Nebraska, and then into Kansas. I was excited about going to Kansas because we were going to visit Uncle Jack and my cousins. Uncle Jack was Daddy's older brother and Uncle Jack's children were my cousins who I hadn't seen for several years. On the way there, we happened onto the small town of Jetmore, Kansas, which was hidden in a valley. We stopped to get gas, and the gas station owner asked us about California and what we were doing and where we were going. He offered to let us stay behind the gas station for the night. He gave us the restroom key so we could use the facilities in the night and told us he hoped to see us in the morning.

The next morning he pointed out a nearby hill, asking if we had noticed it. The hillside had "Jesus Saves" on the side of it, written with letters made from white rocks. The letters were probably forty or fifty feet tall. The man told us that he and his church members had put the rocks there, carrying them up the hillside and placing them to make the words. Then he started telling us how Negroes were black because they sinned and that the Bible taught that Negroes were inferior and asked us what we believed. He had heard that everyone in California was not only a hippy (as he gave us the once-over) but that we all practiced free love. He had also heard that white girls might even marry Negro men and that was against God's plans. Would we like to come to a Bible class to hear more about how this was against God's plans?

This seemed a bit much for a free night's stay where we had been entrusted with a bathroom key. We thanked him and headed towards Wichita, where we visited Uncle Jack, Aunt Bernie and my cousins. David and I had a great visit, they all loved the camper, and we enjoyed hearing my cousin Greg play jazz. Greg was still a teenager, but he was a great musician. I wondered if Greg Richter would ever make it as a jazz musician. He and my other cousins, Rose and Blake, had grown up so much in the few years since I had seen them. It was hard to believe the changes in all of us.

After our visit, David and I headed through Missouri, Arkansas, Mississippi, and Alabama. And the south started to take hold of me…it was so green and was like traveling through a forest. Much of the time it was David and I and our truck on lonely two-lane roads, getting a feel of America and this vast country and what it was like. Our truck had overheated so frequently in Nebraska that David had used our cutting torch to remove the front grill of the truck. That way the radiator was exposed to more air and stayed cool. Before we left California, we had custom-built the truck seat, removing the standard cab seat and making a wooden seat with foam cushions and vinyl psychedelic covers. That left space for a torch, tanks, and welding equipment to be stored in the cab of the truck. We traveled snuggled together on our comfortable custom-built seat, with Indigo sitting on our shoulders.

We went through small, dusty towns that looked impoverished, where we felt like the only white people in the town, and our truck with California license plates stood out like a beacon. Everywhere we went we talked with people, had coffee in the cafés, and listened to how their lives were and we shared with them about how things were in California. Most people were friendly and kind.

However, some country roads got a little spooky. There were roads with small houses and beautiful quilts hanging on their roadside picket fences, and it was common to see signs hanging on the fences next to the quilts: "Yankees Welcome," or "Jesus Saves," or "Moonshine Kills," or "Yankee Go Home." We began to see confederate flags, and hand-written signs, "The South Will Rise Again." We visited little country stores where the matchbook covers had "Moonshine Kills" printed on them with a local phone number to report illegal stills and moonshine. How odd and foreign that was to me, as if we had traveled back in time to the era of national prohibition. And there were beginning to be stores and towns that we went into where the local white people looked at us suspiciously and did not talk or greet us, but asked us instead when we would be leaving.

In one town we stopped at a gas station and were filling our gas tank when two sheriff cars pulled up, pinning us in. They asked what we were doing in their town and why we had left California and if we were rabble-rousers coming to rile up the niggers, because if we were we had better turn right around and leave town. I told them that this was America and we had a legal right to travel wherever we wanted and that they couldn't tell us to leave town. Then both sheriffs got out of their cars, came over to our open window, and asked us to get out of the truck. We did, and they kept us there, questioning and acting like stereotypical redneck southern sheriffs. They finally told David and me that we had better be gone by sunset or that we would regret it.

I was outraged. This was America. They couldn't get away with such intimidation. We should call the ACLU. We weren't going to let them bully us like that! The phone book at the gas station had no number or information for the ACLU. We called the telephone operator from the phone booth and asked her to look up the number of the ACLU for us. She asked us what that was. We said, "American Civil Liberties Union," and asked for the number. She said that we must be the rabble-rousing hippies that she had heard about and that she wasn't giving us any number for the northern Communist groups and that she was telling the sheriff that we had called for the number.

David and I sat on the curb in that little southern town, talking and discussing and debating if we should stay or leave. The sun was going down, and a parade of pick-up trucks was beginning to slowly pass our parked camper. We decided that our lives were more important than providing amusement to a group of rednecks who were looking to cause trouble and fearful of change. We didn't want to be found hanging from some tree or our truck burned up somewhere with us in it. So we left town just before sunset. The small town disappeared into the distance and into the sunset. The sky turned from pink to bluish-green, and finally purple, blue and black. Stars came out and we drove the lonely country road in the dark, our windows open to let in the air which was finally cool enough to be comfortable.

For three nights in a row I dreamed about eating fried chicken. I would wake up in the night dreaming that I was eating fried chicken and that I enjoyed it. I didn't even like fried chicken; we had not grown up on fried foods and I had seldom had fried chicken. Besides, David and I were vegetarians and we were so dedicated to being vegetarians that we did not wear leather or use anything that was a by-product of the slaughterhouse industry. No leather, no gelatin, nothing with rennet in it…. and now after three years of vegetarian food, mostly raw food and no dairy products I was dreaming of fried chicken. I told David about my dream, and he said he had heard of women craving pickles and ice cream but not chicken, but if that was what I was craving then we better stop and get some.

We went into a southern coffee shop in the mid-afternoon. It was cool and dim inside and the seats in the booth were also cool. There were few customers, as it was between the lunch and dinner shifts. The pink-uniformed waitress served us coffee and asked what we'all were fixin' to get. I told her fried chicken. I then ate the entire fried chicken dinner, and never got sick and after that my craving was over. David and I figured that my body must have just needed the protein and the fat.

We stayed at a campground by a small river one night, and the next morning we went into the campground/truck stop coffee shop for breakfast. I saw on the menu that they were serving something called "grits." Grits? Wasn't grit something that you got under your fingernails or in your gas line or that was just dirty? What the hell was grits? So I asked the waitress, "What's grits?" Well, you would have thought a federal offence had just taken place. She almost shrieked in her surprise, "Honey, ya'll don't know what's grits is? Where ya'll from....California?!?!?" The coffee shop became silent. Everyone was looking at me. I looked at the waitress and said that, no, I didn't know what grits were but please, ma'am, could I have some? Things were looking up until I added, "...with catsup please." "Honey, ya'll don't eat grits with catsup...hey fellas, she don't know what grits are and now she wants catsup with her grits!" I was lectured about grits and butter and honey, and she brought me some white stuff that looked like cream of rice and I gagged it down.

When we got out to the truck I thought David was going to die laughing. I didn't think it was that funny.

That night we pulled into a raucous roadside bar/café/gas station that had a parking lot full of pickup trucks and loud country music blaring from inside. It was the kind of place we tried to avoid, but we had been driving on empty the last twenty miles and had to pull into the first gas station we found. The gas station was shut, but we asked the bartender if someone could unlock the pumps for us. He said sure, but why didn't we have some supper first. I was so tired of hearing country music. I went over to the juke box to see if there were any songs I wanted to select, and a few of the locals who were drunk started to hassle me, pulling at my hair and asking if I was a free-love hippy and why didn't I give them some of that lovin.' It was gross. They were gross. The music was all about standing by your man and crying because your man left you and how sad life was without a man…and these creepy jerks thought they were some prize!

I went back to the bar to find David, and he was paying the bartender for the gas he had been getting while this happened. I felt the eyes of those drunken creeps on me, and then saw that they were not watching me, but that they were watching David pay for the gas. David and I had broken a hundred-dollar traveler's cheque that morning, so the wad of cash that David pulled out of his pocket was thick. I didn't like the way the men were looking at David and the money.

I signaled David that we needed to go, and as we hurried out to the truck I told him what had happened. I was mad at him for not being careful with our money and showing how much cash he was holding. And as we pulled out of the parking lot, we saw those two men get into a car and pull out too.

At first we didn't want to believe that they were following us. We hoped that it was a coincidence that the men left the same time we did and were coincidentally traveling the same direction. After all, this was a two-lane road in the middle of nowhere and there were only two directions to go. Miles down the road, after midnight, we were still being followed, the headlights behind us some times disappearing but then reappearing. There were no other vehicles on the road. I looked at the map and was glad that a highway was coming up in about twenty miles; when we got there and merged onto the highway we were disappointed to see the car was still shadowing us.

We drove in the dark through Alabama and into Georgia, thankful to see the "Welcome to Georgia" sign as we left Alabama. The car followed us until we got to Atlanta, Georgia, and then they were gone. We didn't know if it had been a coincidence or if they had been waiting for us to pull over and go to sleep so they could rob us. Maybe they had finally gotten tired of following us. Perhaps they had sobered up and decided to go home.

We pulled into the driveway of Margaret Horton's house just as dawn was breaking. David's mother didn't know we were coming, but when she got up that morning and saw the home-build camper with the California license plates parked in her long, shady driveway, she couldn't wait to see us.

We stayed in Atlanta for several weeks. We visited David's dad, Wilf, and spent time with David's sister, Jennifer, who was staying with Margaret until college started in the fall. And we went on day trips to the Great Smokey Mountains and took the boat to water ski at Lake Allatoona and Lake Lanier. And when a friend of David's mom offered the use of her cabin in the Georgia Mountains, we headed out there for a visit; David's mom, his sister Jennifer and the two of us.

Georgia was hot and humid, and as we left the highway and headed down a country road the lushness of the plants testified to the almost-tropical southern climate. After driving several hours we turned onto a dirt road, and the road was hemmed in on both sides by kudzu. Kudzu is a non-native, invasive plant and it was choking out many native plants. It could grow at least a foot in just one day; in fact, many people called it "the foot-a-night" plant. As we drove down the dirt road, we were soon driving over kudzu. We drove past what we realized was a car completely covered with kudzu. I had made the mistake of saying what a beautiful plant it was, as it reminded me of a morning glory plant without the flowers. But as we traveled and saw entire cabins overgrown with kudzu I realized what a threat this plant was, and why the locals hated it. It was strangling the native plants and changing the environment.

We finally got to the cabin, and then saw with disappointment that it was not really a cabin, but a trailer, and that it had been broken into. There was a pair of men's work boots outside the door, and someone had been living there. No one was there at that moment, and because we did not want to drive down the desolate rutted and unlit road in the dark, we decided to stay and hope that the person did not return.

The trailer was unbearably hot inside, but the bugs outside made it too miserable to sit outdoors. Never in my life have I spent a night in woods that were so noisy! There were frogs and cicadas, and the cicadas sounded like a high-pitched buzzing hum with a rhythm like sawing wood by hand. The woods must have been full of dog packs, because the barking of dogs continued all night long. It was hot, it was humid, there was no place comfortable to go, and it was so noisy that I couldn't even hear myself think. The mattress was stinky and I started imagining a crazy chainsaw murderer would show up at the door, because after all he had been staying there and didn't want us there. It was a horrible night!

The next morning was cooler outside, and we saw that all around the trailer were day lilies and other beautiful blooms, including azaleas and rhododendrons. But I was really glad when we decided to go back to Atlanta and not spend another night at the trailer. I had seen a part of the south that let my imagination run way too wild!

That day at Margaret's house we got a long-distance phone call from Simon. He had called my parents and they had given him Margaret's phone number. Tommy was sick, and

Simon was worried about Tommy. The doctors thought that Tommy had meningitis and had performed a spinal tap to diagnose it, but it wasn't meningitis. Simon was waiting for the doctors to tell Tommy what was the matter, and Simon was afraid that Tommy was going to die. Simon also said that when he called for the phone number my mom said that Daddy's allergies had become extreme and Daddy had been taken to the emergency room twice for adrenaline shots due to allergic reactions. I called my parents to make sure things were okay, and then David and I decided that it was time to head home.

On the way home to California from Atlanta, David and I stopped at a rest stop along a road in Mississippi. We needed to get a part for the truck, and got in a stupid fight about how much money we had remaining and what route we were going to take home. David said he would go to the next town and get the part and come back later to get me, leaving me at the road stop. Once he was gone I felt alone and vulnerable, especially when I saw that the trash can near where I was sitting was full of hard-core porno magazines. It got dark and David had still not come back to get me and I wasn't sure what to think.

A trucker pulled in and sat at another picnic table eating his dinner. When he was done he came over and started talking to me. I told him that David and I had fought and I wasn't sure what was going on. The trucker asked me about our truck; when I described it he told me that he had seen farther down the road at another rest stop. So I got in his truck and we went down the highway and found David asleep in our camper. He was about twenty miles away! David said that he had been mad at me but that he was on his way back to get me when he got tired.

I thanked the trucker and got back in our truck with David. We were now traveling west, and the evening sun was bright in our eyes. We drove towards home through Chattanooga and then Nashville Tennessee, and stopped at the

Grand Ole Opry. Westward we drove, seeing Little Rock, Oklahoma City and Amarillo, Texas. But we were almost out of money, and were to the point of rationing our dollars to buy gas and nothing else. After leaving Atlanta we had been driving without side trips or stops along the way. In New Mexico we did stop at Taos and some Indian reservations, and we were amazed when we drove through Flagstaff, Arizona, because it was snowing there and it was still summer!

The evening we entered California it was unbearably hot. We had driven through the Mohave Desert and by the time we arrived in Barstow, we were ready to pull over and spend the night. Barstow was hot and loud, noisy from trains and highway traffic. We parked in a restaurant parking lot to grab some sleep, but the heat and the noise kept me awake. A short while after midnight I was finally dozing off when I heard talking outside our camper door. From the conversation I soon realized that there were several young men planning to break into the camper, thinking that there was no one inside and that there might be some valuables. I woke David up by shaking him and put my finger over my lips, indicating for him to say nothing. I pointed to the cab, and slid through the connector into the cab, and David followed me. We had learned to face our truck outward every time we parked, and as we hurriedly left, three young men came running after us, one of them waving a crowbar!

With that close call, we decided to just drive straight home. We went through Bakersfield as dawn was just breaking, through Delano and Fresno, and at Los Banos we turned west. We stopped at Casa de Fruta east of Gilroy for some fresh produce and by afternoon David, Jane, Indigo the cat, and our home on wheels pulled into the commune.

We had traveled nine-thousand miles in nine weeks and spent nine-hundred dollars.

When we got home we found out that Tommy was sick
with syphilis. No one even thought that people still got it. He
was very, very, sick and it was upsetting to all of us.

I went back to work at Fairchild, but I became
increasingly uncomfortable about the circuits I was designing. I
was part of the camera and instrument division, and I often
asked my boss what was the end-product of my designs. I didn't
want to be designing something that was part of the military-
industrial complex, something that would be used in war or in
technology used for killing. My boss became more evasive in his

answers, and one time he told me the circuit would go into a juke box. A juke box?! I couldn't believe that. The rumor mill began to circulate that, in fact, some of our circuits were being used by the military.

When I asked my boss this point blank, his non-answer led me to believe that I was using my hands and brain and energy to create something used for war, so I decided that once the baby was born I would look for another job, and quit working at Fairchild. I was determined that if I stayed in the MOS or mask design field that I would be certain of what I was designing for before I laid my pencil to Mylar again.

But my focus of my future had changed. David and I had traveled nine thousand miles together. We were now ready to travel a different road as we awaited the new life that would be joining us and would transform our lives forever.

W here Have all the Flowers Gone?

"Where have all the flowers gone?" My heart was so touched by the folk singing of the 1960s, of the sensitivity and messages in the songs. It was painful that a folk singer such as Pete Seeger was banned from singing on TV for seventeen years. We were supposed to be a democracy. We were supposed to be allowed political freedom, yet the dream that was promised included lies about racial equality, about economic equality, and about gender equality.

There was great opportunity for the Palo Alto Dreamer to march in peace marches, to go hand-in-hand with the United Farm Workers, not as a spoiled rich kid or as an observer, but as a person whose heart was full of the need for justice, full of the yearning for peace and full of the desire to see world harmony.

World peace meant simply no more war...to be a hippy chick putting a daisy in the rifle of the National Guard and hoping that the guardsman would smile and think and that I might affect his life. So many peace marches throughout my life...there is never an end to war, and as long as there are still wars, there are still antiwar rallies.

The Kezar Peace March...what a incredible mixture of antiwar, music, drugs, making love in the warm sun behind the trees....there was so much passion around stopping the war…and the passion is still there, the hope for peace is still there…and the folk songs still evoke the dream of equality, the dream of peace, the dream of clean air and water.

My second decade was a roller coaster of volunteering, drugs, art, music, and discovering sex and relationships. My family gave me freedom to explore and in so doing allowed me to make mistakes and learn from them. I had gone from worrying about nylons and hair and makeup to traveling to Mexico and Canada and across America.

I lived in a commune and was going to have a baby. I was ready for whatever adventures and relationships and challenges that were sure to come my way. The 1960s and early 1970s had truly been a sparkling time of my life.

The 70 / 80 Transformation

awaited

the

Palo Alto Dreamer

T he second part of the story has been put down on paper.
Part two shared the vibrancy, the intensity,

the hope and the connectedness of

The Sparkling 60s and 70s.

My world had expanded, my culture exploded with sex, drugs,
rock n' roll, and I was committed to social justice. I had great
faith that society would cure generations of social ills.

Again Gretchen said, "Write the next part of your story…
I want to know what happened!"

As I write the next chapter of my life's story, the story of how
my young family worked and struggled to keep social
commitments balanced with careers and children, I find it is
also a reflection of many other people's lives. The political
changes which colored the decade of the 1970s and the early
1980s affected all of us who were caught up in the
transformation of the 1970s and early 1980s.

Part three will be dedicated to David, to my family and
friends, and to those who remember or were part of

The 70 / 80 Transformation

A Palo Alto Dreamer